Pentecostal Spirituality

Pentecostal Spirituality

A Paradigm of Liberation

Shaibu Abraham

CWI

Christian World Imprints

First Published in 2020 by

Christian World Imprints
Christian Publishing & Books from India
C-3, Shop No. 14, Ground Floor
Wazirpur Industrial Area, **Delhi-110052**
cwidelhi2017@gmail.com
www.ChristianWorldImprints.com
Phone: +91 11 41526079

ISBN: 978-93-5148-417-2

Printed in India.

To

All My
Teachers, Colleagues,
Friends and Students

Contents

Preface ix

Abbreviations xiii

Chapter 1: Pentecostal Spirituality: A Paradigm of Liberation 1

Chapter 2: The Full Gospel: Message of Liberation 17

Chapter 3: Holiness: Separation for Liberation 35

Chapter 4: The Baptism in the Holy Spirit: Power for Liberation 53

Chapter 5: Spiritual Gifts: Tools of Liberation 79

Chapter 6: Evangelism and Mission: Methods of Liberation 115

Chapter 7: Worship: Cradle of Liberation 143

Chapter 8: Preaching and Testimony: Communications for Liberation 163

Chapter 9: Eschatology: Urgency for Liberation 183

Chapter 10: Conclusion 205

Bibliography 209

Index 227

Preface

Pentecostal movement is considered as a spiritual movement and emphasises the experience of God through the Holy Spirit in its doctrines and life of its members. Pentecostals insist that every aspect of their faith should be according to the experiences that recorded in the pages of the Bible. Religious observers, sociologists, theologians alike appreciate the movement for its experiential nature of spirituality and observe that Pentecostalism has transformed the spiritual outlook of Christianity as a whole. For instance, Harvey Cox, Donald E. Miller, David Martin, Walter J. Hollenweger, Alister McGrath and a multiple of other scholars who are stalwarts in their own areas, agree with the observation that Pentecostal spirituality is actually a move that bring back the original biblical spirituality and bridges the gap of "ecstasy deficit" of the contemporary world. Moreover, they also insist that Pentecostal movement is a liberative movement around the world, particularly in the Majority World. The observation and research by world renowned agencies like, *The World Christian Encyclopaedia* and *The Pew Forum* term Pentecostal movement as the fastest growing religious movement of the globe, growing fast in the new mission fields, especially in the third world situations. They assert that the movement is liberating thousands of people from their wretched conditions and transforming them for a better future. Keen observations and researches proved beyond a doubt that, more than systematic programmes or methodological approaches in the context, it is the vibrant spirituality of the movement that results in its magnificent growth and transformation of masses.

Pentecostalism is known as a movement of the Spirit, and its spirituality is fundamentally experiencing God and Christ through the agency of the Spirit. Rather than insisting on ecclesiastical structures and a system of elaborate theological dogmas and written liturgy, Pentecostal movement began as a spiritual movement, emphasising on spiritual elements such as 'born again' experience, 'holiness', experience of 'the baptism of the Holy Spirit', spiritual gifts and so on.

These elements of Pentecostal spirituality have facilitated the movement to be a unique entity in the Christendom and attracted millions within its span of hundred years. Its basic Christology (the Full Gospel - Jesus the saviour, healer, Spirit-baptiser, coming king) preached throughout the world effected transformations in the lives of the suffering masses. Similarly, it spirituality of holiness enabled Pentecostal believers to separate themselves from worldly affairs and move toward the perfect likeness of Christ. As a result of holding the spirituality of holiness, early Pentecostals were ready to sacrifice their worldly possessions and comfort for the sake of new found sanctified experience. Besides, this experience created a new vision of spiritual and social realities and propelled them to act against the oppressive systems like racism, caste system, poverty, slavery and other social and cultural issues. Similarly, the experience of the baptism in the Holy Spirit endowed them with power to carry out urgent mission and social ministries which delivered millions. The fervent eschatological expectation of the return of Christ enabled believers to keep themselves holy and prepared and focus on the work of the Kingdom of God.

However, a cursory glance into the contemporary affairs of the Pentecostals denominations in many places, mainly the movement is old or crossed a century mark, the above mentioned liberative spirituality is either in a declining mode or partially lost. This trend is clearly visible even in the third world context where churches are old. Let me narrate my own observations about the movement. I left Kerala, the Indian State at the southern tip of Indian subcontinent where Pentecostalism began simultaneously with the Azuza Street Revival and lived in north India and abroad for a period of time. Having come back to the State of Kerala after a gap of three decades, I could see vast differences in the functioning of the major Pentecostal denominations. I can very well identify the contrast between the earlier shape of the movement and contemporary trends. The most striking element is the palpable spiritual decline in the air. What is unmistakably visible is, disarray among leadership of various Pentecostal denominations, split into various groups and factions and fight for supremacy in hierarchical ladders of the denominations. Petty politics to reach the top, nepotism, personal rivalry, electioneering that is worse than secular politics are norms now. Backstabbing, court cases and even physical violence are carried out without any trepidation. One may argue that such things were present in a certain degree even from the beginning of the movement, but what I feel is, the sheer power of Pentecostal spirituality somehow kept those unruly elements under the lid. However, as of today, the vitality of Pentecostal spirituality is slackened off and the human elements are gaining control over the churches and its leadership.

In such a juncture, it is significant to regain the original vibrancy of Pentecostal spirituality into the fore. It is imperative to reemphasise the very basic components of Pentecostal spirituality such as the full gospel, baptism in the Holy Spirit, holiness, use of spiritual gifts, eschatological expectation, passionate and urgent mission and so on. Focusing on these elements would bring a change in the contemporary scenario of latching on to hierarchical structures, leadership struggles and assimilating into larger cultural and social patterns that ooze out the vitality of the movement. Insisting on the original spirituality will drive the movement straight to its goal of reaching and liberating ordinary people from their predicament and preparing its members for the coming of the Lord.

This book is presented in an effort to persuade Pentecostals to go back to their original spirituality, reemphasising the spiritual elements; to regain the power of the Spirit, holiness, eschatological expectancy and other vital elements as a way of life. This would make the movement a liberative force in a world of oppression, injustice, poverty and suffering. The movement can make a difference only if it regains its sagging spirituality. It is anticipated that this endeavour will help Pentecostal movement to reignite its passion for liberation.

Here I would like convey my love and thanks to my wife, Sheena, who always stood with me in my academic endeavours, constantly praying for me and taking care of all my needs. I also remember my parents, P. M. Mathew and Saramma Mathew, for their constant prayers. I would also love to convey my gratitude to all my colleagues and students, who enriched me with fresh insights on Pentecostal movement in informal talks and class discussions which greatly contributed to this book. Special thanks to *Christian World Imprints* for the speedy publication of the book.

Abbreviations

ABD	The Anchor Bible Dictionary
AJPS	Asian Journal of Pentecostal Studies
Dharma Deepika	A Journal of South Indian Missiological Research
DJG	Dictionary of Jesus and the Gospels
DPCM	Dictionary of Pentecostal and Charismatic Movements
DPL	Dictionary of Paul and His Letters
EPW	Economic and Political Weekly
IBMR	International Bulletin of Missionary Research
IJST	International Journal of Systematic Theology
IRM	International Review of Mission
JEPTA	Journal of the European Pentecostal Theological Association
JES	Journal of Ecumenical Studies
JPT	Journal of Pentecostal Theology
NDBT	New Dictionary of Biblical Theology
NDT	New Dictionary of Theology
NIDPCM	The New International Dictionary of Pentecostal and Charismatic Movements
Pneuma	The Journal of the Society for Pentecostal Studies
WBC	Word Biblical Commentary

Chapter 1

Pentecostal Spirituality A Paradigm of Liberation

Pentecostal movement, since its inception has been claimed to be a spiritual movement. Pentecostals insist that what have been considered as their fundamental doctrines should not stand as mere statements or theoretical construct but to be experienced in personal and communal life. They take strenuous efforts to convey this idea among their members as well as to outsiders. Hence, Pentecostalism is widely understood as an experiential tradition in Christendom. Harvey Cox, the Hollis Research Professor of Divinity at Harvard, describes Pentecostalism as the experiential branch of Christianity *par excellence*. He had famously asserted that the phenomenon of the origin of Pentecostal movement is the sign of return of primal spirituality and the movement fills the "ecstasy deficit" in our postmodern world.[1] He observes that Pentecostals talk about experience "a lot", and persistently emphasize personal experience as "a *sine qua non* of spirituality and the indispensable touchstone of faith."[2] Cox, who worked out a theology for "post-religious" age (*The Secular City*, 1965), changed his standpoint and published the seminal work, (*Fire from Heaven: The Rise of Pentecostal Spirituality*, 1995), seeing the considerable growth of Pentecostal movement and the spiritual fervour it has brought around the globe. He confessed that he was in error to swallow what sociologists and religious observers were predicted, the waning away of religions. The growth of Pentecostal movement worldwide and its effects forced him to

[1] Harvey Cox, *Fire from Heaven: The Rise of Pentecostal Spirituality and the Reshaping of Religion in the Twenty-first Century* (Cambridge, MA: Da Capo Press, 1995).

[2] Peter D. Neumann, *Pentecostal Experience: An Ecumenical Encounter* (Eugene, OR: Wipf and Stock Publishers, 2012), 11.

rethink his earlier conclusion.[3] His observation is that Pentecostalism represents a spiritual restoration of significance and purpose to masses of people whose daily experience is one of despair, injustice, and hopelessness.[4] Cox expresses his feeling about Pentecostal movement and its effect upon the religious scene of today's world:

> The more I read about the Pentecostal-Charismatic tsunami, and the more I participate in and observe its many manifestations, the more convinced I become that, in addition to being a beguiling phenomenon on its own, it also provides an invaluable lens through which to watch the whole religious resurgence. The turn from an emphasis on doctrine to the cultivation of a direct experience of God—as spirit, mystery, or transcendence—can be traced in virtually all the traditions. So, can the change from hierarchical ordering to more participation. The impressive ability of Pentecostals to retrieve, absorb, and transform elements of the indigenous religious cultures into which they move is something happening...[5]

David Martin, a British sociologist too states that the growth of Pentecostalism is the largest global shift in the religious marketplace over the last forty years. In his view, what is occurring on the ground religiously simply does not correspond to armchair predictions of the end of religion. The growth of Pentecostalism raises significant questions about the so-called secularization hypothesis.[6] In a revealing statement, McGrath affirms Pentecostalism as an important recovery of experiential Christianity which may have potential to influence both the religious and especially atheistic West. He states, "it is this form of Protestantism (Pentecostalism) that may be expected to resist erosion by atheism. Pentecostalism is strongly predisposed toward the dispossessed and oppressed, undermining one of the most atheistic critiques of religion—that it oppresses."[7] Miller and Yamamori quoting *The World Christian Encyclopedia* says that in 1900 Europeans and North Americans constituted 80% of the world's Christians, whereas today 60% live in Asia, Africa, or Latin America. "The Southern Hemisphere seems to be fertile soil for growing Pentecostalism, since Christianity is expanding in the developing world while contracting in much of the developed world...It stands to reason that Pentecostalism will

---

[3] Cox, "Preface", *Fire From Heaven*, xv-xvi.

[4] Cox, *Fire from Heaven,* 104.

[5] Harvey Cox, "Foreword", in *Global Pentecostal and Charismatic Healing,* edited by Candy Gunther Brown (Oxford: Oxford University Press, 2011), xx.

[6] Donald E. Miller & Tetsunao Yamamori, *Global Pentecostalism: The New Face of Christian Social Engagement* (Berkeley: University of California Press, 2007), 30.

[7] Alister McGrath, *The Twilight of Atheism: The Rise and fall of Disbelief in the Modern World* (New York: Doubleday, 2004), 194-215.

be a prominent driver of the demographic transformation that is reshaping Christendom."[8]

Central to Pentecostal faith and practice is the concept of encounter and experience of God. Pentecostals embrace a spirituality that expect to touch God and to be touched by God. Pentecostals value experience-based encounters with God because they have the potential to transform believers. They believe that if God initiates an experience, it must be in order to positively transform the individual concerned.[9] The God-experience that Pentecostals claim to, is accomplished through the work of the Holy Spirit. In other words, Pentecostalism is known as a movement of the Spirit, and its spirituality is fundamentally about life in the Spirit. Rather than forming ecclesiastical structures, having systematic doctrines, liturgy, vestments and buildings, Pentecostal movement began as a Spirit movement, emphasising on spiritual elements such as 'born again' experience, experience of the baptism of the Holy Spirit, spiritual gifts and so on. For Pentecostals, spirituality is a lived experience of God through Christ, manifested and experienced through the activities of the Holy Spirit. Archer comments,

> Pentecostals have always emphasized experiential Christianity rather than doctrinal confession. Rather than describe or explain doctrines in the mode of systematic or dogmatic theologians associated with the seminary and scholar, they typically explore them in the biblical narrative and by the testimony of those affected by them. Their theology is praxis-oriented, experiential and oral.[10]

Similarly, Daniel E. Albrecht, while writing on Pentecostal spirituality affirms that "what is most distinctive of Pentecostals is not their theology or their ecclesiastical structure, but rather their sense of experience of God."[11] He continues to asserts that Pentecostalism is a movement of the Spirit and spirituality is fundamentally about life in the Spirit. Pentecostal expect the Holy Spirit to speak to them, to touch their hearts through strong emotions, to reveal something of God to them through ideas and pictures that come to their minds or through dreams, to pray through them in sighs, groans and in unknown languages, and to transform them ever more closely in holiness to the image of Christ.[12] Besides, Pentecostal spirituality affirms a sensitivity to the Holy Spirit. Pentecostals have

---

[8] Miller & Yamamori, *Global Pentecostalism*, 31.

[9] Keith Warrington, *Pentecostal Theology: A Theology of Encounter* (London: T&T Clark, 2008), 26.

[10] Warrington, *Pentecostal Theology*, 15-16.

[11] Daniel E. Albrecht and Evans B. Howard, "Pentecostal Spirituality", in *The Cambridge Companion to Pentecostalism,* edited by Cecil M. Robeck, Jr & Amos Yong (New York: Cambridge University Press, 2014).

[12] Albrecht and Howard, "Pentecostal Spirituality", 425.

developed an affective ability to notice the nuances of the Spirit. Just as the New Testament speaks of the Holy Spirit leading, filling, convicting, comforting, and encouraging Christ's people, Pentecostal spirituality acquainted Pentecostals to be receptive to the activity of the Spirit. Further, Pentecostals have an orientation towards the gifts of the Spirit such as tongues, prophecy, healing, miracles and the like.

Moreover, for Pentecostals, there is no dichotomy between these experiences and their doctrines, life and practices. For them spirituality is integral to their daily life. Pentecostal spirituality affected their past and is effecting transformations in their present. They strongly anticipate the same spirituality would change their future destiny. The joy they inherited through their salvation experience and the empowerment of the Holy Spirit enabled them to envision Christian life as participation in the divine life. This experience is believed to be related to the experience of the early Christian community in the New Testament. Pentecostals view their Pentecostal experience as *normative*, in the sense that it follows the pattern or experience of the early church.

Even though Pentecostals always acclaim their experience, they insist that their experience is fully in accordance with the Bible and they question any experience that is not recorded in the Scripture. For instance, the phenomenon of speaking in tongues for which Pentecostals are known, is not invented by the Pentecostals of the last century. But, as we know, it is a New Testament phenomenon and practiced by the apostles of Jesus Christ and the early church. Even in the history of Christianity we see sporadic occurrences of tongue speaking.[13] Similarly, the practice of supernatural healing was carried out by Jesus himself, as a sign of 'in breaking of the Kingdom of God' and his compassion towards the suffering masses of his time. He also commanded his apostles to heal the sick and cast out demons. The same is in the case of the baptism of the Spirit, prophecy and so on. What Pentecostals claim to experience has biblical and theological validity. Instead of condensing their experiences into a system of doctrines or dogmas, Pentecostals tend to exercise them as lived spirituality of everyday life (Here I acknowledge that it is significant to define and systematise one's experience if possible, for the benefit of others and Pentecostal theologians are doing it). Therefore, ordinary Pentecostals have no qualm in testifying and proclaiming their experiences - the experience of the Spirit baptism, divine healing and God experience in their worship. This communication of spirituality to others placed Pentecostal movement as a Spiritual movement in popular perception.

As we are aware of, there is a difference between being religious and being spiritual, and according to Jacobsen, Pentecostals generally opted for the more spiritual side of that divide. As defined today, "religion" is associated with organized institutionalized faith while "spirituality" focuses on personal values

[13] R. P. Spittler, "Glossolalia", in *NIDPCM,* edited by Stanley M. Burgess (Michigan: Zondervan, 2002), 673-74.

and practices. Religion is seen as promoting norms of belief and behaviour that are codified and standardized for an entire group. By contrast, spirituality is more individualistic, discovered from within rather than learned from the outside. Religion is embodied in doctrines, creeds, and formal liturgies, while spirituality finds better outlet in poetry, song, and dramatic performance.[14] Spittler, while explaining Pentecostal spirituality underlines the same idea:

> Spirituality refers to a cluster of acts and sentiments that are informed by the beliefs and values that characterize a specific religious community. In addition, spirituality focuses on the pietistic habits of ordinary individuals. In contrast to this, theology defines systematized, ordinarily written, reflections on religious experience. For Pentecostals the most significant aspect of spirituality is individual experience which includes not only religious feeling, but also emotions of joy or sorrow.[15]

Pentecostals consider personal experience as the arena of true religion. Quoting Lesslie Newbigin, Spittler describes three broad approaches to Christian spirituality. Protestants view religion as belief, orthodoxy, doctrinal assent—a matter of the intellect whereas the Catholic church think rather in terms of obedience, participation, and religious acts. When it comes to members of the Pentecostal churches, they achieve religious satisfaction through personal experience, and this always brings an emphasis on the Holy Spirit.[16]

It is a known fact that ordinary people look for experiences that they can identify with, stir up their emotions and passions positively and make a difference in their lives. However, doctrines and dogmas that are placed as statements stand aloof from the life of the people (at least in the case of ordinary people). It doesn't mean that doctrines are not useful or ineffective, rather when they exist as a mere statement of our faith, they may not make a strong say upon the lives of the people. If people experience and understand, for instance, sanctification, which is a cardinal doctrine of Christianity in terms of internal and external transformations and a thrust to alter and drive a person into an alternative trajectory, the one who experience it as well as others realise the validity and effect of this fundamental doctrine. Similarly, if participants receive a definite experience of God in their worship, that may transform their life. In other words, the spiritual elements that are experienced in one's life can make a definite change for the better. Christian faith speaks about the direct experience

---

[14] Douglas Jacobsen, *Thinking in the Spirit: Theologies of the Early Pentecostal Movement* (Bloomington, IN: Indiana University Press, 2003), xi.

[15] R. P. Spittler, "Pentecostal and Charismatic Spirituality", in *NIDPCM*, edited by Stanley M. Burgess (Grand Rapids, MI: Zondervan, 2002), 1096-97.

[16] Lesslie Newbigin, *Household of God*, quoted by Spittler, "Pentecostal and Charismatic Spirituality", 1097.

of God through Christ, however, unless experienced concretely, it may continue as a theoretical construct. Those who received such spiritual experiences acted differently than others and transformed people around them. The mystics of the Biblical stories sometimes claimed and acted what were unfathomable and indigestible to others, yet such spiritual experiences elevated them to higher levels of understanding of reality and practices which baffled others (for example, OT prophets and NT apostles).[17] Pentecostal spirituality enables people to experience God and be transformed and liberate others. Pentecostals acted differently and were being ridiculed by others for having the experience of the Baptism in the Holy Spirit, tongue speaking, prophecy, lively worship and neck breaking evangelism and mission. Their spirituality points towards a spirituality that is at par with mysticism of the earlier period of Christianity. Land writes, "Pentecostalism exists in continuity but differentiating discontinuity with other Christian spiritualities ... It is more Eastern than Western in its understanding of spirituality as perfection and participation in the divine life. In this regard, it has much to learn from persons like Gregory of Nyssa, Macarius the Egyptian and St. Symeon the New Theologian. It is both ascetic and mystical."[18]

The vitality of experiential spirituality, thus makes Pentecostal movement into a unique category among Christian denominations. Pentecostal movement, more precisely, Pentecostal spirituality opens a window to the biblical experiences - experience of God in Christ. People experience the divine presence overwhelmingly in the Pentecostal worship services; they speak in tongues, prophesy, experience divine healing and exorcisms. The lived experience of God felt by the early church is experienced right now. People feel happy, they vent out their hurt feelings, pain and suffering; they forget their troubles and move on with life. Alexander appropriately puts it, "People like to feel good. It's better than feeling bad. And Pentecostalism helps people feel good. Pentecostalism

---

[17] The lives of the prophets became signs and parables to the society. They acted the message in their personal lives and became *the* message. Isaiah was asked to go naked and barefoot for three years as a sign and a portent against Egypt and Ethiopia (20:3). Ezekiel was isolated from people and silenced for a long time and he had to lie down on his side 390 days bearing the punishment of the house of Israel. He had to cut down his daily provision of food and drink and to cook the bread on human dung. His loving wife had been taken from him within a period of twelve hours and even he was not allowed to mourn about her (24:15-18). To show the adulterous life of Israel, prophet Hosea had to marry a certain Gomer, a promiscuous woman. The children born were out of illicit relation of Gomer. He was labelled as "a fool" and "a crazy fellow" (9:7), surely alluding to his marriage relation with Gomer.

Similarly, Paul records his own mystical experience: "...I will go on to visions and revelations from the Lord. I know a man in Christ who fourteen years ago was caught up to the third heaven. Whether it was in the body or out of the body I do not know—God knows.. was caught up to paradise and heard inexpressible things, things that no one is permitted to tell" (2 Cor. 12:1-3).

[18] Steven J. Land, *Pentecostal Spirituality: A Passion for the Kingdom* (Sheffield: Sheffield Academic Press, 1993), 30.

'gives voice to feelings — the pain, the joy, the hope for new life.'"[19] Cox claims that people have had the emotion squeezed out of them by modernity's demand for rationality and that we're looking for a way to be whole again; Pentecostalism is an answer to this problem...the Pentecostal spirituality of hope and joy can "enhance an individual's sense of belonging to a community, meet felt needs and bring a greater awareness of and love for both God and one's neighbour". Pentecostalism is appealing because you can actually "feel the love."[20] Having conducted a research among third world Pentecostals, Miller and Yamamori observed that the same joy and love present among Pentecostals impel them to involve in social ministries; they comment:

> The work of doing social ministry is not easy; it requires ministering to people who are often sick, despairing, and living on the margins of society. If one is going to assist these individuals, then one needs hope. And, equally important, one needs to transmit this hope to others with a spirit of joy. Otherwise the task becomes dreary and, for many, unsustainable... they are filled with new hope and desire for a better world. The challenge is to channel these emotions, these feelings, these desires...Christians we have seen a unique quality in many of the people we encountered during our research, which was a residual spirit of joy.[21]

Emotional freedom, hopefulness, and joy seem to be as significant as any other factors in explaining why Pentecostalism is such a fast growing faith. As Alexander puts it, "Pentecostals see themselves as people of the Spirit, and as the song says, "Where the Spirit of the Lord is, there is freedom". Freedom to weep, freedom to dance, freedom to celebrate, and freedom to hope for and experience a better life. No wonder it's contagious."[22] Anderson explains the effects of Pentecostal experience of the divine:

> The emphasis on a personal, heart-felt experience of God through the Spirit is offered to all people without preconditions, enabling them to be "powerful" and assertive in societies where they have been marginalized. They are offered solutions to their felt needs in all their varieties. This will continue to draw people in the majority world to Pentecostal churches. When yours is an all-encompassing,

---

[19] Paul Alexander, *Signs & Wonders: Why Pentecostalism is the World's Fastest Growing Faith* (San Francisco: Jossey Bass, 2009), 146; Alexander quotes Brian McLaren who speaks about Pentecostals in Africa, "Pentecostal joy is itself a revolutionary manifestation of the kingdom of God in the land of HIV, Idi Amin, civil war, genocide, and breathtaking poverty"; Brian McLaren, "Reflections on Amahoro - Africa, May 2007"; http://www. brianmclaren.net.

[20] Alexander, *Signs & Wonders*, 147.

[21] Miller & Yamamori, *Global Pentecostalism*, 221.

[22] Alexander, *Signs & Wonders*, 148-149.

> omnipotent, and personal God who enters into a personal relationship with individual believers, everything becomes a matter for potential prayer. The "born-again" experience focusing on a radical break with the past attracts young people disenchanted with the ways of their parents.[23]

This unique character of Pentecostal movement make it the fastest growing religious movement on the globe. The statistics presented by *The World Christian Encyclopaedia* and other research agencies reveal extensive growth worldwide.[24] It is also an interesting fact that Pentecostalism is growing fast among the third world nations, in Asia, Africa and south American continents. What is unique about the growth of the movement is, it is more acceptable among the poor, disenfranchised and the ordinary people. In India, Pentecostal growth is predominantly taking place among the poorest of the poor - among Dalits and Tribals in interior villages and among slum dwellers and lower class people in the metropolitan cities. The middle class and the wealthy also join the movement as it helps them to relieve the tensions of postmodern life. Moreover, young people are more attracted to the Pentecostal and Charismatic churches where exuberant worship, heart-touching messages and lively fellowship make a better effect on their lifestyle. Miller and Yamamori comments,

> Pentecostalism often attracts people who are suffering from what sociologists refer to as anomie. In large urban metropolitan areas the picture is quite different, with loneliness and normlessness being real problems. Employment is often unstable; housing is precarious; and vices, such as gambling, prostitution, drugs, and alcohol, are typically rampant. Within this context, the attraction of Pentecostalism is obvious: it brings order, stability, and hope to people who are living precarious lives. To their credit, Pentecostal churches often function like surrogate extended families.[25]

It has been also consistently demonstrated that more and more women are attracted to Pentecostal churches. While discussing the Pentecostal growth in tribal areas of the state of Rajasthan in North India, Sarbeswar Sahoo, a sociology

---

[23] Allan Anderson, *To the Ends of the Earth: Pentecostalism and the Transformation of World Christianity,* https://erenow.net/common/to-the-ends-of-the-earth/11.php.

[24] According to the *World Christian Encyclopedia,* Pentecostals/Charismatics growth is projected for A.D. 2025 is around 811 millions. David B. Barrett, George T. Kurian, and Todd M. Johnson, *World Christian Encyclopedia,* 2nd edition (New York: Oxford University Press, 2001), 19. Similarly, a *Pew Forum* study of contemporary Pentecostal and charismatic Christianity observed that Pentecostal and charismatic types of spirituality are renewing existing churches and charting new frontiers; see www.pewforum.org/Christian/Evangelical-Protestant-Churches/Spirit-and-Power.aspx.

[25] Miller & Yamamori, *Global Pentecostalism,* 34.

teacher at Indian Institute of Technology, Delhi (IIT), shows that tribal women have experienced liberative changes in their lives. He speaks about their conversion experience, experience of miraculous healings and transformative changes in socio-economic wellbeing. He summarises his findings:

> Interviews with *adivasi* women testify that they have experienced great transformations in their lives during the post-conversion period. Their marital and family lives have significantly improved and miracle healing (*chamatkar*) has brought both physical cure and mental peace. Conversion to Pentecostalism resulted in a substantial decline in male abuse and alcohol addiction and its ensuing miseries like domestic violence and poverty. In the post-conversion period the husband's role in the family has been positively strengthened and relationship between husband and wife has broadly shifted from suspicion and abuse towards trust, care and respect. Not just in the domestic sphere but also in the public sphere, particularly in the church, women are treated with dignity and are encouraged to lead prayer meetings...[26]

This phenomenon points to a pertinent fact; the most oppressed section of the population, women find Pentecostal movement as a liberating movement. This was true from the inception of the movement. The experience of the baptism of the Holy Spirit and the power received from it unleashed a mission which was also included social ministries to rescue many from their dismal situations. Archer elucidates that the ministry of early Pentecostals, even though most were not directly engaging in social action, brought transformation to the poor and destitute as well as hope to the lower income working class. "We see clear examples of Pentecostal communities' proclaiming the Full Gospel without separating the spiritual from the social or using social ministry as a means to spiritual ministry. ...The vitality of Pentecostalism is its robust spirituality of transformation for those in the margins."[27] Moreover, the effects of Pentecostal spirituality and the conscious efforts of today's Pentecostals around the world has been enacted far-reaching changes among the poor. According to Miller and Yamamori, there is substantial evidence for the "social uplift" associated with Pentecostalism, in that Pentecostals have a competitive economic advantage over their neighbours because of their moral proscriptions against alcohol, drugs, gambling, and womanizing. Without these social evils, believers may produce surplus capital that can then be invested in business enterprises or in the education and welfare of their families. In addition, Pentecostal youths are encouraged to delay their sexual debut, potentially contributing to higher levels of education, especially among young

---

[26] Sarbeswar Sahoo, *Pentecostalism and Politics of Conversion in India* (New Delhi: Cambridge University Press, 2018), 19.

[27] Kenneth J. Archer, *The Gospel Revisited: Towards a Pentecostal Theology of Worship and Witness* (Eugene, OR: Pickwick Publications, 2011), 254.

women. Furthermore, the social networks associated with Pentecostalism create a supportive community that contributes to the social welfare of members.[28] The Pentecostals who intentionally involve in social welfare activities are called "progressive Pentecostals" by Miller and Yamamori. According to them, typically, large churches have cell groups where members are surrounded by people who care for them and their families. Within these churches, it is also possible to have a social role, an identity, as someone who is valued and needed. And some Pentecostal churches, especially large ones, have formal programs to assist people in need. When one is a member of a cohesive church community, the problem of anomie is thus at least partially ameliorated.[29]

Further, there are many social ministries run by progressive Pentecostals as "some of the most innovative social programs in the world."[30] Pentecostals, appear to be particularly effective and powerful when seeking to engage politics from the bottom up, in the developing world especially, given the widespread failure of politics there, Pentecostalism offers a capsule of hope and mobility. This capsule is sustained by moral reform, hard work, opportunity for participation and mutual support, in an alliance with a belief in a providence that will bring salvation here and now as well as hereafter.[31] It is obvious that, on the one hand, Pentecostal movement emphasises on experience of God and on the other, liberate the poor and downtrodden and stand as a liberative movement. Now, certain significant questions need to be asked in relation to its liberative potentials. Why are people attracted to Pentecostalism and how do their lives transform? What are the factors that make Pentecostalism a liberative movement? These questions need to be answered looking at the transformations happening in the lives of the people who joined the Pentecostal movement.

The primary reason for the liberative power of the movement is its unique spirituality. As we have seen, as a religious movement Pentecostalism focus more on spirituality than doctrines, structures or administration. A close observation would clearly reveal that it is the spiritual constituents of Pentecostal spirituality that bring liberation and transformation to the people. Major constituents of Pentecostal spirituality such as the full gospel, the baptism in the Holy Spirit, healing and exorcism, worship, mission and so on effect the transformation. My own research in Indian context to understand the Christology of Pentecostals showed that it is these constituents of Pentecostal spirituality that are effecting

---

[28] Miller & Yamamori, *Global Pentecostalism*, 44.

[29] Miller & Yamamori, *Global Pentecostalism*, 34.

[30] Miller & Yamamori, *Global Pentecostalism*, 17.

[31] Calvin L. Smith, "The Politics and Economics of Pentecostalism: A Global Survey" in *The Cambridge Companion to Pentecostalism*, edited by Cecil M. Robeck, Jr & Amos Yong (New York: Cambridge University Press, 2014), 200.

liberative changes among the people.[32] A person who joins a Pentecostal church undergoes considerable changes through these elements. For instance, a person hears the message of the full gospel - Jesus as saviour, healer, sanctifier, Spirit baptiser and the coming king - some way or the other affected spiritually, mentally and physically. One may receive Jesus as saviour, breaking with the past life, change one's life radically, establish a new vista in life, in the family and surrounding. It is demonstrated that the conversion experience enacts inner transformation of the person which is also the key to social transformation. This is why conversion and incorporation into the community of faith cannot be seen apart from the transformation of society. That is, "the rebirth of a person by the Spirit is the anticipation of the transformation of the cosmos" (cf. 2 Cor 5:17; Rom 8:21).[33]

A person who experiences the baptism of the Spirit, receives 'the power from on high', becomes a transformed person and a new perception of reality dawns upon him. A person filled by the Spirit of God is impelled by that same Spirit to cooperate with God in the work of evangelism and social action in the anticipation of the new creation.[34] A person who receive miraculous healing is not only physically transformed but a new direction is created in his life and his surroundings. It has been emerged that when people are healed of their sickness and delivered from evil powers, their life standard has been improved significantly. They feel empowered and ready to face forces of society which stand against them.[35] Similarly, when someone is delivered of evil spirits, it is not mere deliverance but complete *shalom* prevails in individual and family life, leaving behind the spiritual world once they dreaded. Instead of the fear of the spirits, now the person enjoys the close proximity of the presence of Jesus and of the Holy Spirit, that bring joy and wellbeing. This assurance of permanent safety and fearlessness permeate the spiritual and physical realms, ultimately bring liberation and transformation. The awareness that a believer has power and authority over demonic forces impel the person to rescue others of the same predicament, thus becoming an agent of liberation.

In Asian context, especially in India, most of the occasions people are attracted to Christianity not due to the sense of sin or guilt but the struggles such as sickness, evil spirit infestation or the evil effect of certain cultural practice.[36]

---

[32] Shaibu Abraham, *Pentecostal Christology: Empirical Approach in Indian Context* (New Delhi: Christian World Imprints, 2019), 85-127.

[33] No Author, "Evangelization, Proselytism and Common Witness: The Report from the Fourth Phase of the International Dialogue 1990-1997 between the Roman Catholic Church and Some Classical Pentecostal Churches and Leaders", *AJPS* 2/1 (January 1999): 105-151.

[34] Veli-Matti Kärkkäinen, "Spirituality as a Resource for Social Justice: Reflections from the Catholic-Pentecostal Dialogue", *AJPS* 6/1 (2003): 85.

[35] Abraham, *Pentecostal Christology*, 92-93.

[36] Stanley M. Burgess & Gary B. McGee, "Signs and Wonders", in *NIDPCM,* edited by Stanley M. Burgess (Michigan: Zondervan, 2002), 1068.

Here these elements of Pentecostal spirituality come into play for attracting the masses to Pentecostalism and liberating them. The attention to spiritual gifts and power encounters with evil forces have proven to be greatly helped in alleviating the suffering of the ordinary people. According to Burgess, this dimension has contributed to the gradual 'Pentecostalisation' of much of the Third-World Christianity in worship and ministry.[37] Miracles are not mere events that bring recovery of one's health or simply a desirable change of circumstances, rather they are the signs of divine intervention in the ordinary realm. Moreover, supernatural elements are considered as the gifts of the Spirit operating through the members for the benefits of larger society.[38] The *charismata* equip believers to move beyond their ability in this world of spiritual as well as physical bondages, rescuing people through healing their body and mind and bringing them to the kingdom of God. Therefore, these gifts can be essentially considered as means of liberation.[39] They are also widely used for church growth.[40] It is believed that power encounter as opportunities to demonstrate the might of God through dramatic healings, casting out demons and divine protection, and when people see God's miraculous interventions, they believe.

In Asian context, however, the missionary message and practice brought the western worldview, causing a clash with the non-western worldview of the mission fields. According to Wonsuk Ma, this often resulted in 'split-level Christianity' or a syncretistic one. In contrast, when Christ is preached through the power of the Spirit in non-western worldview, it easily opens the minds of people and raises an expectation for God's miraculous work.[41] Ma explains it,

> Healing or the supernatural work of God causes a 'wow' effect in the mind, and it causes a 'crack' in their tight worldview reinforced by community life in a tribal setting. A tangible experience of the power of God brings changes in numerous areas of personal, family and even community life. Such a healing or miracle plays a decisive role in a mass conversion or people's movement.[42]

Similarly, the Spirit experience in the Pentecostal worship may impart a new insight about the presence and power of God. Pentecostal preaching, the

---

[37] Burgess & McGee, "Signs and Wonders", 1068.

[38] Young-Gi Hong, "Church and Mission: A Pentecostal Perspective", *IRM* XC/358 (July, 2001): 300.

[39] Shaibu Abraham, *Pentecostal Theology of Liberation: Holy Spirit and Holiness in the Society* (New Delhi: Christian World Imprints, 2014), 37-39.

[40] C. Peter Wagner, *Your Spiritual Gifts Can Help Your Church Grow* (California: Gospel Light, 2001).

[41] Wonsuk Ma, "Full Circle Mission: A Possibility of Pentecostal Missiology", *AJPS* 8/1 (2005): 20.

[42] Ma, "Full Circle Mission", 20-21.

powerful communication of biblical stories can change the lives of the people for better. Evangelism and mission carried out in the power of the Spirit bring transformation and liberation. The ordinary members are empowered to venture into the unknown and the Spirit gives them power to proclaim the message; the community becomes a channel of liberation in the society, even though the members face struggles.[43] They form an alternative community in the midst of a hostile and oppressive culture.

Even though, the same experiential nature of spirituality is cherished and advocated today, it seems that the places where Pentecostalism is a century old, these constituents of Pentecostal spirituality have been considerably declined. The structure and form of the church take precedence in many of the Older Pentecostal denominations than the lived experience of God. Emphasis placed on the spirituality in the early period of the movement is not fully seen today. For instance, the early Pentecostals were known for their holiness lifestyle. Pentecostals' long cherished idea of holiness that emphasized integrity in intentions and actions has been turned out to be more on outward appearances and dress codes. Personal and communal holiness that infused through the work of the Spirit and the power that bestowed by the baptism of the Holy Spirit are being diminished considerably. In today's Pentecostal churches both in leadership and among laity, elements lacking personal integrity and moral uprightness are increasing. Many of the practices which were considered to be unholy earlier, slowly creeping back into the movement. The fraternal feeling and egalitarian attitudes are replaced with superiority and caste feeling. In Pentecostal denominational settings, hierarchy is the norm now. Hierarchy in the leadership and struggle for positions in the denominational structures supersede the power of the Spirit which was considered indispensable. Clashes for leadership and struggle for supremacy result in court cases and even physical violence. Pentecostals sacrificed their long cherished holiness ideals on the altar of selfish interests and worldliness.[44] Even though, similar impious elements and leadership struggles were part of the early Pentecostalism, a strong emphasis on spirituality had somehow overcome those tendencies. However, in the contemporary setting, Pentecostal spirituality is not in full play as of early period and therefore, human elements are on the rise. Moreover, the growth potential that the early Pentecostalism had shown is not visible. Although, Pentecostal mission is rapidly growing in newer mission fields, growth in the older places are plateaued. For instance, Margaret Poloma's research on the Assemblies of God (*The Assemblies of God at the Crossroads*, 1989)

---

[43] Samuel Solivan, *The Spirit, Pathos and Liberation: Toward an Hispanic Pentecostal Theology* (Sheffield: Sheffield Academic, 1998).

[44] Nonetheless, still there are lot of people holding the original spiritual fervour, personal holiness and integrity of life in the Pentecostal movement. I believe that their presence in the movement keeps the movement going forward and not allowing to fall into the fate of some of other denominations that were also begun by reformation and revivals.

shows that how charismatic experiences such as speaking in tongues, healing, and prophecy are related to the growth of the Assemblies of God. However, the success of the denomination and its move toward a more stable, bureaucratic, and hierarchical organization contribute to specific tensions, inconsistencies between beliefs and practices. Moreover, its accommodation to the larger culture, support of conservative politics, ambivalence toward women in ministry, and a fear of the experiences that contributed to its growth, some way or the other, retarded its growth and renewal. Poloma was pessimistic about its future as the denomination became more focused on the qualities of rationalization over charisma. Later, however, in a second book, Poloma finds some hope for the denomination, especially among those congregations who are experiencing new waves of divine love with the result of a renewed commitment to engaging the community in some benevolent way.[45] It is obvious that the future of Pentecostal movement is largely depend on its spirituality.

Therefore, in the following pages, we shall explore some of the significant elements of Pentecostal spirituality to unravel and understand their liberative power among the masses and to regain the original health of the movement. They are namely, the Full Gospel, holiness, the baptism of the Holy Spirit, spiritual gifts, evangelism and mission, worship, preaching and testimony, and eschatology. In the following eight chapters, we shall briefly explore these elements, to fully understand how do they propel the movement into a global force and liberate and transform people from various cultures, languages, religions, castes, class, and tribes. Each constituent part is explained with its origin and development; besides, a biblical and theological account of its validity is presented in order to demonstrate its liberative power. At the end of each chapter, a few suggestions are proposed to recapture the original spiritual fervour of the spirituality.

The readers may approach the chapters in any order since each chapter is self contained and explained independently; however, reading in the sequential order may make better sense. This work is an effort to introduce Pentecostal spirituality to wider audience who do not have a deeper knowledge about Pentecostal movement and its spirituality. This is also meant for new generations of Pentecostals as well as for outsiders to give a glimpse of the liberative power of Pentecostal movement's spirituality and its relevance in the twenty first century where oppression of the poor and their suffering are not heard with a compassionate hearing. This is presented in a simple and readable language, avoiding all theological jargons, so that it can be read and understood by ordinary believers, those who are interested in Christian spirituality and anyone having concern for the poor and suffering populace. At the same time, the topics are dealt

---

[45] Michael Wilkinson, "Sociological Narratives and the Sociology of Pentecostalism", in *The Cambridge Companion to Pentecostalism*, edited by Cecil M. Robeck, Jr & Amos Yong (New York: Cambridge University Press, 2014), 236-237.

with systematic and scholarly manner and therefore can be useful for theological students and Pentecostal scholars for further research. I am aware of the fact that a lot have been written about Pentecostal spirituality but my intention is to present Pentecostal spirituality as *a paradigm of liberation* in the third world situations. One more word is warranted; let me confess that I am a Pentecostal by faith and with sympathy I have treated the topics to present them to the wider audiences. Simultaneously, I have tried to highlight some of the negative tendencies crept into the Pentecostal spirituality so as to bring a balance to the discussions. Here it is expected that readers will find it beneficial academically and spirituality to capture the original spirituality of Pentecostal movement.

Chapter 2

The Full Gospel Message of Liberation

The Full Gospel or Fourfold Gospel, which portrays Jesus Christ as the saviour, healer, Spirit baptizer and the soon coming king, is one of the most significant elements of Pentecostal spirituality that steered the Pentecostal movement forward in its growth, consolidation and mission. This is also sometimes known as the "Fivefold Gospel" adding one more element, Jesus as the sanctifier. All over the world the classical Pentecostals use this Christological notion in their worship services, especially in sermons and in evangelistic endeavours such as open-air meetings and outreaches. For Pentecostals, Pentecost is the core theological symbol of Pentecostal theology, and its theological narrative is the Full Gospel.[1] The full Gospel is the fourfold (fivefold) devotion to Jesus Christ and the Pentecostal movement developed this doctrine from the background of the Holiness movement and various evangelical revival strands of the nineteenth century.[2] Later, Pentecostal leaders adopted this doctrine and used it effectively

[1] Wolfgang Vondey, Pentecostal Theology: Living the Full Gospel (London: Bloomsbury T&T Clark, 2017), 6.

[2] Donald W. Dayton, *Theological Roots of Pentecostalism* (London: Scarecrow Press, 1987), 19. The 'statement of truth' of the Pentecostal Fellowship of North America (PFNA) calls it full Gospel and draws attention to 'healing for the body' as well as 'holiness' and baptism in the Spirit. For detailed description, see Dayton, *The Theological Roots,* 15-28; Donald Dayton, "The Rise of the Evangelical Healing Movement in Nineteenth Century America", *Pneuma* 4/1 (1982): 1-18; Also see Melvin E. Dieter, "Wesleyan Holiness Aspects of Pentecostal Origins", in *Aspects of Pentecostal-Charismatic Origins,* edited by Vinson Synan (New Jersey: Logos International, 1975), 67-69; A.B. Simpson, *The Fourfold Gospel: Jesus as Saviour, Sanctifier, Healer and Coming King* (Orlando, FL: Bridge-Logos, 2007); C. Nienkirchen, "Simpson, Albert Benjamin", in *NIDPCM,* edited by Stanley M. Burgess (Michigan: Zondervan, 2002), 1069-70.

in Pentecostal evangelistic campaigns.[3] Allan Anderson explains it, "The Full Gospel as it came to be known in Pentecostalism, included a message of a personal, experiential, and exclusive salvation from sin through a "born-again" or conversion experience; an instant, distinctive experience of holiness following conversion known as sanctification; the practice of healing the physically sick through prayer and laying on of hands; the baptism in the Spirit empowering for witnessing including speaking in tongues; and a sense of the imminent, pre-millennial return of Christ. Fundamental to all activities was the conviction that this "full gospel" had to be preached.[4]

From the beginning of Pentecostal movement this message has been considered as a fundamental doctrinal position and its core spirituality. Besides, throughout its spread worldwide, the full gospel acted as the Christology of the movement. The spirituality of the full gospel- salvation, healing and baptism of the Holy Spirit through Jesus Christ- not only unleashed spiritual deliverance to the masses but also brought social and economic liberation for many. This message propelled Pentecostalism into a libreative force that transformed the lives of millions of poor and downtrodden in the Third World nations. Therefore, it is significant to explore its origin, liberative potentials, the theological and Christological imports to appreciate its worth and effect to bring a new lease of life to the century old movement, which we will do in the following pages.

The Origin of the Full Gospel

The Full Gospel or Fourfold Gospel that the Pentecostal movement adhere to, had been acquired from the revival stream of nineteenth century Protestantism in the United States. This revival is also the precursor to the origin of the Pentecostal movement. In the early part of the 19th century, the United States experienced a tremendous surge of religious fervour among Protestants, as revivals became popular in various parts of the country. The revival movement began at the beginning of nineteenth century and by 1820, membership rose rapidly among the Baptist and Methodist congregations. By 1840, the revival peaked out. However, later in 1850's vibrant leaders like Charles Finney and others emerged with more reforms in churches. Charles Finney became the leading figure in the revival movement and a pioneer of the formation of the doctrine of the Baptism of the Holy Spirit, which became the cornerstone of the Pentecostal movement and

---

[3] Raymond L. Cox, *The Four-Square Gospel* (Los Angeles: Foursquare Publications, 1969), 9. For example, Aimee Semple McPherson, founder of the International Church of the Foursquare Gospel summarises it in characteristic Pentecostal style: Jesus saves us according to John 3:16. He baptises us with the Holy Spirit according to Acts 2:4. He heals our bodies according to James 5:14-15. And Jesus is coming again to receive us unto himself according to 1 Thess. 4:16-17.

[4] Allan Anderson, *To the Ends of the Earth: Pentecostalism and the Transformation of World Christianity*, https://erenow.net/common/to-the-ends-of-the-earth/ (accessed on 30/07/19).

its theology.[5] Finney's preaching had a great impact among the ordinary people where he emphasised Christ's redemptive sacrifice for the removal of sin and guilt of humanity. Further, he reiterated that by accepting Christ as saviour one can achieve holiness in one's personal life and that is termed as baptism in the Holy Spirit.[6] There were other prominent leaders and authors such as R. A. Torrey, A. J. Gordon, D. L. Moody, Adoniram Judson, and Andrew Murray. Their powerful ministry among the ordinary people and writings resulted in the formation of the Holiness Movement which became the immediate predecessor to the Pentecostal movement. These leaders' emphasis on the redemptive work of Christ in removing the sins and bestowing sanctification, created an atmosphere in the formation and establishment of doctrine of the Full Gospel.[7] Moreover, they also underlined the need of Christians to engage in social ministry to improve the world around them in consonance with their faith. Following this call, many were involved in active social activities such as anti-slavery, temperance, moral and prison reform and aid to the poor.[8]

However, it was Albert Benjamin Simpson, founder of the Christian and Missionary Alliance, who coined and popularised the doctrine of the Fourfold Gospel. Simpson's Fourfold Gospel heralded that it is Christ who is the saviour, sanctifier, healer, and coming king. Raised as a strict Scottish Presbyterian in Canada, Simpson was attracted as a teenager to Puritan devotional writings. He incorporated holiness ideas into his Reformed faith and was filled with the Holy Spirit, which became a turning point in his ministry. Later he was re-baptized by immersion and experienced faith-healing of his chronic heart disease.[9] Having personally experienced the baptism of the Holy Spirit and miraculous physical

---

[5] Although, A. B. Simpson is known for the formation of the Fourfold Gospel, according to Bernie Van De Walle, it was not only Simpson but also the ministry of other leaders contributed to the formation of this Christology. Bernie Van De Walle, "A. B. Simpson's Fourfold Gospel: Both Product and Critique of Late Nineteenth-Century Evangelical Theology"; https://www.academia.edu/33060050/A._B._Simpson_s_Fourfold_Gospel_Both_Product_and_Critique_of_Late_Nineteenth-Century_Evangelical_Theology (accessed on 5/7/19).

[6] Roland Wessels, "The Spirit Baptism, Nineteenth Century Roots", *Pneuma* 14/2 (Fall, 1992): 127-157.

[7] "The fourfold Gospel, rather than belonging solely to the Christian and Missionary Alliance, was instead the practical experience and commonly-held experience and theology of late nineteenth-century evangelicalism in general. Rather than being the peculiar theology of A. B. Simpson, the fourfold Gospel was, to a greater or lesser degree, also the spiritual biography and theology of the leading lights of late nineteenth-century American evangelicalism including such luminaries as D. L. Moody, Adoniram Judson, and Andrew Murray"; See, Van De Walle, "A. B. Simpson's Fourfold Gospel".

[8] Donald W. Dayton, "Christian Perfection to the Baptism of the Holy Ghost", in *Aspects of Pentecostal Charismatic Origins*, edited by Vinson Synan (New Jersey: Logos, 1975), 46-47.

[9] http://www.cmalliance.org/about/history/simpson (accessed on 5/7/19).

healing, Simpson popularised the foundation of the doctrine of the Fourfold Gospel.[10]

As we glance into his life and ministry, we can unmistakably see the development of the Fourfold Gospel and its liberative potentials. At the age of 30, Simpson left Canada to pastor a Presbyterian Church in Kentucky, and later a Church in New York City of the same denomination. He was earnest in ministering to the large number of immigrants pouring into the city, nonetheless, met with great opposition from the leadership of his church. Simpson's heart was broken and eventually resigned his prestigious pastorate and set out to establish the Gospel Tabernacle, a church in the heart of the city, where all—the poor, homeless, sick, and displaced—would be welcome. Simpson's ministry to New York's immigrants caused him to have a great burden for the poor and a thirst for the unreached masses throughout the world.[11] He held evangelistic meetings, ran several rescue missions, preached at the jails, had meetings for sailors, opened an orphanage and a home for unwed mothers, provided a dispensary for the poor, and started the Missionary Training School.[12] Moreover, his personal healing experience from a chronic illness wrought a deep-rooted faith in Jesus Christ as the healer and generated a passion for divine healing services. Thus, his life, spiritual experience and ministry largely contributed to the popularisation of the Fourfold Gospel and that in turn became a tool of liberation.

As we closely investigate into the elements of the Fourfold Gospel, it is obvious that he was thoroughly and deeply Christo-centric and his Christology was highly experiential and also thoroughly biblical. Not only that, its presentation was down to earth and appealing to the common people. Coupled with his holiness mooring and the power received through the baptism of the Holy Spirit, the Fourfold Gospel turned out to be a potent weapon that liberated ordinary people not only of their sinful condition but also of their wretched situation in that era. His exposition of the elements of the Fourfold

---

[10] The formulation of Simpson's Fourfold Gospel of Jesus as Saviour, Sanctifier, Healer, and Coming King mirrored the life, faith and experiences of his spiritual journey. Simpson experienced Jesus as Saviour as a result of his Reformed and Puritan roots, coupled with the reading of Walter Marshall's Gospel Mystery of Salvation (1692) in 1858. In 1865 he was ordained and then served prestigious churches in Hamilton, Ontario, and Louisville, Kentucky. In 1873, at the age of 30, Simpson left Canada to pastor the Chestnut Street Presbyterian Church in Louisville, Kentucky, and later the Thirteenth Street Presbyterian Church in New York City. He then began his involvement with the "sanctified, Spirit-filled, higher and deeper" life in 1874 upon reading William E. Boardman's the Higher Christian Life (1858). Next in 1881, Simpson continued his spiritual journey by being "miraculously" healed of a chronic heart disorder during a vacation at Old Orchard Beach, Maine. He was subsequently baptized by immersion in February 1882 in a Baptist Church in New York City. Then, he organized and opened an interdenominational Gospel Tabernacle Church in New York. http://www.cmalliance.org/about/history/simpson.

[11] http://www.cmalliance.org/about/history/simpson.

[12] https://healingandrevival.com/BioABSimpson.htm (accessed on 5/7/19).

Gospel present ample evidences of the persuasive power of this Christology. Simpson elaborates the salvation receives through Christ in his book,

> Salvation delivers us from Satan's power and kingdom. God hath "delivered us from the power of darkness and translated us into the kingdom of His dear Son". Salvation delivers us from much sorrow and distress in life. It brings a glorious sunlight into the life and drives away those clouds of depression and gloom which overwhelm us. Salvation comes to us by the righteousness of Jesus Christ. He perfectly fulfilled for us every requirement of the law...Every moment He held steadfastly in the path of obedience, and His perfect grace and obedience are the price of your salvation. Salvation comes to us through the death of Christ. His obedience is not enough. He must die. His crucifixion is the atonement for our sins. Salvation comes through the resurrection of Jesus Christ from the dead, which was God's seal of His accomplished work and the pledge of our pardon. Salvation comes through the intercession of Jesus at the right hand of the Father. He is our Great High Priest there, where He ever liveth to make intercession for us, and thus keeps us in continual acceptance.[13]

Similarly, Simpson also greatly emphasised the divine healing comes through Christ. It is obvious that the divine healing he experienced significantly contributed to the notion of Jesus as the healer. The belief that Jesus as saviour was universally accepted by all the denominations of that time, nevertheless, a firm faith and practical application of Jesus as the healer was considered to be out of mode. Yet, Simpson very strongly asserted that divine healing is also a part of the redemptive work of Christ and can be accessed today:

> Divine healing is part of the redemption work of Jesus Christ. It is one of the things He came to bring. Its foundation stone is the cross of Calvary. "He redeemeth thy life from destruction". Surely that healing comes from Himself alone. "By His stripes we are healed". That is the redemption work of Christ. You have a right to it, beloved, for His body bore all the liability of your body on the cross. Take it and love Him better, because it came from His stripes. I love to think of that word as being in the singular number, stripe. That is the Greek meaning. His body was so beaten that it was all one stripe. There was not an inch of His flesh but was lacerated for us....Jesus is our healer because He has bought healing for us with His stripes. It is a part of His purchased redemption on Calvary. "Surely, He hath borne our sicknesses and carried our pains."[14]

---

[13] Simpson, *The Fourfold Gospel.*

[14] Simpson, *The Fourfold Gospel.*

For Simpson, Christ not only enacts our salvation but Christ is our salvation. Regeneration is nothing but the vitality of the indwelling Christ himself overflowing to the believer. It is not that Christ brings along with him something called vitality but he himself is vitality. The same hold true for other aspects of the fourfold Gospel. Simpson insisted on the person of Christ. The Fourfold Gospel proclaimed that the indwelling Christ himself regenerates and sanctifies and we should long for him. Simpson reminded the late nineteenth century Evangelicalism that the proper subject of longing and sole provision for Christian life is nothing other and nothing less than Christ himself.[15]

However, it needs to be noted that the Fourfold Gospel was not a systematic Christology encompassing all the aspects of person and work of Christ. Rather it was a popular Christology that penetrated into the hearts and minds of the masses and persuaded them to receive the benefits wrought by Christ. Bernie Van De Walle calls it a "contextually located pastoral Soteriology" than a full-blown systematic Christology and delineates the point,

> Fourfold Gospel is an inadequate Christology. There are various ways in which person of Christ is so much more than just saviour, sanctifier, healer and coming king. It was not intended as a full-blown systematic Christology. Rather than a systematic Christology, the Fourfold Gospel is, instead a contextually located pastoral Soteriology. The fourfold Gospel does not enumerate and investigate all of the various aspects of Jesus Christ. Instead, the fourfold Gospel identifies how he is the all-sufficient provision for the complexity of human need.[16]

Nevertheless, Simpson is considered as a proto-Pentecostal and the Fourfold Gospel became the Pentecostal Christology of early Pentecostals in the beginning of the next century. Besides, many of the adherents of the Christian Missionary Alliance too joined the Pentecostalism. Charles Nienkirchen underlines this fact and explains that many of the early Pentecostals were from the Christian Missionary Alliance and of course, naturally the Full Gospel formed the basic theological mooring, in particular a handy Christology for the early Pentecostals that became a rallying point all over the world;

> The year 1906 was accounted as the year of the Azusa Street revivals which are considered by some as the beginning of modern Pentecostalism. The close personal and theological affinities between the Alliance and Pentecostalism made this a difficult period for the Alliance. Estimates are that as many as one-third of the Alliance

---

[15] Walle, "A. B. Simpson's Fourfold Gospel".

[16] Walle, "A. B. Simpson's Fourfold Gospel".

constituency, including many important churches and prominent leaders, joined Pentecostal movement in the decade following 1906.[17]

Obviously, the powerful outpouring of the Holy Spirit and the resultant enthusiasm for evangelism and mission was not bereft of a definite Christological message. The Fourfold Gospel turned out to be a potent Christological narrative with which gospel message is spread "at end of the earth", accompanied by healing, exorcism and other miraculous events. This in turn transformed the spiritual condition of millions of people in nations, languages and religious groups but also positively impacted the social and economic circumstances, especially in the Majority world.[18] Thus, the Fourfold Gospel turned out to be a message of spiritual liberation as well as an instrument of social and economic transformation for many. Having said this, we shall now delve into the essential theological significance and transformative potentials of this Christological message. Here we are going to concentrate on one of the elements, Jesus the saviour; other themes such as healer, baptiser of Spirit and so on, will be treated elsewhere.

The Full Gospel: A Popular Pentecostal Christology

The theme, Jesus as the only saviour and incomparable to others are the central tenet of Pentecostal movement. Although, Pentecostalism emphasises Spirit baptism and the gifts of the Spirit, all these important doctrines are thoroughly dependent on the bedrock of Christology which exalts Christ as the saviour, healer and coming king. These Christological notions Pentecostals intimately experience through the work of the Spirit in their personal and community lives. Consequently, they are eager to proclaim Jesus as saviour and have no qualms in presenting Jesus as unique. Such dissemination of the message of the full gospel transformed the life of the people. As already discussed, the Christological affirmation in the fourfold Gospel was wholeheartedly assimilated by the early Pentecostals and applied to their lives and mission.[19] The early Pentecostal journals and literature are full of these claims. *The Pentecostal Evangel* boldly asserts, "He had been made or ordained a Saviour...Christ was manifested to undo, to nullify,

---

[17] Charles Nienkirchen, *A. B. Simpson and the Pentecostal Movement* (Peabody, Mass: Hendrickson, 1992).

[18] Richard Shaull and Waldo Cesar, *Pentecostalism and the Future of the Christian Churches* (Michigan: W. B. Eerdmans, 2000); Donald E. Miller & Tetsunao Yamamori. *Global Pentecostalism: The New Face of Christian Social Engagement* (Berkeley: University of California Press, 2007); Shaibu Abraham, *Pentecostal Theology of Liberation: Holy Spirit and Holiness in the Society* (New Delhi: Christian World Imprints, 2014).

[19] Simpson, *The Four-Fold Gospel*, 31; They believed and practiced what Simpson said, "Christ is called the 'mighty to save', because no matter how weak or how wicked the sinner may be, He is able to save him to the uttermost' and 'Salvation comes by confessing Christ as the Saviour".

to destroy the works of the devil."[20] They were convinced about the efficacy of the blood of Christ in salvation, "No blood, no mercy. No blood, no protection."[21]

Early Pentecostals strongly emphasised the divinity of Jesus and affirmed Jesus as "the only true God". Again, *The Pentecostal Evangel* comments: "The General Council, with the Christian Alliance and all other real Evangelical Christians, believe strongly in the Deity of Jesus Christ."[22] Whenever there were any attacks against the deity of Christ from liberals, there was a reaction from the Pentecostals. Commenting on the liberal attitude of some denominational theologians, *The Pentecostal Evangel* quotes a liberal view against Jesus and reacts against it strongly: "They patronizingly speak of Him as a great man and a great teacher, and so forth. I have a clipping concerning a certain professor in a Baptist college in Missouri. This professor states, 'I do not subscribe to the deity of Jesus, nor to His vicarious death and intercessory work. I do not worship Christ or pray in His name, I do not believe that He is divine. I cannot accept the statements in the Bible concerning his pre-existence, and I do not believe that Christ is infallible or that He is a safe one to follow'. I suppose he prefers to follow his own gigantic mind. This statement from a man, who has been training the preachers of the coming generation, shows how things are going in the religious world."[23] Another article says, "But I desire to exalt my Jesus as a divine Christ...He was in the form of God, He was equal with God. He is God."[24] Moreover, they considered Jesus as the only way to salvation and proclaimed this conviction.[25] The name of Jesus is above every name and holds the power to overcome anything in the world,[26] because he has risen from the dead and dwells in us through the power of the Spirit.[27]

In addition, while the Pentecostal movement emerged in the scene, the western Christianity was under the onslaught of theological relativism and higher criticism. Nonetheless, this did not deter the early Pentecostals from the task of proclamation. It is interesting to observe that when the Western Protestantism and theology were reeling under the burden of liberalism, Pentecostalism was

---

[20] No Author, "Our Jesus", *The Pentecostal Evangel* 492 (14 April 1923): 1.

[21] No Author, "When I See the Blood I will Passover You", *The Pentecostal Evangel* 493 (21 April 1923): 1; No Author, "The Power of the Blood", *The Pentecostal Evangel* 495 (5 May 1923): 1.

[22] No Author, 'The Only True God', *The Pentecostal Evangel* 324-325 (24 January 1920): 6-7.

[23] No Author, "What Think ye of Christ", *The Pentecostal Evangel* 496 (12 May 1923): 6.

[24] W.T. Gaston, "What Think ye of Christ", *The Pentecostal Evangel* 496 (12 May 1923): 6.

[25] No Author, "The Only Way", *The Pentecostal Evangel* 499 (2 June 1923): 1; "There is one way only into this place of, safety, this house of defence, this strong habitation, this fortress of the redeemed: I am the Way, the Truth, and the Life, no man cometh unto the Father but by Me"; No Author, "He That Climbeth Up Some Other Way, the Same is a Thief and a Robber", *The Pentecostal Evangel* 402-403 (23 July 1921): 3.

[26] Smith Wigglesworth, "The Power of the Name", *The Pentecostal Evangel* 480-481 (20 January 1923): 2.

[27] Wigglesworth, "Our Risen Christ", *The Pentecostal Evangel* 490 (31 March 1923): 2.

steadily growing and embraced the theological position that Jesus is the saviour and the only true God. This is all the more true in the Third World situation where multi-religious settings stand against this confession and proclamation. The emergence of the concept of religious pluralism, or the idea of many ways for salvation, did not deter Pentecostals from professing Jesus to be the *only* Saviour.

The Full Gospel: A Functional Pentecostal Christology

One of the unique features of Pentecostalism is its insistence in applying the work of Christ in every aspect of believers' lives. What is read in the Bible has to be experienced in life, in their contextual circumstances. This leads Pentecostals to appropriate Jesus' actions in the Gospels literally. Jesus has healed many, so healing is available even today. Jesus has provided for the poor, so his ability to provide for believers is still anticipated and experienced. Archer explains:

> When Pentecostals read Scripture, they do so from within their cultural-contextual worldview. They read Scripture as the marginalised people of the latter rain. At the centre of the dramatic narrative is Jesus, the divine-human Messiah. Jesus is a mighty miracle worker empowered by the Holy Spirit.[28]

As of today, most of the Pentecostal theologians rightly emphasise that Pentecostalism is more Jesus-centred than Spirit-centred.[29] This is because Pentecostal proclamation revolves around the "Full Gospel" in which Jesus is proclaimed as saviour, (sanctifier), healer, Spirit-baptiser and the soon coming king.[30] A glance into the elements of the Full Gospel suggests that they are closely related to soteriological aspects and, hence, point toward a functional Christology. These elements have been intimately appropriated and proclaimed in everyday experiences of ordinary Pentecostals.

According to Dayton, the unique theology of Pentecostalism is neither tongue-speaking nor sanctification but the Full Gospel which provides a historical and theological pattern to analyse the movement.[31] The theological heart of Wesleyan Pentecostalism is the Full Gospel and as a result, Pentecostal theology should be structured around these central tenets. A theology based on the Full

---

[28] Kenneth J. Archer, *The Gospel Revisited: Towards a Pentecostal Theology of Worship and Witness* (Oregon: Pickwick Publications, 2011), 42.

[29] Keith Warrington, *Pentecostal Theology: A Theology of Encounter* (London: T&T Clark, 2008), 34.

[30] It is to be noted that different people use the terms 'fourfold' or 'fivefold' interchangeably but denote the same idea. See A. B. Simpson, *The Fourfold Gospel*; Dayton, *The Theological Roots,* 15-28.

[31] Dayton has shown that Pentecostalism borrowed a fourfold-devotion to Jesus Christ as Saviour, Spirit Baptizer, Healer, and Coming King from the Holiness movement and other evangelical strands. Dayton, *The Theological Roots,* 15-28; Dayton, "The Rise of the Evangelical Healing Movement", 1-18.

Gospel can reveal the ways in which Pentecostalism, as a movement, is both similar to and dissimilar from other movements within Christendom.[32] Similarly, Kärkkäinen argues that a valid Pentecostal theology is to focus on Jesus Christ as the centre of the Full Gospel and is a methodological gateway to a balanced theology.[33]

However, the unique Pentecostal contribution to this doctrine was the addition of a Pentecostal flavour and a new theological direction. Macchia rightly captures the essence: "What was unique was how these themes formed a "gestalt" of devotion in the Spirit to Jesus that reconfigured evangelical piety and gave Pentecostalism its Christological centre as well as its theological cogency and direction."[34] The provision of bodily healing through the atonement and by the gift of the Spirit became one of the main theological emphases of the Pentecostal movement. Dayton considers "the Divine Healing Movement" of the nineteenth century as one of the "theological roots of Pentecostalism."[35] Horton, in his *The Gifts of the Spirit,* says that divine healing is the only way of healing open to believers and authorised by the Scriptures.[36] Early Pentecostals were convinced of this aspect and practised the divine healing in the name of Jesus in their daily life including exorcism.[37] Here it is obvious that Christology and Pneumatology are interwoven in that, whatever Christ is, he is in the Spirit: Jesus Christ as the Saviour, healer and so on. And conversely, whatever the Spirit effects in the believer's life, be it salvation, healing or Spirit-baptism, it is the work of the Lord, Jesus Christ.[38] Consequently, the full gospel is a functional Christology focused on the work of Christ for the believers.

The Full Gospel: A Pentecostal Spirit Christology

It is alleged by non-Pentecostals that Pentecostalism emphasises the baptism of the Spirit, spiritual gifts and the other miraculous so much so that Christology

[32] John Christopher Thomas, "Pentecostal Theology in the Twenty-First Century: 1998 Presidential Address", *Pneuma* 20 (1998): 3-19, 17.

[33] Veli-Matti Kärkkäinen, "David's Sling: The Promise and Problem of Pentecostal Theology Today: A Response to D. Lyle Dabney", *Pneuma* 23 (2001): 147-152.

[34] F.D. Macchia, "Pentecostal Theology", in *NIDPCM,* edited by Stanley M. Burgess (Michigan: Zondervan, 2002), 1123-1124.

[35] For detailed descriptions see Dayton, *The Theological Roots*, 115-141; Kimberly Ervin Alexander, *Pentecostal Healing: Models in Theology and Practice* (Dorset, UK: Deo Publishing, 2006), 8-63.

[36] Allan Anderson, *An Introduction to Pentecostalism* (Cambridge: Cambridge University Press, 2004), 232.

[37] For example, Charles Parham wrote in 1902: "Christ did not leave his believing children without signs...Neither did he send forth his servants to preach vague speculative theories of a world to come, but with mighty power for the relief of suffering humanity: feeding the hungry, clothing the naked; healing the sick; casting out the devils..". Quoted in Dayton, *The Theological Roots*, 24-25.

[38] Kärkkäinen, "David's Sling", 147-152, 152.

pushed into the background. The early Pentecostals were accused of the theological error of forsaking the all-sufficiency of Christ and following a Gnostic spirituality, due to their emphasis on Spirit baptism.[39] However, it is clear that the early Pentecostals emphasised the supremacy of Christ more than the Spirit baptism. For instance, Allan Anderson puts the record straight:

> ..the focus of Pentecostals in seeing Jesus as saviour is always Christocentric—"coming to Jesus," "receiving Jesus"—and a lifestyle conversion and a radical break with the past or the "world" is a prominent part of their "full gospel" proclamation and implicit theology. In fact, some suggest that as a result of their central Christology, Pentecostals might have a limited Trinitarian framework. Be that as it may, Pentecostals identify with the evangelical "born again" movement whose essential message is that "Jesus saves", expressly declaring the life-altering nature of Christian conversion, and the invitation to "sinners" is "Let Jesus come into your heart."[40]

From the beginning of the movement, leaders have been insisted the supremacy of Christ. For instance, Seymour was categorical about the vitality of Christology and exhorted the people by saying, "Now, do not go from this meeting and talk about tongues, but try to get people saved". McClung asserts, "Seymour, and subsequent Pentecostal leaders since him, had a strong Christology which centred more on the Giver than the gift."[41] According to Macchia, Pentecostals have never meant to sever Spirit empowerment from the supremacy of Christ in salvation. He contends, "After all, Pentecostals have always emphasised that Christ is the baptiser in the Spirit."[42] Pentecostals understand that Christ acts here and now through the work of the Spirit. Christology in Pentecostalism is, therefore, rightly termed pneumatological Christology, and this dimension of Christology has been rightly emphasised by Pentecostalism from the beginning. Land, while speaking about Pentecostal spirituality affirms that, "Pentecostal spirituality is Christocentric precisely because it is pneumatic; its fivefold Gospel is focused on Christ because of its starting point in the Holy Spirit...In Pentecostal spirituality, Jesus Christ is the centre and the Holy Spirit is the circumference."[43] Thus,

---

[39] Frank D. Macchia, "The Struggle for Global Witness: Shifting Paradigms in Pentecostal Theology", in *The Globalization of Pentecostalism*, edited by M.W. Dempster, B.D. Klaus & D. Petersen (Carlisle: Regnum, 1999), 13.

[40] Anderson, *To the Ends of the Earth.*

[41] Stanley H. Frodsham, quoted in L. Grant McClung jr., "Truth on Fire: Pentecostals and an Urgent Missiology", *Society for Pentecostal Studies Annual Meeting Papers (1985)* (Cleveland: Society for Pentecostal Studies, 2006): 5, C.D. Rom.

[42] Macchia, "The Struggle for Global Witness", 15.

[43] Stephen J. Land, *Pentecostal Spirituality: A Passion for the Kingdom* (Sheffield: Sheffield Academic Press, 1993), 23.

the Full Gospel functions as the central narrative conviction of the Pentecostal community.[44]

Pentecostals embrace the Full Gospel, which places Jesus and the Spirit at the centre of God's dramatic redemptive story. The proclamation of the Full Gospel is the declaration of the redemptive activity of God in Christ Jesus and the Holy Spirit to the community.[45] These confessional-doxological statements flow out of the redemptive encounter with the living Word, Jesus Christ, who is present in their community through the powerful presence of the Holy Spirit.[46] In line with this Pentecostal orientation, Archer argues that to uphold the identity of Pentecostal theology, it is essential to articulate it "Pneumatologically and organise it around the fivefold Gospel."[47] Furthermore, according to Archer, a Pentecostal theology can avoid the Christo-monistic tendency of Reformation theology of the Word by affirming and addressing the missional role of the Spirit, in conjunction with the missional role of Jesus. Thus, he affirms that "Spirit Christology would more correctly reflect the Pentecostal story and scriptural testimony."[48] Thus, it could be suggested that Pentecostal Christology is basically a functional Christology of the Full Gospel with a pneumatological emphasis.

The Full Gospel: A Liberative Spirituality

In the early days of Pentecostal movement, the Full Gospel was a powerful and handy tool for testimony in the hands of ordinary believers, of their Pentecostal faith to outsiders. In Pentecostal conventions, open-air meetings and evangelistic campaigns, the full gospel was the subject of preaching. The Pentecostal movement in the state of Kerala, in India has been grown into a considerably large community attracting thousands of adherents from other denominational churches and other religions was due to the propagation of the gospel message that Jesus is the saviour and healer.[49] I still have the vivid memory of my childhood days, Pentecostal preachers would elaborate the stories of miraculous healings, exorcism and second coming of Jesus in a dramatic way in worship services and outdoor meetings. They would expound Jesus as saviour and healer from the gospel passages along with true incidents of salvation and healing experiences of people who joined Pentecostal churches to convince the audiences. Often recipients of healings from incurable illnesses, those who have been delivered of evil spirits and other

[44] Kenneth J. Archer, "A Pentecostal Way of Doing Theology: Method and Manner", *IJST* 9/3 (July 2007): 312.

[45] Archer, "A Pentecostal Way of Doing Theology", 312.

[46] Archer, "A Pentecostal Way of Doing Theology", 312.

[47] Archer, "A Pentecostal Way of Doing Theology", 301-314.

[48] Archer, "A Pentecostal Way of Doing Theology", 314.

[49] K. E. Abraham, *K. E. Abraham, A Servant of Jesus Christ: Autobiography,* Translated by Finny Jacob (Kumbanad, Kerala: India Gospel Outreach, 2016).

problems would testify their stories to convince the listeners. These proclamations focused on bringing people into a personal relationship with Jesus Christ. In every gospel meeting audiences would be invited to receive Christ as their personal saviour and leave their sinful way of life. The divine healing in the name of Jesus is emphasised and sick people were being prayed for healing. It was a customary practice in earlier days that the theme of the last day of the message of a convention should be of the second coming of Jesus.[50] Such expositions of work of Christ attracted people from all faiths, especially from denominational churches where personal salvation experience or divine healing were not so emphasised. Since these Christians knew the Bible stories, they would accept gospel message and join healing prayers to become Pentecostal believers.[51] Besides, people from other faiths, especially Dalits and Tribals, the untouchable people of India joined in large numbers in Pentecostal movement due to the healing and exorcism and also by presenting of Jesus as saviour in their own religious and social context.[52] Such miraculous events transformed their life situations and brought them to the main stream of the society.[53] The major reasons for the magnificent growth of the Kerala Pentecostal movement was due to the skilful use of the Fourfold Gospel by the early Pentecostals.

It is not only in evangelistic outreaches and conventions, even in the congregational setting too the exposition of this concept is extensively practiced. The worship services, especially sermons are very often filled with the stories of healing and miracles that come through the powerful work of Christ. Believers are encouraged to put their trust in Christ to be healed of every sort of illness and also exercise their faith to bring healing to others. The testimony session in the Sunday service is full of experiences of healing and deliverances brought by Christ. Even today the Full Gospel is emphasised in the Pentecostal churches. The local church I am part of, the newly joined pastor introduced recital of the Fourfold Gospel for Sunday School children; while they recite their memory verses in the Sunday service, a boy or girl would shout the expression in top voice and others repeat it. I still remember as a Sunday School student in my village church, the same was repeated every Sunday at the end of the Sunday school session.

This is true all over India, in particular in the north Indian rural settings. The gospel message of Jesus as healer, exorcist and saviour continuously shared

---

[50] However, now a days the messages of second coming of Christ is not so often heard in conventions.

[51] Abraham, *K. E. Abraham, A Servant of Jesus Christ*, 119-120.

[52] Abraham, *K. E. Abraham, A Servant of Jesus Christ*, 84 & 99.

[53] P. G. Abraham, *Caste and Christianity: A Pentecostal Perspective* (Kumbhaza, Kerala: Crown Books, 2003), 116-118; Having conducted a study among the Dalit Christians who were joined recently in Pentecostal churches, Abraham notes the response of the people: 1. I have experienced God's deliverance in my trouble. 2. I have experienced God's healing power in my sickness. 3. God had delivered me from devilish attack.

among the general populace by missionaries, evangelists and ordinary believers. This message is all the more relevant in interior villages of north Indian states, where medical facilities are scant, and as a result thousands of people are being incapacitated by prolonging illness.[54] Besides, Jesus as healer and exorcist is popular particularly among Tribal and Dalit population, where people are affected by witch-craft and other harmful religious customs. A large section of the inhabitants suffer because of evil practices and sickness due to poverty. However, the healing and deliverances in the name of Jesus is preached in such situations and a large number of affected people have joined Pentecostal movement through healing and exorcism. The people who experienced divine healing and deliverances from evil spiritual forces readily accept Jesus as saviour and share their testimonies to others which in turn transform their lives.[55] This resulted in establishing new churches in many north Indian villages and the spread of Pentecostal movement in north of India can be attributed to the dissemination of the message of the Full Gospel. Hence, even after a century of its inception of the Pentecostal movement, the Full Gospel is still be termed as the significant constituent of Pentecostal spirituality and holds its value among the Pentecostals.

Although, early Pentecostals were successful in attracting people with the full gospel in a predominantly Christian context, Pentecostal movement faces stiff challenges in multi-religious context like India and other Asian nations. The functional nature of this Christology often portrays Jesus Christ similar to gods of other religious traditions, thus, diminishing the ontological nature of Christology, in particular the supremacy of Christ. Even though, there are certain efforts to uphold this element, Pentecostal theologians in general have not adequately developed a Christology that introduces the person of Christ in ontological terms to uphold the supremacy in a religious pluralistic context.[56] The reason seems to be that early Pentecostals were so deeply involved in the defence of Spirit baptism and glossolalia that Christology had been taken for granted. Moreover, Pentecostals usually just borrow Christological ideas from the Evangelical Theology. However, it is very clear that the theological conception of Pentecostals is significantly different from the Evangelical Theology and Christology, because of the context and the Spirit-experience. Therefore, the Pentecostal theology needs to foray into an ontological Pentecostal Christology to uphold the ontological unity of Christ with the Father, thus having a balanced Pentecostal Christology.

---

[54] See my article, Shaibu Abraham, "Jesus the Healer: Ordinary Indian Pentecostal Christology", *SATHRI Journal* IX/2, (October 2015): 58-74.

[55] See how Christological themes like Jesus the healer, exorcist, saviour and so on, transform the lives of the poor; see my book, Shaibu Abraham, *Pentecostal Christology: Empirical Approach in Indian Context* (New Delhi: Christian World Imprints, 2019).

[56] Ralph Del Colle, *Christ and Spirit: Spirit-Christologies in Trinitarian Perspective* (Oxford: Oxford University Press, 1994) and Abraham, *Pentecostal Christology*, 170-173.

Ontological Pentecostal Christology

As we have seen, the basic mooring of Pentecostal Christology is of a functional Spirit Christology, since the work of Christ is activated and actualised through the power of the Holy Spirit. Therefore, it is significance to construct an ontological Christology to compliment with the movement's functional Christology. Several Pentecostal scholars endorse it and advocate for an ontological Spirit Christology. For instance, Hunter supports Spirit Christology, "so long as Christology and Pneumatology are seen in a Trinitarian structure."[57] Habets holds that a Trinitarian Spirit Christology satisfies the requirements for a biblical Christology when it is seen, not as a replacement for, but as a complement to the existing Logos Christology.[58] His main emphasis is that Spirit Christology needs to be developed from a Trinitarian framework to avoid denying the ontological identity of Christ with God.[59] Therefore, here we shall explore the presentation of Ralph Del Colle, the Roman Catholic Charismatic theologian, since he speaks in Pentecostal terms and advocates a classical Trinitarian position in Spirit Christology.[60]

According to Del Colle, the experiential reality in Spirit baptism among Pentecostals becomes the basis for their spirituality. Pentecostal spirituality is essentially concerned with a communion in which God, the self, the neighbour and all of creation are known in prayer and praise of God, witnessing the risen Christ through the power of the Spirit.[61] Taking this idea forward, Del Colle argues that the "knowledge of God," or "religious affection" appropriate for the Christian, is one that brings transformative conversion and praxis, the presence of God mediated by the risen Lord in the Holy Spirit.[62] What is unique to Pentecostal experience is that this transformation is marked by an experimental effusion of the Spirit as gift and empowerment. Thus, Pentecostalism intrinsically holds that the presence of God is Christologically and Pneumatologically inscribed into our regenerated human faculties. That is, there is no relationship with Christ, without the awareness of the Spirit and vice versa.[63]

---

[57] Harold D. Hunter, "The Resurgence of Spirit Christology", *European Pentecostal Theological Association Bulletin 11* (1992), http://www.fullnet.net/np/archives/writings/epta.html (accessed 1 September 2010); Harold D. Hunter, "Spirit-Christology: Dilemma and Promise", *Heythrop Journal* 24 (1983): 127-140, 266-277.

[58] *Myk Habets,* "Spirit Christology: Seeing in Stereo", *JPT* 11/2 (2003): 216-228.

[59] *Steven M. Studebaker,* "Integrating Pneumatology and Christology: A Trinitarian Modification of Clark H. Pinnock's Spirit Christology", *Pneuma* 28/1 (Spring 2006): 8, 5-20.

[60] Del Colle, *Christ and the Spirit.*

[61] Ralph Del Colle, "Spirit Christology: Dogmatic Foundations for Pentecostal-Charismatic Spirituality", *JPT* 3 (1993): 94.

[62] Ralph Del Colle, "Schleiermacher and Spirit Christology: Unexplored Horizons of the Christian Faith", *IJST* 1/3 (1999): 288-289.

[63] Del Colle, "Spirit Christology", 93.

Consequently, Del Colle proposes a Spirit Christology from a Trinitarian perspective. The true Gospel portrayal of Jesus emerges only when the Christological event is understood to be a thoroughly Trinitarian event.[64] That is, God the Father effects salvation through the Son and in the Spirit; Jesus is both "Son" and "Spirit-bearer". Therefore, the theological elaboration of this idea in the direction of Christian doctrine leads to the construction of Spirit Christology which attempts to represent this reality in the realm of our understanding faithfully.[65] He explains the relevance of Spirit Christology:

> To contemplate the person of Jesus Christ in the light of the Pentecostal-charismatic experience is to explicate the confession of "truly human" and "truly divine" within the ambit of a Spirit anointed and transfigured human being that is God's communicative and salvific relation to humanity. He is the mediator of life, mission and our deepest human identity, what we can describe in the language of election as our calling to exist in graced filial relation to God, the source of all reality.[66]

Thus, Spirit experience can truly contribute to an ontological understanding of Christ because it emphasises both his divinity and his humanity.

According to Del Colle, Trinitarian Spirit Christology proposes that the work of God in Jesus Christ proceeds of the Spirit and is enacted in the Spirit such that the Spirit becomes a gift to humanity in divinizing and missionising power.[67] Moreover, taking the idea of David Coffey, he argues that the Spirit creates, sanctifies and unites the assumed humanity of Jesus to the divine Son, so that the same Spirit as the Spirit of the Son may be poured out as a gift, enacting a regenerated, empowered and transfigured humanity so that in the eschaton God may be all in all (1Cor.15:28).[68] It is significant to note that Pentecostal-Charismatic spirituality contributes to a theological recognition of Trinitarian Spirit Christology because "it apprehends in Spirit baptism/renewal of the living agency and presence of Christ and the Holy Spirit, as co-inhering but distinct, in the full inheritance of Christian initiation."[69] The believer knows Christ to

---

[64] Del Colle, *Christ and the Spirit*, 4; That is, "the relationship between Jesus and God and the role of Christ in redemption cannot be fully understood unless there is an explicitly pneumatological dimension".

[65] Ralph Del Colle, "Trinity and Temporality: A Pentecostal/Charismatic Perspective", *JPT* 8 (1996): 101.

[66] Del Colle, "Spirit Christology", 94.

[67] Del Colle, "Spirit Christology", 106.

[68] Del Colle, *Christ and the Spirit*, 124. Some of the Charismatic and Pentecostal theologians use the Spirit Christology of David Coffey for their Spirit Christologies (Del Colle, Steven M. Studebaker).

[69] Del Colle, "Spirit Christology", 106.

be Baptizer in the Spirit and the Spirit is the *Paraclete* who glorifies Christ in the manifestation of *charismata* and the formation of virtue. Here Trinitarian distinctions are not a matter of speculation but of lived experience and Christian witnessing. Moreover, the Full Gospel is central to the Pentecostal-Charismatic experience that understands Christ as Saviour and Baptizer in the Spirit. In this experience there is an existential awareness of the effusion of the Holy Spirit as gift of the risen *kyrios*.[70] The key issue for a systematic Trinitarian Spirit Christology is whether or not the Son and the Spirit can be distinguished in the Christian experience of grace. The *Christus praesens* is known through the proclamation that effectively announces salvation. Likewise, prayer and petition for the outpouring of the Holy Spirit, the epicletic dimension associated with the *Spiritus praesens* (Lk.11:13; 24:49), implies a distinction from the *Christus praesens*.[71] Thus, the Pentecostal-Charismatic experience reveals the Trinitarian deep structure of Christian faith and theology.

Let me conclude here. The full gospel can be termed as *the* Christology of the Pentecostalism world-wide. Although, obtained from preceding renewal movements, Pentecostalism utilized this Christology to its full potentials and became a spiritual and liberative force. It is not only a popular Christology but also a functional Christology in that ordinary people intimately experience the person and work of Christ in their lives and share it to others. Likewise, it is a Spirit Christology where the work of Christ is actualised through the power of the Holy Spirit. Further, this Christology transformed the lives of many and continues to liberate people from their struggle-some situations. Nevertheless, the movement needs an ontological Christology to have a balanced Christology and also to present Christ in religious pluralistic contexts. Such a balanced Christology will propel the community to be a spiritual and social force in the 21st century.

---

[70] Del Colle, "Spirit Christology", 106-107; Del Colle, "Trinity and Temporality", 111.

[71] Del Colle, "Spirit Christology", 107; Del Colle, *Christ and the Spirit*, 174-179.

Chapter 3

Holiness
Separation for Liberation

The doctrine of holiness or sanctification can be described as one of the most, if not the most, important doctrines of Pentecostal Churches. It forms the basic spirituality of Pentecostal movement all over the world. Pentecostals claim that they are sanctified and therefore live a separated life from the world and the people live in an unholy lifestyle. While non-Pentecostals would indulge in unwanted and immoral activities, the larger society tolerates them; but if a Pentecostal acts similar way, questions are raised by the same people who involve in such immoral activities. Many of the deeds and dispositions of ordinary people, possessed by cultural and social customs, are considered to be unholy by Pentecostals. Pentecostals desist any such ideas and actions that are contrary to their holiness standard. Consequently, this spirituality provided them a unique identity and a special life-style among other Christians and non-Christians. In earlier days, Pentecostals were nicknamed for their separated life and even considered them as nuisance to larger society. But, after a century of the movement, the original vigour and passion for holy life is largely missing in the movement. Integrity in words and actions, a separated way of life and godly character that earned a unique identity for Pentecostals among others are partially missing. Now it seems that Pentecostals are also similar to others, and most of Pentecostal denominations have become mirror images of the denominations they have once separated from. Therefore, it is imperative to regain the lost traits of holiness Pentecostals cherished from the beginning of the movement. Here we shall explore briefly the origin, development and implication of this spirituality that liberate and transform millions all over the world.

Pentecostal Doctrine of Holiness

The *Dictionary of Pentecostal and Charismatic Movement* terms holiness as the doctrine of "sanctification" or "Christian Perfection" which denotes completeness, or wholeness, of Christian character, including freedom from sin. The word *holiness*, which is most widely used today, refers to perfection of soul. Holiness originates in conversion and covers the whole span of the Christian experience in constant growth and cleansing. It is a state of separation and purity wherein souls move toward the perfect likeness of Christ.[1] This doctrinal position has a strong base in the scripture and has its emphasis on personal holiness. In biblical understanding, holiness refers to *separation* or *apartness.* It is God's holiness, his transcendent nature and separated existence from all his creations is fundamental to holiness idea in the Bible. The concept of holiness, thus flows out of God's nature itself and exhibited in God's attributes such as his glory, righteousness, justice, mercy, love and so on. In the Old Testament, Israel was called a holy people because of their separation to God from all other nations. They belonged exclusively to the Lord and was not like any other people.[2] They should reflect God's holiness through their moral qualities of righteousness, justice and love in which true holiness consists. Besides, Israel is to be a holy people with a social order which distinguishes it from other nations. They were expected to be "a kingdom of priests and a holy nation". Moreover, this separated status demanded ethical standard from Israel. In the Psalmists and Prophets the divine holiness becomes, above all, an ethical reality convicting men of sin (Isaiah 6:3) and demanding of those who would stand in His presence clean hands and a pure heart (Psalms 24:3). In the New Testament, Christ's people are regularly called saints and holiness is understood in ethical and spiritual terms having high quality of life and conduct. God has chosen and sanctified his people in order to make it a distinct community midst of other nations. The communities of those who believe in Christ are the "temple of God", filled and indwelt by the Holy Spirit (1 Cor. 3:16). The Holy Spirit has taken up abode in the heart of every regenerate person, and sanctification is going on there. The church of Jesus Christ is a people set apart for the Lord, enjoying his special presence and favour (1Peter 2:9-10). Therefore, Christians are exhorted to imitate Jesus in every aspect of their life (Phil 2:5). Thus, the New Testament closely connects holiness with moral qualities which the holy God demands from his people.

Pentecostals consider this aspect of holiness as an integral part of their life and spirituality. Frequently quoted Bible verses in relation to holiness among Pentecostals are: "Therefore let us go on toward *perfection...*" (Heb. 6:1); "...

---

[1] C.W. Conn, "Christian Perfection, (A Pentecostal Perspective)", in *DPCM,* edited by S.M. Burgess & G.B. McGee (Michigan: Zondervan, 1988), 170.

[2] For example, Deuteronomy 7:6 reads, "For you are a people holy to the Lord your God; the Lord your God has chosen you to be a people for his own possession, out of all the peoples that are on the face of the earth".

make you *complete* in everything good so that you may do his will..." (Heb. 13:21); "...holiness without which no one will see the Lord" (Heb. 12:14); "....as he who called you is holy, *be holy* yourselves in all your conduct; for it is written, "You shall be holy, for I am holy" (1 Pet. 1:15-16); "For this is the will of God, *your sanctification*..." (1 Thess. 4:3); "...let us cleanse ourselves from every defilement of body and of spirit, *making holiness perfect* in the fear of God" (2 Cor. 7:1). This understanding of holiness, is actualised in the Pentecostal movement through the development of doctrine of sanctification. For many Pentecostals, the experience of sanctification has signified the seeking all the will of God for one's life, loving the Lord with a whole heart and joyfully bearing burdens without grumbling or complaining. In sanctification, the believer learns to walk in perfect love and to exist in harmony with the will and nature of Christ.[3]

This biblical position of holiness was imparted to Pentecostals by the Holiness revival movement of the late nineteenth century and had played a prominent and unique role in the formation of the spirituality of holiness. The Holiness movement of the nineteenth century began as a Renewal movement within the Methodist Church. It was an attempt to recover both the religious fervour of the previous century and John Wesley's teaching of a second work of grace in the life of the believer. In addition, a concerted effort was extended to recovering the faith of the primitive church, and this, in particular, opened the door for the miraculous gifts of the Spirit to be manifested. Beginning in the Methodist Church, this Renewal movement eventually exerted an influence on almost every denomination in America.[4]

Historical Roots of the Doctrine of Holiness

Most Pentecostal historians agree that the origin of the Pentecostal movement in America is the outpouring of the Holy Spirit in 1906 in Azusa Street, Los Angeles. It was William J. Seymour, a Negro holiness evangelist, who became instrumental in the hand of God.[5] The outpouring of the Spirit was apparently so intense that within a short time the revival fire spread around the world. As we trace back the history and holiness doctrine of the Pentecostal movement, we come to the conclusion that there were many factors behind the scene. Out of them, the Wesleyan holiness revival played a major role in the formation of the doctrine of holiness and baptism of the Holy Spirit in the Pentecostal movement. According

---

[3] Cheryl Bridges Johns, *Pentecostal Formation: A Pedagogy Among the Oppressed* (Eugene, OR: Wipf and Stock Publishers, 2010), 93.

[4] Eddie L. Hyatt, *2000 Years of Charismatic Christianity* (Florida: Charisma House, 2002), 125.

[5] Leonard Lovett, "Black Origins of the Pentecostal Movement", in *Aspects of Pentecostal Charismatic Origins,* edited by Vinson Synan (New Jersey: Logos, 1975), 125; Walter J. Hollenweger, "The Black Roots of Pentecostalism", in *Pentecostalism After a Century: Perspective on a Movement in Transition,* edited by Allan H. Anderson & Walter J. Hollenweger (Sheffield: Sheffield Academic Press, 1999), 40-44.

to Klaude Kendric the Holiness Movement made two contributions that prepared fertile ground from which modern Pentecost could ultimately spring. First, it introduced a new interest in "spiritual experience" subsequent to the experience of salvation, and second, it produced the phenomena which included "tongues."[6] Well-known Pentecostal observer Walter J. Hollenweger comments, "John Wesley, the founder of the Methodist Church, had already made a distinction between the sanctified, or those who had been baptised in the Spirit, and ordinary Christians."[7] Even though, this had a negative effect of abstaining from the world, the concept was meant to be an expression of the force of God's Spirit in the world.[8] Here we shall briefly look into the Wesleyan holiness to trace more fully the growth of doctrine of holiness in the Pentecostal movement.

Development of the Doctrine of Holiness

For Wesley, sanctification, considered as a whole, is a process of development which begins at the very moment a person is justified. Christian perfection is the completion of sanctification begun at regeneration. In his own words,

> It is nothing more nor less than that habitual disposition of the soul which, in sacred writings, is termed holiness; and which directly implies, the being cleansed from sin, "from all filthiness both of flesh and spirit", and by consequences, the being endued with those virtues which were also in Christ Jesus; the being so "renewed in the spirit of our mind", as to "be perfect as our Father in heaven is perfect..." Perfection in the sense of infallibility does not exist on the face of the earth.[9]

While narrating the history of the Holiness–Pentecostal tradition, Vinson Synan summarises Wesley's doctrine in the following way: Christian perfection involved two separate phases, namely conversion (or justification), then Christian perfection itself (or sanctification). In the first experience, though sins are forgiven, Christians retain a "residue of sin within". This remaining "inbred sin" was the result of Adam's fall and had to be dealt with by a "second blessing, properly so-called". This purifies the believer of inward sin and brought a "perfect love" toward God and humanity.[10] It is the Alders-gate experience that convinced Wesley that sanctification is special a work of the Holy Spirit other

---

[6] Klaude Kendric, *The Promise Fulfilled: A History of Modern Pentecostal Movement* (Springfield: Gospel Publishing House, 1961), 33.

[7] Walter J. Hollenwenger, *The Pentecostals* (Minneapolis: Augsburg, 1977), 21.

[8] Bridges Johns, *Pentecostal Formation*, 69.

[9] Quoted in Lovett, "Black Origins of the Pentecostal Movement", 128. John Wesley's doctrine of Christian holiness can be seen in the *Plain Account of Christian Perfection* (1767).

[10] Vinson Synan, *The Holiness-Pentecostal Tradition: Charismatic Movements in the Twentieth Century*, 2nd edition (Michigan: Eerdmans, 1997), 6.

than conversion. Robert G. Tuttle endorses the same idea, "…the nature of the Aldersgate experience convinced Wesley that sanctification (like justification) was granted in an instant."[11] On 24 May 1738, at a small Moravian meeting in Aldersgate Street in London, Wesley felt his "heart strangely warmed" while listening to the reading of Luther's preface to Romans by William Holland. He described the event in his journal:

> In the evening, I went very unwillingly to a society in Aldersgate Street, where one was reading Luther's preface to the Epistle to the Romans. About a quarter before nine, while he was describing the change which God works in the heart through faith in Christ, I felt my heart strangely warmed. I felt I did trust in Christ, Christ alone for salvation, and an assurance was given me that he had taken away my sins, even mine, and saved me from the law of sin and death.[12]

Modern scholars do not agree as to the exact nature of this experience, but history attests to the fact that nothing in Wesley was left untouched by it. The warmth of his experience united with that of his brother Charles and another member of Holy Club (George Whitefield) to produce the flame of the Evangelical Revival and catch the attention of London, Bristol and the press.[13]

Wesley never taught "sinless perfection" but a perfection of motives and desires. Total "sinless perfection" would come only after death. In the meantime the sanctified soul through careful self-examination, godly discipline, methodical devotion, and avoidance of worldly pleasures, could live a life of victory over sin. This internal perfection could be attained instantly as a "second work of grace", although it was usually preceded and followed by a gradual "growth in grace". Though he disagreed with John Fletcher, his most trusted adviser, who argued that the second blessing was in reality a "baptism of the Holy Spirit" as well as a cleansing experience, at the end of his life Wesley was convinced of Fletcher's position.[14]

The Wesleyan movement became so influential that in later stage the Holiness Movement evolved out of the Methodist churches emphasising more on holiness. The Holiness Movement had begun in the 1830's with the establishment of the Tuesday Meeting for the Promotion of Holiness in 1835 by Phoebe Palmer and her sister, Sarah Lankford. Eventually, word of these successful prayer meetings inspired similar gatherings around the country, bringing Christians of many denominations together to pray. Phoebe became the most

---

[11] Robert G. Tuttle Jr., *John Wesley: His Life and Theology* (Michigan: Zondervan, 1978), 341.

[12] https://www.christianitytoday.com/history/people/denominationalfounders/john-wesley.html (accessed on 25/09/19).

[13] T. R. Albin, "Wesley, John", in *New Dictionary of Theology,* edited by Sinclair B. Ferguson & David F. Wright (Leicester: IVP, 1988), 719.

[14] Vinson Synan, *The Holiness-Pentecostal Tradition,* 6-7.

influential woman in the largest, fastest-growing religious group in America. At her initiation, an estimated 25,000 Americans were converted.[15] Phoebe Palmer had a surprising impact on the theology of the holiness movement. She taught that once consecration was complete the believer should then exercise faith and lay claim to entire sanctification which was later termed as "baptism of the Holy Spirit". She is considered as the link between the Wesleyan revivalism and modern Pentecostalism, and strongly influenced the formation of denominations like The Church of the Nazarene, The Salvation Army, The Church of God, and The Pentecostal-Holiness Church.[16]

Holiness through the Baptism in the Holy Spirit

As explored earlier, Wesley's "second grace of work" or the doctrine sanctification was developed into the baptism of the Holy Spirit by prominent leaders of the Holiness movement. According to Donald Dayton, the first sustained development of the doctrine of holiness through Spirit Baptism took place in America, in Oberlin Perfectionism around the 1850's. Its two great leaders were evangelist Charles Finney, who became the first theology professor at Oberlin College, and Asa Mahan, the college's first president.[17] Finney's revival methodology was the shaping influence on Methodist theology in the Pentecostal churches and formed the major historical bridge between primitive Wesleyanism and modern Pentecostalism. His theology included an experience subsequent to conversion which he called the baptism of the Holy Ghost in which a believer is "baptised into the very death of Christ and by this baptism be slain and buried and planted and crucified and raised to a life of holiness in Christ". Furthermore, ministers without this baptism with the Holy Ghost will remain "spiritually inefficient, in bondage to sin and lust."[18] Thus, it is evident that Finney was thinking of the Spirit baptism as a gift of sanctification to be sought.

In Asa Mahan we can see greater emphasis on this aspect of Spirit baptism as he himself refers to those two great doctrines (i.e., "Christian perfection" and "baptism of the Holy Ghost") which were the theme of his life for many years. His book, *Baptism of the Holy Ghost* (1870) bears strong evidence to the emergence of holiness through the baptism of the Holy Spirit. According to Donald Dayton, Mahan's earlier book, *Scripture Doctrine of Christian Perfection,* like Wesley's *Plain Account,* is basically oriented to Christ for the work of sanctification. But, in the *Baptism of the Holy Ghost,* the Spirit becomes primary. Christ himself was

---

[15] https://www.christianitytoday.com/history/people/moversandshakers/phoebe-palmer.html.

[16] https://www.christianitytoday.com/history/people/moversandshakers/phoebe-palmer.html.

[17] Donald W. Dayton, "Christian Perfection to the Baptism of the Holy Ghost", in *Aspects of Pentecostal Charismatic Origins,* edited by Vinson Synan (New Jersey: Logos, 1975), 46-47.

[18] Roland Wessels, "The Spirit Baptism, Nineteenth Century Roots", *Pneuma* 14/2 (Fall, 1992): 127-157.

dependent upon the "indwelling, and influence, and the baptism of the Holy Spirit, the same in all essential particulars as in us."[19] Furthermore, a new emphasis was given on the empowering of the Holy Spirit. It is also very significant that the gift of the Spirit moves into the centre of his attention.[20] The same idea also can be seen in the lives and writings of John Morgan, D.L. Moody, Reuben A. Torrey, Phoebe Palmer, Daniel Steele, Henry Cowles and many others.

While narrating the background of the modern Pentecostal revival from the Holiness Movement, Klaude Kendric describes the holiness through "baptism of the Holy Spirit" this way,

> The scriptural phrase 'baptism of the Holy Spirit', which was to have an important significance in the Pentecostal movement, was popularised as the name for the experience of sanctification, or 'second blessing'. All who came under the influence of the Holiness ministry became familiar with 'spiritual baptism' with its emphasis upon cleansing from sin. Many claimed to receive such an experience and testified that it changed their entire Christian outlook.[21]

The experience of sanctification and consequent personal transformation, thus became a dominant spirituality.

Holiness: A Spirituality of Liberation

One of the distinctive features of the Holiness Movement was that it emphasised personal holiness which we have seen, as well as communal holiness. The church was considered as a spiritual communion of the sanctified and saved, as opposed to the traditional teaching of the church as a visible institution. Some followers of the Holiness movement considered the institutional church as an exoteric entity and it belongs to the neophytes and the unregenerate. They were against flamboyant life style, had concern for simplicity, and affirmed radical equality expressed in avoiding honorific titles in favour of "Mr" or "Brother". The movement also emphasised equality of women and their equal opportunity in ministry.[22] Furthermore, they also emphasised ministry among the poor. For instance, A. B. Simpson, the founder of the Christian and Missionary Alliance, left socially elite churches to minister among the poor of the inner city slums.[23] Peace was another common theme. The movement opposed the

---

[19] Dayton, "Christian Perfection", 47-48. Mahan also emphasises prophecy as the power of utterance for the edification of the church and the conversion of the sinners.

[20] Dayton, "Christian Perfection", 50-51.

[21] Kendric, *The Promise Fulfilled,* 33.

[22] Donald W. Dayton, "The Holiness Churches: A Significant Ethical Tradition", *Religion Online,* https://www.religion-online.org/article/the-holiness-churches-a-significant-ethical-tradition/ (accessed on 26/07/19).

[23] Dayton, "The Holiness Churches: A Significant Ethical Tradition".

military chaplaincy, advocating "tax resistance", and also called for the abolition of capital punishment.[24]

Moreover, holiness through the baptism of the Holy Spirit has brought a new outlook of social concern in holiness movement. Issues such as slavery, women's rights, child labour, slum conditions and illiteracy were addressed by many adherents of this movement. For example, Dieter speaks about a holiness evangelist, William Jones, preaching and discussing about the plight of immigrant workers, illiterates, ex-slaves and other downtrodden masses.[25] Wesley himself was very specific about the social aspect of mission along with spiritual formation.[26] Timothy Smith, historian of this period, observes that "Oberlin immediately became the vital centre of Christian reflection and action aimed at the liberation of black people from slavery and racism, of women from male oppression."[27] The holiness revivals developed largely out of a cry against the "embourgoisement of Methodism" or a perceived abandonment of Methodism to the cause of the masses and the quest for personal piety.[28] Jeffrey T. Snell also asserts the fact that the Holiness movement emerged historically as a protest against Methodist compromise on the question of slavery.[29]

Cheryl Bridges Johns explains this revolutionary attitude in terms of sanctification: The experience of sanctification brought about a new moral and social sensibility. Sanctification became a process of consciousness-raising whereby people answered God's call to a holy life and to co-operate with God in the transformation of the society. Reality was to be critically perceived and injustice was to be the object of reflection and action guided by the Holy Spirit.[30] Thus, the Holiness Movement not only ushered a paradigm shift in the in existing Christian denominations but also added renewal in the doctrine of holiness and practices.

The adherent who subsequently branched out from the Holiness Movement had a highly conscientised awareness of social realities around them and laboured to alleviate the pain and suffering of the masses. For instance, the Salvation Army saw itself as a living critique of bourgeois churches, revealing the sickness and pain of society and daring to side itself with the oppressed. Dominant in the holiness

---

[24] Dayton, "The Holiness Churches: A Significant Ethical Tradition".

[25] Melvin E. Dieter, "The Wesleyan / Holiness and Pentecostal Movements: Commonalities, Confrontation, and Dialogue", *Pneuma* 12/1 (spring, 1990): 57.

[26] Randy L. Maddox, "Visit the Poor: Wesley's Precedent for Wholistic Mission", *T F Views* (January, 2001): 37-50.

[27] Bridges Johns, *Pentecostal Formation*, 66.

[28] Bridges Johns, *Pentecostal Formation* 65; Donald. W. Dayton, *Discovering an Evangelical Heritage* (New York: Harper & Row, 1976), 151.

[29] Jeffrey T. Snell, "Beyond the Individual and into the World: A Call to Participation in the Larger Purpose of the Spirit on the Basis of Pentecostal Theology", *Pneuma* 14/1 (Spring, 1992), 52.

[30] Bridges Johns, *Pentecostal Formation,* 65-66.

revival was a utopian vision of reality. Christians were to be instruments of the ushering in of the kingdom of God. According to Cheryl Johns, this movement preceded the 'social gospel movement' of the early twentieth century but differed in several key areas.[31]

The Pentecostal Movement which emerged from the Holiness Movement in the next century (1900's) wholeheartedly assimilated the above mentioned holiness spirituality - both personal and social - and carried forward the spiritual and social implications of this revolutionary concept.[32] The initial members of Pentecostal movement were from the Holiness movement who received the baptism of the Holy Spirit which we shall discuss later. By emphasising holiness, Pentecostal Movement became a revolutionary entity among the poor, downtrodden and the black population in America. The same passion and commitment was transmitted world over. Besides, the Pentecostal Movement was deeply committed to personal holiness which rejected all the vices existed among other denominational churches.

Early Pentecostals were eager to propagate and establish the doctrine of sanctification and resultant holiness spirituality. Early Pentecostal literatures, and magazines such as *The Pentecost, The Apostolic Faith, The Pentecostal Evangel* and so on, abounded with various aspects of holiness; the significance and need of sanctification, effects and character of a sanctified person and so on. *The Pentecost* explains concept and effects of sanctification: "Sanctification means cleansing from all sin, a pure heart and a right spirit; the motives, desires, aims single to God's glory, a heart of pure, unsullied, unselfish to man and to God. Hence, it is deliverance from envy, jealousy, peevishness, bigotry, licentiousness, pride, etc."[33] *The Apostolic Faith* also sounds similar and explains the urgency, need and effects of sanctification;

> God is calling His people to true holiness in these days. He says in 2 Tim. 2:21: "If a man therefore purge himself from these, he shall be a vessel unto honour, sanctified and meet for the Master's use". He means for us to be purged from uncleanness and all kinds of sin. Then we shall be a vessel unto honour, sanctified and meet for the Master's

---

[31] Bridges Johns, *Pentecostal Formation,* 66; Unlike the social gospel movement, the Holiness movement sprang from among the poor. The Holiness movement held a high view of Scripture, interpreting literally passages which dealt with both social and personal piety. The Holiness movement viewed sin and evil as very real and present realities. Redemption was to begin with a changed heart, but it was not to end there.

[32] Steven J. Land asserts the fact, "Had there been no eighteenth century Wesleyan and nineteenth century Holiness movements there would have been no twentieth century Pentecostalism; and Pentecostalism is at any rate inexplicable without this theological heritage". Stephen J. Land, *Pentecostal Spirituality: A Passion for the Kingdom* (Sheffield: Sheffield Academic Press, 1993), 49.

[33] *The Pentecost*, vol. 1, No. 2 (Sept, 1908): 7.

> use, and prepared unto every good work. Sanctification makes us holy and destroys the breed of sin, the love of sin and carnality. It makes us pure and whiter than snow.[34]

Similarly, another piece of writing explains the nature of sanctification and how to experience it:

> Sanctification is the second work of grace and the last work of grace. Sanctification is that act of God's free grace by which He makes us holy. Sanctification is cleansing to make holy. The disciples were sanctified before the Day of Pentecost. By a careful study of Scripture you will find it is so now. "Ye are clean through the word which I have spoken unto you". (John 15:3; 13:10); and Jesus had breathed on them the Holy Ghost (John 20:21, 22).[35]

In addition, they were aware of the fact that holiness is indispensible for a victorious Christian life. "The Sanctification brings victory over the world, the flesh, and the devil in the individual life, because there is supplied enough of the divine nature for this purpose. The Spirit inbreathed, as in the case of the eleven apostles (John 20:22) sustains against these and soul forward with desire, purpose and hope until the full earnest of the inheritance is really obtained."[36] When holiness possesses a person, it brings Christian character, especially humility; True holiness is possessed. The closer a man lives to God the smaller he looks in his own eyes, and the bigger God looks to Him. He loses sight of himself and sees only Jesus Christ. There is no saying "I am holy", but rather "He is holy and I am wretched". Paul counted himself the least of the apostles and said he was the greatest of sinners. Jesus was so real to him that he could not see any righteousness in himself. In all the glorious writings of Paul, you never find the words "I am holy" or "I am sanctified."[37] Moreover, they had differentiated between justification, sanctification and baptism of the Spirit, "Justification makes men honest toward their fellow men. Sanctification makes men profoundly honest toward God. The baptism empowers such by setting fire to such honesty so that the dishonest tremble in their very presence."[38]

Besides, the effect of sanctification totally altered the perception and actions of the early Pentecostal believers. Sanctification brought a new awareness of divine justice and resulted in conscientisation. Bridges Johns explains it, "In sanctification, orthopathy, as it refers to right affections, is joined with orthopraxis. One's nature is altered and one's affections reflect the heart of God. This leads not just to

---

[34] "Sanctified on the Cross", *The Apostolic Faith,* vol. 11, No. 13 (May, 1908): 2.

[35] *The Apostolic Faith, January,* vol. 1, No. 12 (January, 1908): 2.

[36] A.S. Copley, "Sanctification", *The Pentecost,* vol. 1, No. 2 (Sept, 1908): 7.

[37] *The Pentecost,* vol. 1, No. 2 (Sept, 1908): 4.

[38] *The Pentecost,* vol. 1, No. 2, Sept, 1908): 7.

personal piety but also to social transformation in as much as the eschatological goals of the Kingdom are paralleled in a social level."[39] Consequently, among the early Pentecostals, racial segregation and gender difference were being blurred; Bartleman said, "The colour line was washed away in the blood."[40] Eddy L. Hyatt comments on this revolutionary attitude, "The Azusa Mission reflected the original interracial character of the Pentecostal movement, which had been hampered by the segregationist policies and customs of the South. Many of the races were meeting at Azusa Street, and an amazing unity of the Spirit had become obvious."[41] The original Azusa board of directors reflected both racial and gender diversity. This board, which signed ministerial credentials and laid hands on the candidates, consisted of seven women and five men. Five of the women were white, and two were black. Of the five men, four were white, and one, Pastor Seymour, was black.[42]

Following the same holiness paradigm, early Pentecostals in Kerala brought a new standard in their life-style; whatever stood against their idea of holiness were rejected or abandoned. Many of them destroyed their *araknut* and *vettilla* plants,[43] their life's earning; some left their old jobs which were not according to the new vision of holiness they achieved through sanctification. While I was a teenager, I knew a disabled person, running a very small shop, selling cigarettes, *beedies* and *paan* for his survival. However, when he had a Pentecostal experience, he left the denominational church he belonged to, abandoned the sale of all such items even jeopardising his small income that supported a large family. I know some faithful people who, out of their passion for holiness, abandoned luxuries, even discarded the use of cosmetics like talcum powder and face creams. Some for the sake of their Pentecostal faith forfeited their rightful ancestral property and some were thrown out of their homes. Besides, early Pentecostals discarded the use of ornaments and still the practice continues. They were mockingly called by others as "the separated ones" and a "sect", since they refused to indulge in many of the things done by their compatriots. Watching movies, loose talk, smoking, and vices which were silently allowed in other churches are prohibited or rejected in Pentecostal churches. Actually it is not a prohibition as such but as one experiences the joy of salvation and the holiness through the baptism of the Spirit, naturally such things move away from a sanctified life. When a person experiences sanctification, whatever is cherished as valuable in worldly terms becomes worthless. Besides, the holiness outlook created new social vision among the Pentecostals. In Indian context caste system is a deep-rooted malaise which

---

[39] Bridges Johns, *Pentecostal Formation*, 94.

[40] Hyatt, *2000 Years of Charismatic Christianity*, 145.

[41] Hyatt, *2000 Years of Charismatic Christianity*, 145.

[42] Hyatt, *2000 Years of Charismatic Christianity*, 145.

[43] The nut and leaves of these plants are used for making *pan*, a compound for chewing to get a mild intoxication. The Kerala Pentecostals consider its use as unholy.

segregated a section of Indian population into untouchables and non-humans. A century ago, the caste-consciousness in Kerala society was so blatant that Dalits and other untouchables were not even allowed to tread through streets. The lower castes and Dalits were not allowed to enter into houses of higher castes and they had no right to pray in the temples and churches.

However, the outpouring of the Spirit and growth of Pentecostal movement brought a sea change in the situation. In Pentecostal churches, Dalits, Syrian Christians, people from other faiths were all welcomed and worshipped together. They sat together, ate together, prayed together and shared their joys and sorrows, even their meagre financial resources in the new-found community. It was neither by a conscious effort nor by a meticulous social programme the initial Pentecostals were achieved equality, but instead as a result of the joy they experienced and the freedom that brought by the Spirit of God (2 Corinthians 3:17-18); there was a total transformation in their spiritual and social outlook. Since most of the people joined the movement in the initial stage were the poor, uneducated or semi-educated and from lower strata of the society, it was impossible to develop an egalitarian social agenda by them. This was possible only because of the experience of sanctification, as we have seen, created a paradigm shift in their attitude and disposition. Hence, for Pentecostals, the doctrine of holiness became their life and a community forming spirituality.

Nevertheless, after a century of its inception, Pentecostal movement has come to a stage where it has rather wittingly or unwittingly lost its original holiness fervour that has given it a unique identity and spiritual strength. Personal holiness that comes through the experience of sanctification upheld by the early adherents is largely lacking. Members lacking personal integrity, moral consciousness and truthfulness are slowly increasing in the movement. To climb the church hierarchy and to win the denominational elections, leaders and pastors stoop down to any extent - bribing people, even resorting to verbal abuse and physical violence. There is no spirit of forgiveness or reconciliation. Financial misappropriations, moral failings, court cases are rampant in the denominational settings. People with money power and influence come to the leadership position with the help of coterie created by them. Now Pentecostals reached a stage where they are not much different from older denominations they have left. Such changes have largely been due to the better economic status of the Pentecostals. Developing economic prosperity, the infiltration of social and moral nuances of the larger society have taken their toll on the movement. This is increasingly affecting Pentecostals in countries where economies are getting stronger and wealth is becoming more widespread. This trend is largely visible in places where the movement became old.[44]

[44] Keith Warrington, *Pentecostal Theology: A Theology of Encounter* (New York: T & T Clark, 2008), 212.

Moreover, although Pentecostals run a number of charity works and social emancipation programmes, the original fervour and power of holiness that attracted the poor and downtrodden into the churches have knowingly or unknowingly waned away. The egalitarian force of the movement that had in the beginning is largely missing. In the beginning of the movement anyone irrespective of caste, creed or colour, could enter into a Pentecostal church and become part of it. But, today Pentecostals have built up "thick walls" around them and becoming a closed community. The social dimension of holiness by the power of the Spirit is not so pervasive as it was earlier.

Today, Pentecostals make an effort to follow certain holiness practices that have been seen in their previous generations, but it seems that many of these practices are just an imitation of early Pentecostals' life styles, without understanding its true value and implications, thus following them like traditions. For instance, early Pentecostals in Kerala totally rejected the use of ornaments, as a sign of their inner transformation, simplicity and rejection of worldly desires and luxuries. Similarly, they insisted on wearing white dresses as a mark of their inner purity exhibited outward. After a century, Pentecostals still continues the same, but conveniently discarding the simplicity and high spiritual and moral standard. Now most of the Pentecostals in Kerala are rich and enjoy all the luxuries like their neighbours and even indulge in blatant exhibition of their wealth without any qualms. Although the real meaning, power and value of these spiritual overtures are lost in transition of the movement, still some insist on these practices without knowing what they have lost. Moreover, some mistake the holiness ideals with some of the cultural elements and practices such as dress-code, shaving away of moustaches, and so on, unwittingly abandoning the personal integrity and social responsibilities.

Furthermore, all over the world among Pentecostals, holiness is sometimes marginalized because it has interpreted "separation from the world" as a refusal to engage critically with contemporary culture, and the emphasis on personal piety has muted any call for social justice.[45] It seems that in the name of holiness Pentecostals shut themselves up from the stark social realities – poverty, injustice, and oppression – for which they are commissioned. Dempster asserts the fact that "many Pentecostal groups with their heritage of *status quo* quietism, unwittingly serve the cause of oppression."[46] Additionally, in reacting against what is perceived as legalism among those who proclaimed holiness at the turn of the twentieth

---

[45] J. Ayodeji Adewuya, "Holiness: Reclaiming the Doctrine", *Issues in Contemporary Pentecostalism*, edited by R. Keith Whitt & French L. Arrington (Cleveland, Tennessee: Pathway Press, 2012), 271-272.

[46] Murray W. Dempster, "Pentecostal Social Concern and the Biblical Mandate for Social Justice", *Pneuma*: 9/2 (Fall, 1987), 142.

century, Pentecostals today appear to have, in a proverbial sense, "thrown out the baby with the bathwater". Legalism seems to have been replaced with libertinism.[47]

As we have seen from the history of the Holiness movement and Pentecostal movement, this spirituality was a revolutionary paradigm for the people involved. As Pentecostal movement is a century old and reached a juncture where the movement has lost some of its cherished spiritual heritage, mainly holiness, it is significant to regain it. To achieve this, Pentecostal movement should go back to its roots and rediscover its original passion for holiness. Here I shall endorse few steps to be taken to recover the lost holiness spirituality but they are neither arbitrarily imposed nor the final word; it is the responsibility of individuals and community to take a conscious call to come back to the original spirituality.

First of all, because of their holiness spirituality, the early Holiness followers and Pentecostals had on the one hand, totally separated from the impurities of the world and its contaminating philosophies and structures, on the other hand, they were fully involved in society in the business of rescuing the lost and the poor. They had a strong conviction that they were a unique and separated people for the Lord and his mission. Therefore, they had no time and resources to spend on worldly affairs. Their encounter with Christ and the "strangely warmed heart" in them created an utopian vision of personal and social holiness. Therefore, they were ready to refuse anything that stood against their conviction and inculcated attitudes and characters that were of high standard. They insisted on cleansing of themselves and rejecting of all filthiness of the flesh and the spirit. For them the experience of sanctification or the baptism of the Holy Spirit was not only a source of power but rather primarily a high level of moral standard that comes through consecration. Pentecostals everywhere testifies that sanctification experience changed their outlook towards oneself and others. Thus, it is a paradigm of transformation and is achieved through the work of the Spirit, therefore, Pentecostals should actively strive for sanctification.

Besides, it is also important to understand that though, the Holy Spirit bestows holiness in us, we should also strive to be holy in our intentions, words and deeds through personal examining, cleansing and personal walk with the Lord.[48] We must cooperate with the Spirit for growing in holiness. Wayne Grudem underlines that the role that we play in sanctification is both a *passive* one in which we depend on God to sanctify us, and an *active* one in which we strive to obey God and take steps that will increase our sanctification. The New Testament very clearly speaks about this aspect of striving for divine character in us. For instance, Paul tells his readers, "*Yield yourselves to God.*" (Rom. 6:13), and "Present your bodies as a living sacrifice, holy and acceptable to God" (Rom. 12:1). Paul realizes that we are dependent on the Holy Spirit's work to grow in sanctification, because he says, "If *by the Spirit* you put to death the deeds of the body you will live"

[47] Adewuya, "Holiness: Reclaiming the Doctrine", 272.

[48] See Conn, "Christian Perfection (A Pentecostal Perspective)", 169-180.

(Rom. 8:13).[49] Here Paul acknowledges that it is "by the Spirit" and also by us. It is commanded to believers to mortify the deeds of the flesh.

There are many aspects to this active role that we are to play in sanctification. We are to "*Strive...for* the *holiness* without which no one will see the Lord" (Heb. 12:14); we are to "*abstain from immorality*" and so obey the will of God, which is our "sanctification" (1 Thess. 4:3). John says that "everyone who hopes in him *purifies himself* as he is pure" (1 John 3:3). This kind of striving for holiness may involve great effort on our part, for Peter tells his readers to "*make every effort*" to grow in character traits that accord with godliness (2 Peter 1:5).[50] Therefore, both divine and human elements work together to achieve Christian perfection.

Secondly, Pentecostals did not invent the doctrine of holiness to suit their personal or communal agenda, nor they intended to perpetuate their hegemony and carry forward their movement with this doctrine, among the plethora of Christian denominations existing at that time. Rather the holiness spirituality was a gift from above, fully a biblical concept, although some may disagree on some of the details of this doctrine.[51] With the biblical testimony, early Pentecostals were strongly convinced that they were chosen and separated for God and sent out to be a catalyst for transformation in the society. The church has to be a community that implants the foretaste of the reign of God where divine characters are shared among their compatriots. Therefore, Pentecostals ought to go back to the scripture to recover the lost zeal and attracting power of holiness.

Thirdly, the sanctification and the liberated experience received from it is not a well thought out human agenda. The sanctification is the free gift of God, actualised through the work of the Spirit in personal as well as social life. In Pentecostalism now a days, the works of the Spirit is predominantly emphasised in terms of "signs and wonders" rather than formation of holy life, thus, lack of Christian character formation. Pentecostals should realise that the power of the Spirit is bestowed upon us primarily for holiness and secondly for power for mission. As a result of sanctification and consecration, the power of the Holy Spirit is imparted on us to move out for mission, enacting miracles, which will transform others. Therefore, Pentecostals need to insist on waiting for the intervention of the Spirit.

Fourthly, some Pentecostals in the name of holiness draw away from the God-given responsibilities in their society. They consider the society as so corrupt and unredeemable that it is a waste of energy and time to involve in any reform

---

[49] Wayne Grudem, *Systematic Theology: An Introduction to Bible Doctrine* (Leicester: IVP, 1994), 654.

[50] Grudem, *Systematic Theology*, 654-657; Many specific passages of the New Testament encourage detailed attention to various aspects of holiness and godliness in life (see Rom. 12:1–13:14; Eph. 4:17–6:20; Phil. 4:4–9; Col. 3:5–4:6; 1 Peter 2:11–5:11; et al.).

[51] For instance, some may question, including Pentecostal theologians, the idea that equates sanctification and baptism of Holy Spirit. Warrington, *Pentecostal Theology*, 207.

activities. Their understanding is that, "it is futile to paint a ship that is sinking". They tend to be individualistic in holiness and secure behind the self-made walls of individualistic holiness. However, it should be conveyed that the real holiness is actualised through service to others as early Pentecostals did. What the 19th century Pietist and social activist Christoph Blumhardt once remarked is right, "one must convert twice: once from the world to God, but then a second time from God back to the world to serve the kingdom of God."[52]

Obviously, it is good to have well defined social strategies and programmes and encourage Pentecostals to carry them out. However, in the Third-World situations where most of the Pentecostals are very poor and live in haphazard conditions, they may be unable to involve actively in social ministries. Even some people accuse Pentecostals of other-worldly and lacking in social awareness. However, as Peterson affirms, contrary to the critique that Pentecostals do not adequately demonstrate a social conscience, typically congregations provide social welfare service to needy families, the sick, the abused and the aged. Consequently, several observers have remarked that "Pentecostals do not have a social policy, they are a social policy."[53] In line with Peterson's assessment, what I am suggesting here is, listen to voice of the Spirit and wherever the Spirit leads, be willing to involve there. The Holy Spirit is the agent of sanctification and also gives power for service with a concept of mission being grounded in historical experience but with consequences which go beyond present history. The Holy Spirit enables a person to experience the paradox of suffering and the power of renunciation to enable to side with the oppressed.[54] The social ministry does not necessarily be done with huge demonstrations or actions, but instead can be carried out penetrating into the roots of the problems by the power of the Spirit. Therefore, Pentecostals can bring great transformation, by listening to the Spirit and striking a balance between the individual aspects of holiness in which strict personal integrity and faithfulness maintained and social aspects of holiness through ministry to others.

Fifthly and finally, the early Pentecostals were ready to forfeit their wealth, position and even highly successful ministerial credentials for the sake of holiness. Through the sanctification experience they learned to become humble and dedicated themselves for the service of others. But if we look into Pentecostal churches and leadership today, situation is entirely different. People do anything to become popular or climb up the hierarchical order of the denominations. Many of the leaders are with inflated egos, superiority complex and ready to trample on their opponents in the denominations. Here there is a great need of

---

[52] F. D. Macchia, "Pentecostal Theology", in *NIDPCM,* edited by Stanley M. Burgess (Michigan: Zondervan, 2002), 1130.

[53] Douglas Petersen, *Not by Might nor by Power – A Pentecostal Theology of Social Concern in Latin (America.* Oxford: Regnum, 1996), 119-120.

[54] Bridges Johns, *Pentecostal Formation,* 100.

the experience of sanctification and a earnest desire to develop Christ's character, especially Christ's humility among the Pentecostals.

Let us conclude our discussion here; holiness is one of the most important factors of Pentecostal spirituality. It provided the movement a unique identity among other denominations and impelled the movement into worldwide. Early members of Pentecostal movement were ready to forfeit many of their cherished possessions for the sake of holiness. Besides, the experience of sanctification transformed their life and lifted them to a higher pedestal of moral and spiritual life. It also propelled them to involve actively in their society to rescue many who were poor and downtrodden. However, after century, the original fervour for holiness is somewhat lost and which resulted in the degeneration of the spiritual standard of the movement. Rather than giving emphasis on internal aspects of holiness such as personal integrity, humility and so on, Pentecostals stay more upon the external aspect of holiness. Therefore, it is imperative to go back to the biblical paradigm of holiness to recover its original spirituality to revive the movement to be an agent of transformation in today's world.

Chapter 4

The Baptism in the Holy Spirit Power for Liberation

The doctrine of the baptism in the Holy Spirit can be termed as the most fundamental doctrine and the basic spirituality of the Pentecostal movement. This vital spirituality is the very reason for the origin and marvellous growth of the movement worldwide. Pentecostals believe that the Spirit-baptism is firmly rooted in the New Testament teaching and was the experience of disciples of Jesus and the early church, for purpose of special service for God. For instance, Myer Pearlman while expounding the Bible doctrines in a Pentecostal perspective, underlines the general understanding of Pentecostals. The Holy Spirit energises "human nature for special service for God, and issues in an outward expression of a supernatural character...In the New Testament this experience is designated by such expressions as falling upon, coming upon, being poured out, being filled with, which expressions convey the thought of suddenness and super-naturalness. All these terms are connected with the experience known as the Baptism with the Holy Spirit."[1] By embracing the phenomenon of the outpouring of the Spirit in the book of Acts, Pentecostals consider themselves as the successors of the early church and claim the original New Testament spirituality in their life. T. B. Barratt presents this concept succinctly:

> The Pentecostal revival seeks to return as much as possible to the doctrine, faith and practice of original Christianity in all manners…

---

[1] Myer Pearlman, *Knowing the Doctrines of the Bible* (Springfield, Missouri: Gospel Publishing House, 1981), 312.

> What really distinguishes us from the other ones in this way is our definite claim to be baptized in the Holy Ghost in the same way as the 120 on the day of Pentecost, a Spirit baptism accompanied by the speaking in tongues.[2]

Pentecostals also consider it as a normative Christian experience and assert that all can attain the baptism of the Spirit. While all the Evangelical groups consider regeneration in a person is enacted by the Holy Spirit, Pentecostals teach the baptism of the Holy Spirit as a second grace or experience other than regeneration in Christian life. The main argument is drawn from the Book of Acts. The disciples on the day of the Pentecost were already, by our present understanding and use of the term, Christians. They had already confessed Jesus as the Christ (Matt. 16:16), been pronounced clean (John 15:3), been told that their names were written in heaven (Luke 10:20), and had forsaken all to follow him (Matt. 19:27). Thus, their reception of the Spirit at Pentecost is seen as subsequent to their regeneration.[3] This understanding of the Spirit-baptism well stated in The "Statement of Fundamental and Essential Truths" in the Constitution and By-laws of the General Conference of the Pentecostal Assemblies of Canada:

> The baptism in the Holy Spirit is an experience in which the believer yields control of himself to the Holy Spirit (Matt 3:11; Acts 1:5; Eph 5:18). Through this he comes to know Christ in a more intimate way (John 16:13-15), and receives power to witness and grow spiritually (2 Cor. 3:18; Acts 1:8). Believers should earnestly seek the baptism in the Holy Spirit according to the command of our Lord Jesus Christ (Luke 24:49; Acts1:4-8). The initial evidence of the baptism in the Holy Spirit is speaking in other tongues as the Spirit gives utterance (2 Cor. 3:18; Acts 1:8). This experience is distinct from, and subsequent to, the experience of the new birth (Acts 8:12-17; 10:44-46).[4]

> Early Pentecostal writings are replete with references to Spirit-baptism and the reception of power for witnessing. Donald Gee, a noted British Pentecostal wrote the following:

---

[2] Nils Bloch-Hoell, *The Pentecostal Movement: Its Origin, Development, and Distinctive Character* (New York: Humanities Press, 1964), 1-2.

[3] David Petts, "The Baptism in the Holy Spirit: The Theological Distinctive", in *Pentecostal Perspectives*, edited by Keith Warrington (Carlisle, Cumbria: Paternoster Press, 1998), 99.

[4] Quoted in Bradley Truman Noel, *Pentecostalism, Secularism, and Post Christendom* (Eugene, Oregon: Wipf & Stock Publishers, 2015), 37; Also see, Myer Pearlman, *Knowing the Doctrines of the Bible* (Springfield, Missouri: Gospel Publishing House, 1937), 309; Robert P. Menzies, "The Distinctive Character of Luke's Pneumatology", *Pneuma* 25 (Fall 1991): 18; J. Rodman Williams, "Baptism in the Holy Spirit", in *NIDPCM*, edited by Stanley M. Burgess (Michigan: Zondervan, 2002), 354.

> It is the Spirit-filled, Spirit-led, and Spirit-empowered Christian who truly possesses dynamic power for witnessing. We have derived the word dynamite from the Greek word *dunamis,* used in Acts 1:8. The power of the gospel sometimes acts with blessed explosive force. Opposition to God's word is sometimes hard as granite and needs the explosive nature of dynamite before the preaching can make any impression. The need is for dynamic power.[5]

We can summarise this doctrine or spirituality with following distinctive elements that is expounded in Pentecostal doctrinal system. First, it is an experience that is fully in accordance with the New Testament teaching. Second, it is a second grace or experience distinct from and subsequent to regeneration or new birth. Third, it is an enduement of supernatural power for mission. Fourth, the experience of the baptism in the Holy Spirit is accompanied by "tongue speaking" which is considered as the initial sign of receiving it.

However, in the beginning of the movement, the manifestations of the Pentecostal experience of Spirit-baptism was deemed as exhibition of excessive emotionalism or vulgarities by non-Pentecostals and even termed as demonic. Pentecostals were termed as "holy rollers" or "holy jumpers", as the lunatic fringe in the Christendom and ridiculed for their new found spirituality. However, the emergence of the Charismatic movement in the denominational churches and the significant growth of Pentecostalism in various nations of the world, even surpassing the Protestant churches have changed this attitude. Now non-Pentecostals also accept and appreciate this spirituality and extensively use in their life and mission. Besides, the transformation that brought by Pentecostal movement to the poor, disenfranchised, and downtrodden can be attributed to this doctrine. This experience of the Spirit emphasised by Pentecostals forms a unique spirituality that liberates and transforms people all over the world. In the following pages we shall see a glimpse of the development of this doctrine and how it becomes a driving force for the growth of the Pentecostal movement and liberates and transforms people of every walk of life.

Origin of the Doctrine of the Baptism in the Holy Spirit

The origin of the doctrine of the Spirit-baptism can be traced back to John Wesley (1703-1791) and his doctrine of Christian perfection. Wesley was a clergy in the Anglican Church. Along with his brother Charles Wesley and some others, he began a religious study group that was derisively called the "Methodists" because of their emphasis on methodical study and devotion. This group was also known as the "Holy Club" as they frequently had holy communion and fasting. On May 24, 1738, in Aldersgate Street, London, during a Moravian meeting where Luther's

---

[5] David A. Womack (ed.), *Pentecostal Experience: The Writings of Donald Gee* (Springfield, MI: Gospel Publishing House, 1993), 37.

preface to the commentary to the Letter of Paul to the Romans was being read, Wesley had a strange spiritual experience in which his "heart strangely warmed". This instant spiritual experience transformed Wesley's intellectual conviction into a personal spiritual experience and had a great impact in the formulation of his theology of Christian perfection which also includes an "instant experience of sanctification".

Wesley formulated that sanctification takes place at the point of regeneration and continues for whole life. However, Wesley added a new dimension in the doctrine of sanctification that there should be a "second blessing" or a "crisis experience" which cleanses a person from "inbred sin", all the filthiness of spirit and body. This internal perfection could be attained instantly as a "second work of grace."[6] This is termed as entire sanctification. Wesley himself explains it:

> But, does God work this great work in the soul gradually or instantaneously? Perhaps it may be gradually wrought in some...but it is infinitely desirable, were it the will of God that it should be done instantaneously; that the Lord should destroy sin "by the breath of his mouth", in a moment, in the twinkling of an eye. And so he generally does; a plain fact, of which there is evidence enough to satisfy any unprejudiced person. Thou therefore look for it every moment! Look for it every day, every hour, every moment!.. If you seek it by faith, you may expect it as you are; and if as you are, then expect it *now.*[7]

In this second experience, a believer is endued with the virtues of Jesus Christ and renewed in spirit and mind. However, in his formulation of the doctrine of Christian perfection, he did not claim an absolute sinless perfection but the experience leads to perfect love for God and one's neighbour, primarily in service of others. Wesley believed in entire sanctification as a work wrought by God in an experience subsequent to salvation. This is the first step in the formation of the Pentecostal doctrine of the baptism of the Holy Spirit as a second work of grace.[8]

However, Wesley's followers emphasised more on the "crisis" aspect of the experience, and eventually his doctrine of Christian Perfection, which also includes gradual process of sanctification, was reinterpreted as a crisis experience that yields instant results. It is Wesley's designated successor, John Fletcher who spearheaded the second blessing or crisis moment into the "baptism of the Holy Spirit". Conversion was understood less as a process, and more as a crisis experience, gained in a moment of time. Fletcher was keen on using the phrase but Wesley appears to have resisted it. Wesley insisted that "the phrase in that

[6] Vinson Synan, *The Holiness-Pentecostal Tradition: Charismatic Movements in the Twentieth Century* (2nd edition) (Michigan: Eerdmans, 1997), 6-7.

[7] Quoted in Truman Noel, *Pentecostalism, Secularism, and Post Christendom*, 15.

[8] For a detailed description of this doctrine, see the chapter on holiness.

sense is not scriptural and not quite proper; for they all "received the Holy Ghost" when they were justified.[9] However, Fletcher was not fully convinced by Wesley's argument, instead he wanted to differentiate between those who baptised with the power of the Spirit and not. He comments,

> You will find my views on this matter in Mr. Wesley's sermons on Christian Perfection and on Scriptural Christianity; with this difference, that I would distinguish more exactly between the believer baptized with the Pentecostal power of the Holy Ghost, and the believer who, like the Apostles after our Lord's ascension, is not yet filled with that power.[10]

Even though Wesley disagreed with John Fletcher in this matter, who argued that the second blessing was in reality a "baptism of the Holy Spirit" as well as a cleansing experience, at the end of his life Wesley was convinced of Fletcher's position.[11] Fletcher's ideas were, thus, the beginning of the development of the doctrine of the baptism in the Holy Spirit as a distinct experience different from conversion and was later co-opted by Pentecostal movement when it emerged in the scene in the subsequent century.

In 1784, John Wesley sent a delegation to Baltimore, Maryland in America to formally organize the Methodist Churches with the purpose of reforming the continent and spreading scriptural holiness.[12] This resulted in the dissemination of the Wesleyan doctrine of Christian perfection all over America. The early pioneers of American Methodism were faithful to Wesley's theology and therefore taught a doctrine of Christian Perfection that was consistent with his definition. However, the doctrine taught by Holiness preachers during the nineteenth century was much closer to Fletcher's version of it. This change in perspective transpired in the form of a "revival movement."[13]

By the beginning of the nineteenth century the Wesleyan doctrine of Christian perfection was neglected in the Methodist churches. However, by 1820-30's there was resurgence of this doctrine with more emphasis on baptism of the Holy Spirit that emphasised by John Fletcher. It was Phoebe Palmer (1807-1874), along with her sister Sarah Lankford spearheaded this movement. In 1835, Lankford began holding "Tuesday Meetings for the Promotion of Holiness" in

---

[9] Donald W. Dayton, *Theological Roots of Pentecostalism* (Grand Rapids, Michigan: Baker Academic, 1987), 50.

[10] Dayton, *Theological Roots of Pentecostalism,* 50.

[11] Vinson Synan, *The Holiness-Pentecostal Tradition,* 6-7.

[12] Quoted in Vinson Synan, *Holiness-Pentecostal Movement in the United States* (Grand Rapids, Michigan: Eerdmans, 1972), 20.

[13] Allan Thomas Loder, *An Examination of the Classical Pentecostal Doctrine of the Baptism in the Holy Spirit: In Light of the Pentecostal Position on the Sources of Theology* (Allan T. Loder, 2000), 30.

her parlour. By 1839, Palmer became the leader of this group, and began teaching a "shorter way" to holiness. According to Palmer, one could skip the process of sanctification altogether and be instantly sanctified through the "baptism of the Holy Ghost". She believed that one receives this second blessing if one totally consecrate to God by "placing all on the altar;" and by exercising his or her faith by "taking God at his word", and claiming what he has promised. Later Palmer began to use terms and language that sounds like early Pentecostals to explain her doctrine of Christian Perfection. In 1859, she published *The Promise of the Father,* in which she referred to holiness as "power from on high". She also began to use the phrase "baptism of the Holy Spirit", which she viewed as synonymous with entire sanctification.[14] Palmer's revival movement resulted in the formation of the Holiness movement and which in turn enabled the development of Pentecostal doctrine of Spirit-baptism in later stage.

Another significant development in relation to the doctrine of the baptism of the Holy Spirit in America occurred through the life, ministry and theology of Charles Finney (1792-1875). He emerged as the best-known revivalist in the United States and probably did more to prepare the way for Pentecostalism than any other. Finney was a lawyer and had a question on his assurance of salvation. On October 10, 1821, he headed out into the woods near his home town Adams, New York, to find God. He was so desperate that he said, "I will give my heart to God, or I never will come down from there". Having reached in the woods, he knelt by a log and wrestled with God in prayer, and had an encounter with God in which he experienced such forceful emotion that he questioned those who could not testify to a similar encounter. He narrates the experience of his encounter,

> The Holy Spirit ... seemed to go through me, body and soul. I could feel the impression, like a wave of electricity, going through and through me. Indeed it seemed to come in waves of liquid love, for I could not express it in any other way.[15]

The next morning itself he resigned his job and later became an ordained minister of the Presbyterian church. In 1825, Finney had powerful ministry in New York. He rode from town to town with the message of salvation, that resulted in great spiritual awakening. The whole area where Finney was then preaching has been referred to by historians as the "Burned-over district"; a reference to the fact that the area had experienced so much spiritual awakening that the district

---

[14] Henry Knight iii, "From Aldersgate to Azusa: Wesley and the Renewal of Pentecostal Spirituality", *JPT* 8 (1996): 86; see Phoebe Palmer, "The Way of Holiness", in *The Devotional Writings of Phoebe Palmer,* edited by Donald W. Dayton (New York: Garland Publishing, 1985), 37-38.

[15] https://www.christianitytoday.com/history/people/evangelistsandapologists/charles-finney.html (accessed on 27/07/19).

had been burned-out.[16] In 1835, he moved to the state of Ohio, became the professor of Oberlin College and later selected as its second president and there he developed his theology. Consequently, his personal divine encounter, ministry experiences and academic pursuit surely had a definite impact on his doctrine of the baptism of the Holy Spirit.

Finney further developed the doctrine of Phoebe Palmer and others and laid a new emphasis on the doctrine of Spirit-baptism. He asserted that Spirit-baptism was not only essential for sanctification, but also for *empowerment for* service. According to Gresham, Finney's later discussions of the baptism in the Holy Spirit revolved around those two themes: sanctification and usefulness. The baptism was presented either as a cleansing, liberating experience or as an act of empowerment for ministry.[17] Moreover, Finney emphasized the crisis aspect of the second blessing experience and reiterated that the experience enables the believer to continually obey God's law, and also empowered him or her to "... prevail with God in prayer and with people through preaching and witness."[18] Finney explains it, "If filled with the Spirit, you will be useful. You cannot help being useful. Even if you were sick and unable to go out of your room, or to converse, and saw nobody, you would be ten times more useful than a hundred of those common sort of Christians who have no spirituality."[19]

Later, in the 1870s he began to teach that sanctification is not a gift from God, but rather an act of consecration on the part of the believer. The baptism in the Holy Spirit, on the other hand, is a gift that is universally promised and proffered to Christians under this dispensation.[20] Finney was the first one clearly to state the baptism in the Spirit was not an experience of sanctification at all, but was exclusively an enduement of power for service.[21] Thus, he abandoned the traditional understanding of the second blessing as "entire sanctification", and redefined it as "an enduement of power for service". Consequently, Finney proposed that Spirit-baptism be made a mandatory qualification for involvement in any church-related office. He believed that this experience was so absolutely necessary for "a supernaturally effective ministry" that one could not expect success without it.[22]

---

[16] https://www.christianitytoday.com/history/people/evangelistsandapologists/charles-finney.html.

[17] John L. Gresham, *Charles G. Finney's Doctrine of the Baptism in the Holy Spirit* (Peabody: Hendnckson, 1994), 15.

[18] Gresham, *Charles G. Finney's Doctrine,* 15.

[19] E. E. Shelhamer, (ed.). *Finney on Revival* (Minneapolis: Bethany House Publishers, 1974), 114, quoted in Noel, *Pentecostalism, Secularism, and Post Christendom,* 27.

[20] Loder, *An Examination of the Classical Pentecostal Doctrine*, 37.

[21] Roland Wessels, "The Spirit-Baptism: Nineteenth Century Roots", *Pneuma* 14/2 (Fall 1992), 142.

[22] Loder, *An Examination of the Classical Pentecostal Doctrine*, 38.

Along with Finney, the life, ministry and the writings of leaders such as Asa Mahan, John Morgan, D. L. Moody, Reuben A. Torrey, Daniel Steele, Henry Cowles and many others helped to firmly establish the doctrine of the Spirit-baptism in the American scene. In Asa Mahan (1799-1889), who was Finney's colleague and the first president of Oberlin College, we see a deeper conviction in the Spirit-baptism. He emphasised the idea of "power" as the major theme of the second blessing experience and the power was granted for service.[23] His book *The Baptism of the Holy Ghost* (1870) presents doctrine of "entire sanctification" in terms of a "Pentecostal experience" and was adopted both by many within the holiness movement as well as others and understood as an endowment of power.[24] Similarly, Dwight L. Moody (1837-1899), another well known revivalist of the nineteenth century, also became instrumental in deeply establishing this doctrine. However, he believed that this gift, which is granted for "service", should not be limited to those in church-related offices only rather, it is the privilege of every believer. The rank and file of the Church need this baptism of the Holy Spirit just as much as the preacher.[25] He made a distinction between the "indwelling" of the Spirit and "Spirit-baptism". He maintained that the Spirit indwells in every believer "in some sense and to some extent" at conversion, but that there is a second experience "...entirely distinct and separate from conversion and assurance". This second experience is another "receiving" of the Spirit as he comes to dwell within us "in power."[26] In his own words:

> The Holy Spirit dwelling in us is one thing; I think this is clearly brought out in Scripture. And the Holy Spirit upon us for service is another thing....I think it is clearly taught in Scripture that every believer has the Holy Ghost dwelling in Him.... But I want to call your attention to another fact. I believe, today, that though Christian men and women have the Holy Spirit dwelling in them, yet He is not dwelling within them in power.[27]

Thus, the life, ministry and writings of these leaders enabled this vibrant doctrine and spirituality to be entrenched in the Christian churches in those times. Besides, this doctrine did not exist as a theoretical construct, rather embraced by many and brought revolutionary changes in spiritual and social landscape of the Western world. It was not only a spiritual renewal but the spirituality of the Spirit-baptism also transformed the social landscape in terms of creating equality

---

[23] Dayton, *Theological Roots of Pentecostalism*, 13.

[24] Dayton, *Theological Roots of Pentecostalism*, 14.

[25] Loder, *An Examination of the Classical Pentecostal Doctrine*, 38.

[26] Loder, *An Examination of the Classical Pentecostal Doctrine*, 38; Dwight Lyman Moody, *Moody: His Words, Work, and Workers*, edited by W.H. Daniels (New York: Nelson & Phillips, 1877), 398; Also see, https://archive.org/details/cu31924052629643/page/n13 (accessed on 27/07/19).

[27] Quoted in Noel, *Pentecostalism, Secularism, and Post Christendom*, 27.

among the blacks and whites, social ministry and unity among churches as we have seen in previous chapters. These spiritual reformers were also impacted the lives of ordinary people. The religious scene was getting ready for the formation of the Pentecostal movement. As Dayton highlights, these developments were a necessary prelude to what would follow. "Once 'crisis' overwhelms 'process' to make sanctification primarily an event occurring at a definite point in time and once the teleological thrust of Christian perfection is transmuted into an initiatory experience that usually follows rapidly on conversion, the stage has been set for the re-emergence of the Pentecostal formulation of the Spirit-baptism."[28] Moreover, the development that the Spirit-baptism was for the endowment of power and the power was meant for service, prepared the way for the emergence of Pentecostal movement and its most vital doctrine and spirituality in the next century. Just as Richard Lovelace has pointed out, by the end of the nineteenth century it was widely assumed that all mature Christians should duplicate Finney's experience of Spirit-baptism. It remained only for Charles Parham to add the teaching that tongues was the initial evidence of the baptism in the Holy Spirit, and the Classical Pentecostal movement was launched.[29]

The Baptism of the Holy Spirit and the Beginning of Pentecostalism

In the previous pages we have briefly explored the development of the spirituality of the baptism of the Holy Spirit and its effects on existing Christian denominations in 18th and 19th centuries. This spirituality brought dramatic changes in the spiritual atmosphere in terms of doctrine and practices. There was an earnest hunger and thirst for personal spiritual renewal and ecclesiastical reformation. The people who were revived by the Holiness movements, were seeking for further spiritual experiences. Such an expectancy among the Christians was satisfied by the emergence of a new renewal movement in the spiritual horizon; surely, that was the Pentecostal movement.

There are differing views and opinions regarding the origin of the Pentecostal movement whether its exact date of formation or leaders. However, one thing is obvious and definite; it is the doctrine of the Spirit-baptism and the supernatural phenomena accompanied with it enabled the movement to kick-start itself. More than any leaders or any set principles, it was the outpouring of the Holy Spirit and the revolutionary transformation people experienced catapulted the movement world over. In the following pages, therefore, we shall explore the powerful manifestation of the Spirit and its effects on the origin of Pentecostal movement and the consolidation of the doctrine and spirituality of the baptism in the Holy Spirit.

---

[28] Dayton, *Theological Roots of Pentecostalism*, 70.

[29] Richard Lovelace, "Baptism in the Holy Spirit and the Evangelical Tradition", *Pneuma* 7/3 (Fall 1985): 119.

Most histories date the beginning of the movement to January 1, 1901, when Agnes Ozman spoke in tongues at the Bethel Bible School in Topeka, Kansas, operated by former Methodist preacher Charles F. Parham.[30] It was Parham who subsequently formulated the "initial evidence" teaching that is central to the theology of most of the classical Pentecostal churches of the world. However, the Pentecostal movement received its greatest impetus from the Azusa Street revival of 1906-9 led by William J. Seymour, a black Holiness preacher from Texas. This revival launched Pentecostalism into a worldwide movement. From Azusa Street, the movement spread throughout the world through the mission's newspaper, *The Apostolic Faith,* and by the pilgrims who flocked to Los Angeles to experience tongues.

Born in Muscatine, Iowa, on June 4, 1873, Parham was greatly suffered by physical illness.[31] At age of nine, he was stricken with rheumatic fever —a condition that plagued him throughout his life despite long periods of remission. With the first bout of rheumatic fever, he felt a call to the ministry. Having survived a particularly severe attack of rheumatic fever in 1891 and miraculous healing, he reaffirmed his ministerial call and also developed a firm belief in the doctrine of divine healing. In 1893 he quit school to assume a pastorate of a Methodist church. Enamoured with the theology of the Holiness movement and spurred by his college experience with divine healing, Parham left the Methodist Church in 1895 to assume an independent ministry.[32]

In October 15, 1900, Parham obtained an unfinished mansion on the outskirts of Topeka and opened a Bible school with about 36 students, most of whom had been ministers from other denominations in the area and shared with Parham his intense desire for a new Pentecostal blessing.[33] Parham gave his students an assignment to diligently search for the evidence of Spirit baptism in the book of Acts and left town for a meeting in Kansas. When he returned, he was eager to see the results of the assignment. Anticipation now filled the house as 75 people gathered together for the evening Watch Night service on January 1, 1901. One of the students in the meeting was 30 year old Agnes N. Ozman. During the

---

[30] *The New Dictionary of Pentecostal Movement* (NIDPCM) recognises Charles Parham (1873-1929) as the founder of classical Pentecostal theology and Pentecostal movement. He inter-connected the basic doctrines of the Pentecostal movement that later defined the movement, such as sanctification, divine healing, *Premillennialism*, and the baptism of the Holy Spirit evidenced by *glossolalia*. Parham's efforts gave Pentecostalism a definable theological corpus and instilled within the movement a fervent missionary emphasis. J. R. Goff Jr., "Parham, Cahrles Fox", in *NIDPCM*, 955. However, if we consider the Pentecostal movement as liberative movement, it is William Seymour would fit for the founder of the movement.

[31] Goff Jr., "Parham Charles Fox", 955-957; also see Douglas Jacobson, *Thinking in the Spirit: Theologies of the Early Pentecostal Movement* (Indianapolis: Indiana University Press, 2003).

[32] Goff Jr. "Parham, Charles Fox", 955.

[33] Roberts Liardon, *Azuza Street Revival: When the Fire Fell* (Shippensburg, PA: Destiny Image Publishers, 2006), 71-72.

service, Ozman went up to Parham and asked him if he would lay hands on her so that she would receive the Spirit baptism. At Ozman's persistence and although Parham himself had not spoken in tongues, he laid hands on the student. Parham narrates what happened next:

> I had scarcely repeated three dozen sentences when a glory fell upon her, a halo seemed to surround her head and face, and she began speaking in the Chinese language, and was unable to speak in English for three days.[34]

On the evening of January 3, while Parham was preaching at a free Methodist church in Topeka, the Spirit fell on the students at the Bethel school. When Parham arrived back at the school, a student met him at the door and led him to the prayer room. Inside he encountered twelve students who were sitting, standing, kneeling, and all speaking in tongues. Overwhelmed by what he saw, Parham fell to his knees and started praying and praising God. While praying, he was also filled with the Holy Spirit and began to speak in other tongues. Here is how Parham described the experience in his own words: "Right then and there came a slight twist in my throat, a glory fell over me and I began to worship God in a Swedish tongue, which later changed to other languages and continued."[35]

In December 1905, Parham moved his Bible school to Houston and there Charles Parham and William J. Seymour (1870-1922) met. William J. Seymour was born May 2, 1870, in Centerville, Los Angeles. Seymour was the eldest son of Simon and Phillis Seymour. His father was a brick maker. We do not know details of his childhood; but what we do know is that by mid 1894 Seymour could be found in Indianapolis, Indiana. Seymour arrived there in the middle of this period of growing racial concerns. Seymour served as a waiter at three different hotels during this period. He was converted in a "coloured Methodist Episcopal Church" in Indianapolis, where he became a member for a period of time. Seymour left Indianapolis most probably in late 1899 or early 1900 and moved to Cincinnati, Ohio. Seymour's testimony to Shumway, who had done research on Seymour, notes that while he was in Cincinnati he contracted smallpox and lost his sight in one eye. Seymour connected this event with God's judgment on him for not entering the ministry earlier. Seymour then came to the Houston area in 1905, where, in August of that year, Mrs. Lucy Farrow, an African-American widow and the founder of a small black congregation, handed the reins of leadership over to him. Farrow encouraged Seymour to study with Parham and learn of the baptism in the Holy Spirit at his Bible school.[36] The Jim Crow laws of the day

---

[34] Liardon, *Azuza Street Revival,* 74.

[35] J. R. Goff Jr., "Topeka Revival", in *NIDPCM*, 1147-1149.

[36] Cecil M. Robeck Jr., "Seymour, William Joseph", in *NIDPCM*, 1053-58; Jacobson, *Thinking in the Spirit,* 61-62.

prevented blacks and whites from congregating together;[37] therefore, there were no blacks allowed in the school. Parham was reluctant to admit Seymour, but sensing Seymour's great spiritual hunger, he eventually allowed him to attend. Parham did not allow him to sit in the classroom with the white students but in an adjoining room where, through an open door, he could listen the teachings on the Holy Spirit baptism. Despite the impositions from Parham, Seymour was not deterred, and because of the intensity of his spiritual hunger, he did extremely well in school. "Later he would be able to recite Parham's teachings word for word."[38] Seymour was consumed with a passionate desire for God. His own words show his spiritual hunger:

> Before I met Parham, such a hunger to have more of God was in my heart that I prayed for five hours a day for two and a half years. I got to Los Angeles, and there the hunger was not less but more. I prayed, "God, what can I do?" The Spirit said, "Pray more". "But Lord, I am praying five hours a day now". I increased my hours of prayer to seven, and prayed on for a year and a half more. I prayed to God to give what Parham preached, the real Holy Ghost and fire with tongues with love and power of God like the apostles had.[39]

In January 1906, Seymour asked permission to move to Los Angeles and Parham gave Seymour the money for the train trip, and then in a momentous act, he laid hands on the kneeling Seymour and sent him on his way. Little did they know at that time that Seymour's trip would strike a match and set off a new blaze of Pentecostal fire.[40] Shortly after Seymour's arrival in Los Angeles, he preached his first sermon at Sister Hutchin's church on Santa Fe Avenue. His theology on the Holy Spirit would clash with hers because that church believed they had already been sanctified and received the Holy Spirit. The clash came to a head when he was finally locked out of the church.[41]

---

[37] Jim Crow was the name of the racial caste system that operated primarily, but not exclusively in Southern and border states, between 1877 and the mid-1960s. Jim Crow was more than a series of rigid anti-black laws; it was a way of life. Under Jim Crow, African-Americans were relegated to the status of second-class citizens. These heinous laws enforced separate use of water fountains, public bathhouses, and separate seating sections on public transport. The Jim Crow laws represented the legitimization of anti-black racism. Sadly, discrimination and segregation were also prevalent in the churches, and many Christian ministers and theologians taught that whites were the "chosen people", blacks were cursed to be servants, and God supported racial segregation. Many in those days did not believe that blacks even had a soul.

[38] Liardon, *Azuza Street Revival,* 92.

[39] Eddie L. Hyatt, *2000 Years of Charismatic Christianity* (Florida: Charisma House, 2002), 142.

[40] Liardon, *Azuza Street Revival,* 72-79.

[41] Liardon, *Azuza Street Revival,* 95.

Then he came to North Bonnie Brae Street and had meetings in the home of Mr. and Mrs. Richard Asberry in February 1906. During that time, Edward Lee, a janitor employed at the First National Bank, asked Seymour to pray for his ailing health. Seymour went there, anointed him with oil, and he was healed. Then Lee asked him to pray for the baptism of the Holy Spirit. Even though Seymour had not personally received the experience, he prayed for Lee, and Lee immediately began speaking in tongues.

Later in the meeting, Seymour began to tell the story of Mr. Lee's healing and his infilling of the Holy Spirit. As soon as Seymour finished, Lee raised his hands and began to speak in tongues. The entire group dropped to their knees as they worshiped God and cried out for the baptism. Then, six or seven people lifted their voices and began to speak in another tongue. Jenny Evans Moore, who would later marry Seymour, fell to her knees from the piano bench as one of the first to speak in tongues. For three days they celebrated. The news spread quickly bringing crowds that would fill the Asberry's house and the yard surrounding their home. It was on the third night, on April 12, 1906 that Seymour would finally experience his own encounter with the Holy Spirit.[42]

Seymour's friends quickly located a vacant, two-story, whitewashed, wooden frame building at 312 Azusa Street. And on April 14, 1906, they had their first meeting in a building that had been a Methodist church and then had been sold and remodelled; the top half as apartments. A. G. Osterburg, a boss for a local construction company, paid several men to help renovate the building. Volunteers swept the floors and whitewashed the walls. J. V. McNeill, a devout Catholic and owner of the largest lumber company in Los Angeles, donated lumber for the cause. Sawdust was placed on the floor, and planks were nailed to wooden barrels for uses as pews. Two empty crates were nailed on top of each other to act as Seymour's pulpit.

Frank Bartleman, who was one of the leaders and participants, later narrated the happening of the Azuza street:

> Friday, June 15, at "Azusa", the Spirit dropped the heavenly chorus' into my soul. I found myself suddenly joining the rest who had received this supernatural "gift". It was a spontaneous manifestation and rapture no earthly tongue can describe. In the beginning this manifestation was wonderfully pure and powerful. ...No one could understand this "gift of song" but those who had it. It was indeed a "new song", in the Spirit.[43]

Four days after the opening of the Azusa Street mission, on April 18, the great earthquake of 1906 shook the foundations of San Francisco. Combined with the fire that erupted during the earthquake, the city of San Francisco was

---

[42] Liardon, *Azuza Street Revival,* 96-97.

[43] Liardon, *Azuza Street Revival,* 33.

almost totally destroyed. Considering the apocalyptic size and destruction of the earthquake, along with the religious fervour in Los Angeles, the stage was set for a Holy Spirit eruption.[44]

While narrating the history of the Azuza Street revival in testimony, Bartleman who was there at the beginning of the revival, best described those early days also in his book:

> Brother Seymour generally sat behind two empty boxes, one on top of the other. He usually kept his head inside the top one during the meeting, in prayer. There was no pride there. The services ran almost continuously. Seeking souls could be found under the power almost any hour of the day or night. The place was never closed nor empty. The people came to meet God—He was always there. Hence, a continuous meeting. The meeting did not depend on the human leader. God's presence became more and more wonderful.[45]

Bartleman continues to portray the powerful manifestations of the Holy Spirit and how people encountered God's presence:

> In the early "Azusa" days both heaven and hell seemed to have come to town. Men were at the breaking point. Conviction was mightily on the people. They would fly to pieces even on the street, almost without provocation. A very "dead line" seemed to be drawn around "Azusa Mission", by the Spirit. When men came within two or three blocks of the place they were seized with conviction.[46] We had no human programme. The Lord Himself was leading. We had no priest class, nor priest craft. We did not even have a platform or pulpit in the beginning. All were on a level. The ministers were servants, according to the true meaning of the word. We did not honour men for their advantage, in means or education, but rather for their God-given "gifts"...... No subjects or sermons were announced ahead of time, and no special speakers for such an hour. No one knew what might be coming, what God would do. All was spontaneous, ordered of the Spirit.[47]

Under "the power of the Spirit", people spoke in tongues, interpreted, prophesied, cast out demons, healed innumerable diseases, wrote in tongues, saw visions, played musical instruments without any previous training. Someone might be speaking, suddenly the Spirit would fall upon the congregation. God

---

[44] Liardon, *Azuza Street Revival*, 103; Frank Bartleman, *How Pentecost Came to Los Angeles: As it was in the beginning*, 2nd edition (Los Angeles: F. Bartleman, 1925), 28.

[45] Bartleman, *How Pentecost Came to Los Angeles*, 34.

[46] Bartleman, *How Pentecost Came to Los Angeles*, 32.

[47] Bartleman, *How Pentecost Came to Los Angeles*, 34-35.

himself would give the altar call. Men would fall all over the house like the slain in battle, or rush for the altar en-masse, to seek God. The scene often resembled a forest of fallen trees. Then, in a burst of "glory", they would "come through" to salvation, or sanctification, or baptism in the Spirit, with shouts and songs of praise, speaking in tongues, leaping, running, jumping, kissing, and embracing one another.[48]

There was marked changes in the attitude of the people who were the early participants. Instead of racial prejudices, hatred and ego of those times which segregated people apart, a divine love that unites everyone flowed by the power and manifestations of the Spirit;

> In that old building, with its low rafters and bare floors, God took strong men and women to pieces, and put them together again, for His glory. It was a tremendous overhauling process. Pride and self-assertion, self-importance and self-esteem, could not survive there. The religious ego preached its own funeral sermon quickly.[49] Divine love was wonderfully manifest in the meetings. They would not even allow an unkind word said against their opposers, or the churches. The message was the love of God. It was a sort of "first love" of the early church returned. The baptism as we received it in the beginning did not allow us to think, speak, or hear evil of any man...We seemed to live in a sea of pure divine love.[50]

Initially, the Azusa Street mission had a multi-racial, multi-ethnic character. The first issue of *The Apostolic Faith* newspaper reported that, "God makes no difference in nationality. "Ethiopians, Chinese, Indians, Mexicans and other nationalities worship together". Other ethnic groups represented at one time or another in those early days were Portuguese, Spanish, Russians, Norwegians, Frenchmen, Germans, and Jews. One of the Azusa leaders estimated that more than twenty different nationalities were represented at the meetings. An eyewitness of the Azuza street observed, "It is noticeably free from all nationalistic feeling. ... No instrument that God can use is rejected on account of colour or dress or lack of education". The ethnic minority groups of Los Angeles found themselves welcome at Azusa, and some would discover there the sense of dignity community denied them in the larger urban culture[51] In the November issue of *The Apostolic Faith* paper Seymour wrote, "The meeting has been a melting time. The people are all melted together...made one lump, one bread, all one body in Christ Jesus. There is no Jew or Gentile, bond or free, in the Azusa Mission. No instrument that

[48] Robert M. Anderson, *Vision of the Disinherited: Making of American Pentecostalism* (Peabody, Massachusetts: Hendrickson Publishers, 1979), 67-68.

[49] Bartleman, *How Pentecost Came to Los Angeles*, 34-35.

[50] Bartleman, *How Pentecost Came to Los Angeles*, 32.

[51] Anderson, *Vision of the Disinherited*, 69-70.

God can use is rejected on account of colour or dress or lack of education. This is why God has built up the work...The sweetest thing is the loving harmony."[52]

According to Bartleman, a large number of people from different continents gathered to experience of the Baptism of the Spirit. "The work was getting clearer and stronger at, "Azusa". It seemed that everyone had to go to "Azusa". Missionaries were gathered there from Africa, India, and the islands of the sea. Preachers and workers had crossed the continent, and come from distant islands, with an irresistible drawing to Los Angeles."[53] A few months after the revival had opened, hundreds were pouring into the little building on Azusa Street. It is reported that as many as 21,300 attended the services, and up to 800 crowded into the building at a time. Every inch big enough for a chair was jammed full. *The Los Angeles Daily Times* reported, "The room was crowded almost to suffocation. Many were seated in the windows and scores who could not enter crowded around the lobby and struggled to view..."[54]

Moreover, there was a great desire for urgent world mission. Many of the newly baptized in the Holy Spirit would feel a call to the mission field. Consequently, men and women were departing for Scandinavia, China, India, Egypt, Ireland, and various other nations. Even Sister Julia Hutchin, who initially locked Seymour out of her mission, came to Azusa, received the baptism of the Holy Spirit, and left for Africa.[55]

Similarly, the Indian subcontinent had witnessed certain revivals which created a context for the origin of Pentecostal movement.[56] These were the revivals that broke out in the states of Tamil Nadu and Kerala in denominations run by CMS and the Mar Thoma Church in 1860, 1873 and 1895. It was John Christian Aroolappen of Tirunalveli, in the state of Tamil Nadu (1860), who was became instrumental in the revival. He was a local catechist trained by Carl T. E. Rhenius, a Prussian missionary sent by the Church Missionary Society in 1814 who worked in Tamil Nadu until his death in 1838. Aroolappen was also tutored by Anthony Norris Groves, an independent missionary from England who had arrived in India in 1833 and been greatly influenced by the millennialism and other teachings of the Plymouth Brethren.[57] Aroolappan happened to read about the revivals in the US, England and Ulster in 1857-59 and greatly inspired by them and earnestly prayed for a movement of the Spirit in India.

---

[52] Liardon, *Azuza Street Revival,* 103-104.

[53] Bartleman, *How Pentecost Came to Los Angeles*, 32.

[54] Liardon, *Azuza Street Revival,* 104.

[55] Liardon, *Azuza Street Revival,*104; Cecil. M. Robeck Jr., "Azuza Street Revival", in *NIDPCM,* 344-350.

[56] For a detailed description see my book, Shaibu Abraham, *The History of the Pentecostal Movement in North India: Unfolding its Social & Theological Contexts* (New Delhi: Christian World Imprints, 2017).

[57] G. B. McGee, "Pentecostal and Pentecostal-like Movements (1860-1910)" in *NIDPCM,* 118.

It was reported that a mighty revival broke out on March 4, 1860 and the outpouring of the Spirit was accompanied by prophecy, *glossolalia*, *glossographia*, interpretation of tongues and intense conviction of sins among nominal Christians. There were dreams, visions, signs in the heavens, and people falling down and/or shaking.[58] This revival resulted in passionate evangelistic activities among the native people, which were neither supported by missionaries nor by western money. There was flood of conversions, which amazed western missionaries who were really struggling to educate the masses and to convert them.[59]

Along with the above revival, another revival broke out in nearby Travencore, in the state of Kerala in 1873 through a disciple of John Aroolappen, named Mathai (*Pandikaran Mathai Upadeshi*) and others, among CMS and other historic churches in Kerala. He came to Kerala with construction workers and preached in many places of the central Travancore. His evangelistic meetings had created intense conviction of sins and a renewed interest in the Bible reading among the Syrian Christians. Phenomena such as "flinging the arms in the air, shaking in every limb, violent contortions, falling on the ground and rolling about" were noted in these revivals and people also spoke in tongues.[60]

Other than these revivals, there were two more revivals in Kerala in the years 1895 and 1908, prior to the coming of western Pentecostal missionaries. These revivals also witnessed similar signs of Spirit movement occurred in earlier; people were being filled with the Holy Spirit, speaking in tongues and other Spirit manifestations such as healings and visions. K. E. Abraham, one of the founding fathers of the India Pentecostal Church (IPC) states in his autobiography that as a nine year old boy he participated in the 1908 revival and witnessed the power of God manifested in many people, but he did not realize what it was.[61] According to him, this revival took place before George Berg, the American missionary from the Azusa Street Mission came to India in 1908.[62] These revivals prepared the ground for the formation of Pentecostal movement, when the people who received the Spirit-baptism from the Azuza Street revival introduced the doctrine of the baptism in the Holy Spirit.

---

[58] McGee, "Pentecostal and Pentecostal-like Movements (1860-1910)", 118-119. Also see, G. B. McGee, "Pentecostal Phenomena and Revivals in India: Implication for Indigenous Church Leadership", *IBMR* 20/3 (July, 1996), 112-114.

[59] McGee, "Pentecostal Phenomena and Revivals in India", 113-114.

[60] Abraham, *The History of the Pentecostal Movement in North India*, 47.

[61] K. E. Abraham, *Yesukristhuvinte Eliya Dasan*, 3rd editon (Malayalam) (Kumbanad, India: K. E. Abraham Foundations, 2001), 12.

[62] Abraham, *Yesukristhuvinte Eliya Dasan,* 62-63. Earlier George berg came to India as Brethren missionary but in February 1908 he returned as a Pentecostal missionary with the Spirit experience. See, Allan Anderson, *Spreading Fires: The Missionary Nature of Early Pentecostalism* (London: SCM, 2007), 95.

The north of India also witnessed some Pentecostal revivals states such as Maharashtra, Gujarat and Punjab. One such was in the Mukti Mission at Kedgaon, near Pune, founded by Pandita Ramabhai, a Brahmin widow who was baptized in 1883 and dedicated her life to ministering to Indian girls and women, especially those who were most vulnerable to neglect and abuse in society. There was a famine in India and the Mukti mission had sheltered many women from villages, especially child-widows. In 1898 she attended a Keswick convention where she asked the assembled to pray for 200,000 Indian women and men to carry the gospel to their non-Christian neighbours. She led prayer services among the residents of her Mukti Mission, and organized them into "praying bands" to undertake evangelistic campaigns in the surrounding villages. Inspired by the 1904 Welsh Revival, the prayer band of Mukti Mission, consisted of orphan girls and child-widows, had been praying for an outbreak of revival in India from the beginning of 1905. The number of girls joined for prayer numbered about 500. In June 29, it was said that power of the Spirit manifested like fire so much so that people ran for water to quench the fire. Minnie Abram, who worked with Ramabhai narrates the experience of one of the senior girls at Mukti received the "baptism of fire:"

> The young woman sleeping next to her awoke when this occurred, and seeing the fire enveloping her, ran across the dormitory, brought a pail of water, and was about to dash it upon her, when she discovered that the girl was not on fire. In less than an hour nearly all of the young women in the compound gathered around weeping, praying and confessing their sins to God.[63]

Edith Blumhofer points out that "three features seemed ubiquitous in this Indian revival: fire (felt and seen), intense joy, and public confession of sin."[64] There was also shaking of the body, visions, dreams and coming under the power of the Spirit. Those who received the visitation of the Spirit were all ordinary women, orphan children and child-widows. Moreover, revival created evangelistic fervour among the recipient of the power of the Spirit. Minnie Abraham wrote, 'Some who have sought the baptism of the Holy Ghost and fire have received the fire only for cleansing, but from Acts 2 we see that the tongue of fire gave power for service, as well as cleansing.'[65]

---

[63] Minnie F. Abrams, *The Baptism of the Holy Ghost and Fire*, (Maharashtra, Kedgaon: Mukti Mission, 1906), 5-6.

[64] Edith L. Blumhofer, "Consuming Fire: Pandita Ramabai and the Global Pentecostal Impulse", in *Interpreting Contemporary Christianity: Global Processes and Local Identities*, edited by Ogbu U. Kalu (Grand Rapids, Michigan, Eerdmans, 2008), 223.

[65] Quoted by Gary B. McGee, "'Latter Rain' Falling in the East: Early-Twentieth-Century Pentecostalism in India and the Debate over Speaking in Tongues", *Church History* 68/3 (1999), 653; See also, Helen S. Dyer, (comp.), *Revival in India 1905-1906* (Akola, Maharashtra: Alliance Publications, 1987), 37-49.

It is obvious from the above stories that the outpouring of the Holy Spirit, which was anticipated by the two centuries of doctrinal developments totally changed the spiritual landscape, bringing forth the spirituality of the Baptism in the Holy Spirit. Moreover, it gave birth to a new spiritual movement that would later grow into a world-wide movement. The people who received the blessing of the baptism in the Holy Spirit not only experienced total transformation in personal life, but also a fervent mission-spirit was created in them. Many of them travelled to far-flung places of the world, as we have seen, and began to spread the spirituality of Spirit-baptism and the supernatural manifestation that accompanied the phenomenon. However, it was not just supernatural manifestations only, but instead the dramatic change that impacted upon the lives of the people needs to be counted as the most significant element of the Pentecostal movement. It impacted the spiritual and social landscape of many nations, people groups and cultures as we see today. Therefore, we shall briefly look into the missional and liberative elements of the spirituality of the Spirit-baptism to better understand its impact today.

The Baptism of the Holy Spirit: Power for a Liberative Mission

The Spirit of God is termed the "Holy Spirit" as the Spirit is the Spirit of holiness.[66] Indeed, the coming of the Spirit upon a person or being "filled" with the Spirit presupposes the holiness which is appropriate of the Holy Spirit. The Pentecostal churches count personal holiness as paramount for Christian life and ministry. However, more than this sanctifying aspect, the fire and wind (at the Day of Pentecost, Acts 2:1ff), "gives power for service" which is as necessary for today as in the first century.[67] The Pentecostal movement from the beginning itself considered the baptism of the Holy Spirit as a post-conversion experience which brings sanctifying effect upon the believers and also empowerment for mission in the world such as is featured in Acts 2 at the Day of Pentecost, especially evidenced by unknown tongues "subsequent" to conversion experience.[68]

---

[66] J. Rodman Williams, *Renewal Theology*, vol. 2 (Michigan: Academie Books, 1990), 141-142.

[67] David T. Williams, "Pentecostal Wind and Fire", *Evangel 9/2* (Summer, 2001): 40.

[68] However Anglican New Testament scholar James Dunn argues in a different way. For him, the baptism in the Holy Spirit is "primarily initiatory and only secondarily as empowering…is never directly associated with the promise of power, but is always associated with entry into the messianic age or body of Christ". Similarly Pentecostal New Testament scholar Gordon Fee also questions the exegetical basis of the doctrine of subsequent empowerment in the book of Acts. However, most Pentecostal scholars, like Robert P. Menzies and Roger Stronstad, forcefully argue that baptism of the Spirit is for empowerment for mission. According to them, Luke portrays the Spirit in Prophetic terms and as the source of power for effective witness, and so Luke's Pneumatology should be distinguished from the Pauline Pneumatology which is associated with conversion-initiation. See Robert P. Menzies, *Empowered for Witness* (Sheffield: Sheffield Academic Press, 2001), 232-243 and Roger Stronstad, *The Prophethood of All Believers - A Study in Luke's Charismatic Theology* (Sheffield: Sheffield Academic Press, 1999), 121-122. J. Rodman Williams, *Pentecostal Reality* (New Jersey: Logos International, 1972), 57-84; Frank D. Macchia, "The Struggle for Global Witness: Shifting Paradigms in Pentecostal Theology", in *The Globalization of Pentecostalism*, edited by M.W. Dempster, B.D. Klaus, D. Petersen (Carlisle: Regnum, 1999), 13.

The Pentecostals see themselves as a direct fulfilment of Joel 2:28. Early Pentecostals believed that the outpouring of the Spirit they had experienced was for the urgent missionary activities. Moreover, through the mission, they were commissioned to bring back the church into the New Testament spirituality. In regard to the vision of the early Pentecostals, Hollenweger observes that the time before the birth of the Pentecostal movement is accordingly painted in dark and hopeless colours and in fact as 'a Babylonian captivity of the church'. Then came the miraculous liberation movement, the Pentecostal communities, to put an end to all strife within Christendom... Prior to the return of Jesus on the clouds of heaven there was only one legitimate goal: the sanctification and unification of the children of God and the evangelization of the world within a generation.[69]

As we have already seen, Pentecostalism began as a shift from a focus on holiness to an outward thrust that involved a dynamic filling and empowerment for witness. This shift, however did not involve the abandonment of holiness. Macchia explains it,

> The earliest Pentecostals viewed holiness as a needed preparation for empowerment. True holiness understood as affections that are shaped by the righteousness of the kingdom-to-come, will be enhanced by the sense of dynamic filling and empowerment for global witness that gifts of the Spirit symbolise. Empowerment for service prevents holiness from becoming self-righteous moralism or merely an isolated sense of distinct Christian identity. On the other hand, the empowerment without holiness and righteousness of the kingdom-to-come, foreshadowed by the messianic ministry of Jesus will be misguided, even oppressive.[70]

This understanding, though unknowingly, shaped the earlier Pentecostal way of life and missionary activities. In Bridges Johns' words,

> The active presence of the Holy Spirit called for a radical equalising of blacks and whites, males and females, the rich and the poor. All people were in need of salvation and all could be participants together of the 'later rain' of the Spirit. It was, therefore, one's standing with God which was important. Thus, Pentecostalism stood as a contrast to the dominant order of its day. It was a subversive and revolutionary movement, not based upon philosophic ideology nor totally upon critical reflection. It was a movement that experienced through the Holy Spirit God's divine liberation.[71]

---

[69] Cheryl Bridges Johns, *Pentecostal Formation: A Pedagogy Among the Oppressed* (Eugene, OR: Wipf and Stock Publishers, 2010), 69.

[70] Macchia, "The Struggle for Global Witness", 16-17.

[71] Bridges Johns, *Pentecostal Formation*, 69.

Vinson Synan also notes the equality and fraternity evolved between blacks and whites through the powerful presence of the Holy Spirit and the weakening of racial prejudice.[72] Pentecostal praxis has exhibited radical concepts of justice and equality often in a world which is antagonistic to the development of either. In the Third World, Pentecostalism embodies the reality that in Christ's kingdom "there is neither Jew nor Greek, slave nor free, male nor female" (Gal. 3.28). Within its ranks, a protest against the oppressive-hierarchial political systems is actualized.

Besides, the early Pentecostal missions endeavours were among the poor, downtrodden and the least of the society. It is actually observed that in most places, in the beginning of Pentecostal movement, the poor and ordinary people are being joined. It is all the more obvious in the third-world situations.[73] Having undertaken a full year of empirical, sociological and theological analysis of the Pentecostal movement in Latin America, Richard Shaull and Waldo Cesar conclude that the movement became both a major liberative force among the poor of the Third-World and a challenge to the historic churches. Shaull comments,

> Moreover, they have demonstrated their ability to reach and convert a vast number of the most impoverished and broken people who, because of their social position, have the strongest desire to exchange the existing order of things in the direction of equality and justice. It is now evident that the passion to this was an integral part of the Pentecostal experience from the very beginning.[74]

It is also true in Indian context. People from Dalit, tribal and economically poor background embrace the Pentecostal movement as it gives them a new vigour and hope for their lives. In a context of poverty, lack of medical facilities, caste discrimination, social and spiritual oppression, many people find Pentecostal movement as a refuge and a source of strength in their existential struggles.[75] The poor are more attracted to and accommodated by the Pentecostal churches in India. "Pentecostal Spirituality, characterised by extended prayer meetings, zealous witnessing, and self-venting aggressive worship through song and dance, has often proved useful in bringing people

---

[72] Synan, *The Holiness-Pentecostal Tradition,* 165.

[73] Donald E. Miller & Tetsunao Yamamori, *Global Pentecostalism: The New Face of Christian Social Engagement* (London: University of California Press, 2007); Richard Shaull and Waldo Cesar, *Pentecostalism and the Future of the Christian Churches* (Michigan: W. B. Eerdmans, 2000); Shaibu Abraham, *Pentecostal Theology of Liberation: Holy Spirit & Holiness in Society* (New Delhi: Christian World Imprints, 2014).

[74] Shaull and Cesar, *Pentecostalism and the Future of,* 211.

[75] See Abraham, *The History of the Pentecostal Movement in North India;* Shaibu Abraham, *Pentecostal Christology: Empirical Approach in Indian Context* (New Delhi: Christian World Imprints, 2019).

out of the clutches of depression, worthlessness, aimlessness in life, fear and anxiety...Herein lies the seed of a profound theology of liberating spirituality. Pentecostalism in India thrives among the poor and downtrodden", observes Reuben Gabriel.[76] *The Oxford Dictionary of the Christian Church* rightly terms Pentecostalism as "originally a religion of the poor."[77] Thus, it is obvious that Pentecostal spirituality as well as mission equip people for missionary task and of course, that is a liberative and transformative mission.

Baptism in the Holy Spirit: The Spirituality of Liberation

"For Pentecostals, Spirit baptism is the unveiling of a new reality and the realisation of an altered consciousness", says Bridges Johns, "Such a consciousness does not allow for a person to become 'submerged in reality'. Rather, the mode of awareness may be described as critical consciousness. However, this critical consciousness is not primarily developed as one learns to abstract reality. It is the result of an encounter with the Creator Spirit who enlists humankind in the unveiling of the lies of the established order."[78] Leonard Lovett also brings out the same idea, "Baptism in the Holy Spirit is perceived as being the spiritual baptism where Jesus the baptiser exercises his sovereign will, control, and possession of us through the person of the Holy Spirit....Experientially then, Spirit-baptism in this context is a radical encounter of the divine with the human spirit. God infuses it with *dunamis,* thus opening the way for transforming vertical discipleship into horizontal responsibility."[79] He continues,

> For "Where the Spirit of the Lord is, there is liberty" is a claim long attested to and affirmed by Pentecostal-charismatic believers...The Spirit is God and God is expressed in community, shattering and renewing, rending and healing, revealing and transforming, lifting and liberating a people unto God. When the human spirit is grasped and energised by the Holy Spirit, it is given the necessary power to go beyond itself enabling it to perform task beyond our normally anticipated human ability and comprehension.[80]

---

[76] Reuben Louis Gabriel, "Reflections on Indian Pentecostalism: Trends and Issues", *Dharma Deepika* 2 (July – December, 2002): 69. Dharma Deepika editorial comments, "Now, several Pentecostal churches are being established in smaller cities and villages [in India]. Drawing spiritual strength from the Bible, insights from local,...and adapting themselves to the pressing needs of the modern age, the Pentecostal movements tend to flourish". Daniel Jeyaraj, "Editorial – Pentecostalism", *Dharma Deepika* 2 (July – December, 2002): 2.

[77] F. L. Cross and E. A. Livingston (eds.), "Pentecostalism", *The Oxford Dictionary of the Christian Church,* 3rd edition, (Oxford: Oxford University Press, 1997), 1254.

[78] Bridges Johns, *Pentecostal Formation,* 95.

[79] Leonard Lovett, "Liberation: A Dual-Edged Sword", *Pneuma* 9/2 (Fall, 1987): 166.

[80] Lovett, "Liberation: A Dual-Edged Sword", 165.

The anointing of the Holy Spirit brings a better understanding of the realities of the society and individuals, and compels believers to seek justice because the Holy Spirit is the Spirit of God who wills justice for the creation that is the work of God's hands.[81] The role of the Holy Spirit is that of one who activates conversion in which a person enters into a new realm, and new level of consciousness. The Holy Spirit is the agent of sanctification and also gives power for service with a concept of mission being grounded in historical experience but with consequences which go beyond present history. The Holy Spirit enables a person to experience the paradox of suffering and the power of renunciation. One is enabled to side with the oppressed and to become a servant of the poor by becoming poor in the spirit (humility).[82] Shaull also says, "…among the Pentecostals today it is the experience of the presence and power of God in the baptism of the Holy Spirit that changes everything and gives life a new direction and a call to mission in the world."[83] Then he describes one of his interviews with a peasant woman,[84] which reveals the importance of this experience;

> She spoke about her early life and struggle…then her first visit to a Pentecostal church…after she started going to the church, she had one overwhelming desire, a "yearning for the baptism of the Spirit", which soon happened to her. It was an experience she found no adequate words to describe: "something so beautiful", "a light noise like wind", the compulsion "to speak something I didn't understand", which left her "feeling the Holy Spirit". From this moment she was a new person, filled with enthusiasm to evangelise also care for her own children as well as those of others, to provide food and clothing for those in need, to visit prisons, and to become a lay worker.[85]

Bridges Johns explains this experience of common believers in a theological category, "The experience of sanctification has created utopian visions among people who do not employ critical-reflective, principled, formal operational thought processes. They have experienced…'imaginal transformation'. By experiencing the holy, there is a creative reorganisation of the imagination (self) and the emergence of a new gestalt. The corresponding action, therefore, is directed by this altered perception of the world."[86] According to Lovett, many of the younger black American Pentecostals have come to believe that the task of liberation, which means freedom from personal hang-ups as well as from bondage

---

[81] Richard J. Mouw, "Life in the Spirit in an Unjust World", *Pneuma* 9/2 (Fall, 1987): 117.

[82] Bridges Johns, *Pentecostal Formation,* 100.

[83] Shaull and Cesar, *Pentecostalism and the Future of,* 195.

[84] The full story of Dona Juliana is mentioned in Shaull and Cesar, *Pentecostalism and the Future of,* 174-176.

[85] Shaull and Cesar, *Pentecostalism and the Future of,* 196.

[86] Bridges Johns, *Pentecostal Formation,* 94.

of the oppressor, cannot be fully accomplished until witnesses are endued with power from on high. They are at home with themes like "saved, sanctified, baptised with the Holy Ghost for liberation."[87]

Thus, for Pentecostals, it is only by the Holy Spirit that a true vision of reality can be perceived. "This vision", according to Bridges Johns, "sees both the spiritual and social needs of humankind. There needs to be no dichotomy between evangelism and social action inasmuch as the same Spirit inspires and unveils the need for both. With such an understanding, the gifts of the Spirit can be understood to include all tasks of life that believers are empowered to undertake. Acts of justice and peace are, therefore, acts of the Holy Spirit."[88]

Murray Dempster, who is a Pentecostal ethicist, asserts that the Spirit baptism provides an angular vision for a social ethic designed to promote social justice in a divided world. Then he uses the argument by Roger Stronstad that the coming of the Spirit at Pentecost has profound implications for integrating the Old Testament conception of social justice into a distinctively Pentecostal social ethic. The Pentecost narrative is the story of the transfer of the charismatic Spirit from Jesus to the disciples. By this transfer of the Spirit, disciples become the heirs and successors to the earthly ministry of Jesus and they would continue to do and teach those things which Jesus began to do and teach. Now the ministry of Jesus placed him directly in the tradition of the law and the prophets. Jesus' proclamation of the gospel as good-news to the poor, the captives and the hungry, demonstrates his continuity with the ethical message of the Old Testament. Hence, "a Pentecostal social ethic grounded exegetically in Luke-Acts is a kingdom ethic made operational within the charismatic community by the empowerment of the Spirit."[89] Thus, the experience of the baptism in the Holy Spirit enables individuals to unite together into a confessing and worshipping community which in turn results in a greater thrust in liberative act.

However, after a century of the Pentecostal movement, the liberative and transformative power of the spirituality of the baptism in the Holy Spirit is in a sliding scale. Though Pentecostals still cherish the Spirit-experience, it is confined to the four walls of the church setup, as a consequence, they are now less capable to become an active force in the society. Even though, Pentecostals claimed to be Spirit-filled, the missionary fervour that energised the early Pentecostals is largely missing today. Besides, there is a wrong tendency among the Pentecostals to personalise the power of the Spirit, at the expense of the community dimension of the work of the Spirit through individuals. This individualistic understanding of the power of the Spirit stands as an impediment to the full-blown involvement in social responsibility. Douglas Peterson raises the problem, "The experience of

---

[87] Lovett, "Black Origins of the Pentecostal Movement", 140.

[88] Bridges Johns, *Pentecostal Formation,* 97.

[89] Murray W. Dempster, "Pentecostal Social Concern and the Biblical Mandate for Social Justice", *Pneuma* 9/2 (Fall, 1987): 146-147.

Spirit baptism and its empowerment of the believer are not fully understood in its content and force through their current biblical understanding. The task of a Pentecostal theology is to provide an interpretive theological structure that would present 'an essential connectedness' between Spirit-baptism and the practice of social justice."[90] Stronstad also delineates the same concern: among the Pentecostals today, the Spirit-experience tend to be individualistic, self-centred, and even narcissistic. The experience of Spirit-baptism is sought as a private blessing, rather than as an empowering for ministry. Far too many Pentecostals have been led to receive the blessing of the Holy Spirit in the prayer room and have never been taught to take the empowering of that gift into the street and market places of society. This focus on experience rather than on service is like selling one's birthright of Spirit-empowered service for the pottage of self-seeking experience and blessing.[91] The reason for this is, as Stronstad puts it, Pentecostals do not fully understand the meaning of the pouring forth of the Spirit upon them. Rather, they are preoccupied with speaking with other tongues and initial evidence. As a result they are not challenged to function in the church and in society as Spirit-baptised, Spirit-led, Spirit-empowered, and Spirit-filled prophets.[92]

Moreover, instead of having unity and oneness of mind, Pentecostals developed a 'fractured mentality' in the name of Spirit empowerment. "Split churches, independent churches, a multiplicity of denominations, and of split-off denominations abound. Independence and individualism characterise the Pentecostal movement. Often absent is the unity, the all togetherness, the one accord-ness, which characterised the first century prophets."[93] But, according to Dempster, the early church "was liberated by the Spirit from its deeply entrenched biases and differences to experience right within its own *koinonia* a taste of the social justice longed for by prophets past."[94]

Antidote to these tendencies in Pentecostalism today is to re-emphasise the experience of the baptism of the Holy Spirit in its true sense. Pentecostals need to hunger and thirst for "the power from above" and eagerly wait for it as the early Pentecostals did. Moreover, the spiritual virtues such as unity, love and holiness are to be rediscovered to create an atmosphere for the work of the Spirit. It is good to have policies, programmes and strategies. More than all of these, anticipation and preparation for the powerful outpouring of the Spirit is to be emphasised. Pentecostals should recapture the spirit of prayer and intercession, passion for the mission of God and compassion for the poor and the downtrodden.

---

[90] Douglas Petersen, *Not by Might nor by Power – A Pentecostal Theology of Social Concern in Latin America* (Oxford: Regnum, 1996), 203.

[91] Stronstad, *The Prophethood of All Believers,*123.

[92] Roger Stronstad, "Affirming Diversity: God's People as a Community of Prophets", *Pneuma* 17/2 (Fall, 1995): 156.

[93] Stronstad, "Affirming Diversity", 157.

[94] Dempster, "Pentecostal Social Concern", 148.

Let us conclude our discussion here; it is obvious that the baptism in the Holy Spirit as doctrine developed through two centuries totally transformed the spiritual setting in Christendom and facilitated the formation, growth and consolidation of the Pentecostal movement all over the world. Pentecostals firmly believe that the baptism of the Holy Spirit as a doctrine fully based on the New Testament spirituality and to be experienced by all Christians. Besides, the spirituality of Spirit-baptism propels Pentecostals to foray into the unknown languages, cultures, people groups and nations with the liberating and transforming gospel. For Pentecostals, it is not merely a doctrine to be rigorously followed, rather it forms the fundamental spirituality and life transforming event. For them, it is the power for liberation. This spirituality reorganises their lives and also impels them to involve in others' lives and thus, liberate and transforms them. However, lately Pentecostals have lost the original vibrancy and power of the experience of the Spirit-baptism. Therefore, it is significant to recapture the lost spirituality of the baptism of the Spirit to regain the liberative potentials of the movement.

Chapter 5

Spiritual Gifts
Tools of Liberation

A salient feature of Pentecostalism is its belief in the manifestation of spiritual gifts, such as miraculous healing, exorcism, prophecy, and other gifts that are portrayed in the New Testament. Spiritual gifts or *charismata* played an indispensible role in the dissemination and consolidation of the movement around the world, especially in the third-world nations. From the inception of Pentecostal movement, spiritual gifts were operated in full force that liberated and transformed people who were poor, sick, affected by evil spirits and other troubles. The early leaders of Pentecostalism were particular in the use of gifts of the Holy Spirit in mission and evangelism. This strategic use of spiritual gifts proved crucial for the movement which resulted in substantial growth as we see today. In fact, the Pentecostal movement without doubt can be termed as a Spirit movement and the use of spiritual gifts impelled it into a liberative movement.

The manifestation of the power of God is at the heart of Pentecostal doctrine and practice. Giving freedom to the Holy Spirit to work is what has made Pentecostals the fastest growing group of evangelicals in the world.[1] The Pentecostal revival at the beginning of the twentieth century brought a renewal of the power and gifts of the Holy Spirit. The early Spirit-filled believers were faithful to the Great Commission and employed the power of the Spirit, in terms of *charismata,* and as a result, the number of adherents multiplied in millions all over the world. Pentecostals have the astute faith that Christ builds his Church

[1] Opal L. Reddin, *Power Encounter: A Pentecostal Perspective,* edited by Opal L. Reddin (Springfield, MO: Central Bible College Publishers, 1999), 6.

through the gifts and ministries of the Spirit. Peter Wagner, church growth Professor, observed that in all human history "not another non-militaristic, non-political voluntary human movement" has grown as the Pentecostal and Charismatic movement over the past 25 years. He delineates that such a growth is due to the emphasis on the ministry of the Holy Spirit with the attendant "signs and wonders". Moreover, after surveying the church growth literature, all experts agree that the most important factor in church growth is the supernatural power released through "signs and wonders". This is especially true in the Third World countries which have a different world view than the West.[2]

Pentecostals affirm that spiritual gifts are granted by the Holy Spirit and are normative in contemporary church life and ministry.[3] The modern Pentecostal movement has from its inception emphasized Peter's "this is what is spoken" definition of the "last days" as the primary foundation for the empowering aspects of its Pneumatology. Spurred on by this understanding of fulfilment, Pentecostals have steadfastly proclaimed the continuing charismatic nature of the church empowered by the Spirit.[4] The experience of the baptism in the Holy Spirit is an empowering resource that impelled early Pentecostals to engage in mission. Along with the baptism in the Spirit, Pentecostals assumed that the gift of the Spirit would enable them to evangelise the nations. Bruner endorses the same idea, "... when the Holy Spirit permanently, personally, and fully enters the believer's life, the believer becomes eligible for the full equipment of the spiritual gifts. The gifts of the Spirit have their special purpose, in providing a spiritual capability far mightier than the finest natural abilities could ever supply."[5] Moreover, these gifts are freely given to Christians, as an expression of God's power at work in the world today. John Wimber, the leader of Vineyard Movement asserts:

> The gifts of the Spirit are received by impartation. The gifts are given to us and through us to use for others. However, a believer does not *possess* gifts, a believer *receives* gifts from God to be used at special times for special occasions. Gifts are the attestation of the empowering of the Holy Spirit and are vital for an effective ministry. The gifts are the tools which enable one to fulfil the ministry required.[6]

---

[2] C. Peter Wagner, *Warfare Prayer* (Ventura, CA: Regal Books, 1992), 48; Also see, C. Peter Wagner, *Your Spiritual Gifts can make Your Church Grow* (Ventura, CA: Gospel Light Publications, 2012).

[3] Jon Ruthven, *On Cessation of the Charismata: The Protestant Polemic on Post-biblical Miracles* (Sheffield: Sheffield Academic Press, 1993), 14.

[4] Douglas A. Oss, "A Pentecostal / Charismatic View", *Are Miraculous Gifts for Today?*, edited by Wayne A. Grudem (Michigan: Zondervan Publishing House, 1996), 265.

[5] Frederick Dale Bruner, *A Theology of the Holy Spirit: The Pentecostal Experience and the New Testament Witness* (Michigan: Eerdmans Publishing, 1970), 130.

[6] John Wimber, "Signs and Wonders in the Growth of the Church", *Church Growth the State of Art,* edited by C. Peter Wagner, Win Arn & Elmer L. Towns, (Virginia: Liberty University, 1986), 148.

Furthermore, gifts such as prophecy, visions, word of wisdom and knowledge and dreams are significant in our times, affirms Alexander, because through them God reveals the believers the state of the world at large and also about the seemingly less significant events in our daily lives. This also proves that God cares and communicates with us, and that is a reassuring reality to live in. When ordinary people exercise spiritual gifts, it proves that God is not limited to working only through rich, powerful, or highly educated people — God can speak to anyone who is listening, and those who listen can then relay God's message to their friends and the rest of the world.[7] Thus, the exercise of spiritual gifts not only acts as a tool for ministry but also becomes a transforming spirituality for Pentecostals.

The Evangelical missionaries often condemned animistic practices in the Third World mission fields but failed to offer an alternative way of dealing with their problems and fill the vacuum left after animistic practices had been abandoned. However, Pentecostals, because of their awareness of the presence of the dynamic and empowering Spirit within them, exhibit a confidence sometimes lacking in non-Pentecostals, which can be effective in overcoming any sense of inadequacy and powerlessness. The signs and wonders are thus anticipated by Pentecostals involved in mission, enabling them to powerfully engage in the task of presenting the supremacy of Christ and of authenticating the gospel. Anderson describes healing and exorcism as probably the most important part of Pentecostal evangelism and church recruitment, resulting in significant numbers of people coming to faith as they witness the reality of God in their midst.[8] McClung describes it as an evangelistic door-opener, especially where medical aid is limited.[9]

However, from the beginning of the movement, the use of the spiritual gifts had been questioned and even ridiculed by non-Pentecostals. For instance, Pentecostals were condemned by the World Christian Fundamentals Association in Chicago in 1928, calling them as "tongues-talkers and faith healers."[10] The cessationist groups questions the Pentecostals' use of spiritual gifts such as divine healings, prophecies or miracles and accuse Pentecostals having either demonic influence or fake. Paul Alexander points out: "Pentecostal history is full of stories of other Christians and religious people accusing Pentecostals of being demon possessed and working for the devil. Many books have even been written about it, from A. M. Hills' *Pentecost Rejected* (1902) to John MacArthur's *Charismatic*

---

[7] Paul Alexander, *Signs & Wonders: Why Pentecostalism is the World's Fastest Growing Faith* (San Francisco: Jossey Bass, 2009), 129.

[8] Allan Anderson, "Towards a Pentecostal Missiology for the Majority World", *AJPS* 8/1 (2005): 33.

[9] Keith Warrington, *Pentecostal Theology: A Theology of Encounter* (London: T&T Clark, 2008), 251-252.

[10] Warrington, *Pentecostal Theology*, 267.

Chaos (1993)."[11] They hold the position that the spiritual gifts have ceased with the apostles and the formation of the New Testament.[12] The doctrine that miraculous gifts of the Holy Spirit ceased around the apostolic age has evolved over the long expanse of church history, and has found expression in various religious persuasions and philosophical convictions.[13] Moreover, an impressive list of scholars, have similarly asserted and explained the disappearance of the "religion of the Spirit and of power" in the earliest church.[14] These authors are essentially restating the classic Protestant position on this issue, that miraculous spiritual gifts, including prophecy, were in some sense foundational in that they were essential for the initiation and spread of the Christian faith, but, like scaffolding, they were no longer required after the viable structure and doctrines of the church had been established.[15]

However, Pentecostals have a different take on this issue. For instance, Jack Deere correctly diagnosis the logic concerning the origin of the doctrine of cessationism: "No one ever just picked up the Bible, started reading, and then came to the conclusion that God was not doing signs and wonders anymore and that the gifts of the Holy Spirit had passed away. The doctrine of cessationism did not originate from a careful study of the Scriptures. The doctrine of cessationism originated in *experience*."[16] *Actually, the lack* of miracles in Christian experience and in churches led to various attempts in church history to explain them as

---

[11] Alexander, *Signs & Wonders*, 105.

[12] The main proponent of this position in the last century was Benjamin Warfield (1851-1921) and recently John McArthur holds cessationist position. See Ruthven, *On Cessation of the Charismata*. Ruthven counts what R. W. Graves briefly explains about the cessationist position; in cessationist writings the bewildering and imprecise variety of points at which the *charismata* are believed to have ceased, for example, after the writing of 1 Corinthians, the book of Hebrews, or the last New Testament book; at the closing of the canon of Scripture; when the New Testament was 'accepted' or 'circulated'; at the death of the last apostle; the death of the last disciple on whom the apostles conferred a charism; when the apostolic age passed; at the destruction of Jerusalem; when the Church matured in 'love' or in 'doctrine'; until faith was established; 'when the whole knowledge of God designed for the saving health of the world had been incorporated into the living body of the world's thought'. R.W. Graves, "Tongues Shall Cease: A Critical Survey of the Supposed Cessation of the Charismata", *Paraclete* 17 (Fall 1983): 26-27.

[13] Ruthven, *On Cessation of the Charismata*, 8.

[14] Jack Deere narrates an interesting conversation in this regard: Once, in a conversation with a seminary professor, I challenged the rule at his academic institution that would not admit students into the school who spoke in tongues. I reminded him that Paul said, "Do not forbid speaking in tongues". He replied, "That is not the Word of God for today". When I challenged him to prove that biblically, he could not do so. Yet he was confident that 1 Corinthians 14:39 was no longer a part of the Word of God for today. Jack Deere, *Surprised by the Power of the Spirit* (Grand Rapids, Michigan: Zondervan, 1993), 178.

[15] For example Adolph von Harnack, J.N.D. Kelly, Arnold Ehrhardt, Henry Chadwick, Hans von Campenhausen and Jaroslav Pelikan and others; See Ruthven, *On Cessation of the Charismata*, 16-17.

[16] Deere, *Surprised by the Power of the Spirit*, 99.

temporary endowments, not to be expected anymore in the life of the church. However, it is obvious that even a naive reader would never come to cessationist conclusions—in fact, quite the opposite.[17] Gee also conveys the same sentiment: There is no "sound and convincing argument against the continuance of the early Pentecostal phenomena of the Church . . . the Church ceases to enjoy His gifts through her own lukewarmness and unbelief, and not because God arbitrarily withdraws them as unnecessary today."[18]

But, Pentecostals believe that they are doing what Jesus did and what he taught his disciples to do. When we turn to the New Testament, we learn of miracles, acts of raw courage, and explosive evangelism. Kydd portrays the way early Christians appropriated the power and gifts of the Spirit:

> Closer probing gives us the answer that early Christians were people filled with the Spirit and exercising spiritual gifts such as healing, exorcism and prophecy. They were certainly preoccupied with Christ, but they were very much alive to the presence of the Holy Spirit also. The Holy Spirit was among them, leading them to do some very surprising things. He was also at work quietly and inconspicuously helping Christians to spiritual maturity, but He showed Himself in powerful action again and again. The New Testament Christianity was charismatic. It was very common among them that the Holy Spirit would break in upon them with great force.[19]

As it is obvious spiritual gifts are the New Testament norm, we shall look into the use of spiritual gifts by Pentecostal movement world-wide and analyse how they act as tools of liberation. Here we may not be able to treat all the gifts noted in the New Testament scriptures but limit our attention to miraculous gifts such as tongue speaking, prophecy, divine healing, exorcism, and some others. We shall also explore their theological import and missionary potentials.

Spiritual Gifts in Pentecostal Movement

Pentecostals read the Bible as literally as possible and in the light of their Spirit experience. For them, stories and instructions of the Bible are not just history and doctrinal statements but spiritual lessons to be learnt and applied in personal and community life. When a Pentecostal reads the Bible, the biblical world comes alive in his/her life. What is experienced by the Bible characters thousands of years ago, is spiritually experienced here and now. If a person is delivered from a trouble, the same deliverance is anticipated in one's life. If the apostles and early Christians experienced the outpouring of the Spirit, the same powerful

---

[17] Oss, "A Pentecostal / Charismatic View", *Are Miraculous Gifts for Today?*, 264.

[18] Quoted in Bruner, *A Theology of the Holy Spirit*, 131.

[19] Ronald Kydd, *Charismatic Gifts in the Early Church*, (Peabody, MA: Hendrickson Publishers, 1984), 1.

experience of the Spirit is expected in faith; if they had exercised spiritual gifts such as healing, prophecy, exorcism in the first century, those gifts are not ceased but can be exercised today. Pentecostals actually enters into the biblical world, bypassing two thousand years of gap and bring down the same spiritual categories here. The arguments of cessationists and liberal strands of Christian theology that spiritual gifts are either ceased or cannot applicable today, are out-rightly rejected by Pentecostals. Consequently, wherever Pentecostalism has set its roots, spiritual gifts are exercised individually as well as communally. The spiritual categories that are mentioned in the Bible are enacted in faith, thus, healing, exorcism, tongues, prophecy and so on are directly appropriated.

As we turn to the New Testament, the book of Acts describes the stories of great exploits of Jesus' disciples with the power of the Holy Spirit. They had exercised spiritual gifts in churches and mission fields, performing miraculous feats; healing, exorcism, prophecy and other signs. Those experiences and the stories of the explosive growth of the early church function as the blueprint and inspiration for Pentecostal living. Pentecostal theology and hermeneutics take these happenings as interpretive grid and emulates them in life as well as in the missionary endeavours, even though the Protestant theology considers those happenings as only history.[20] As we know, the primary descriptions and detailed explanations of the spiritual gifts are given in Pauline letters, as instruction to the churches.[21] Here the first Epistle to the Corinthian Church (1 Corinthians 12: 8-10) stands prominent in having the details of miraculous gifts. It says,

> For to one is given the word of wisdom through the Spirit, and to another the word of knowledge according to the same Spirit; to another faith by the same Spirit, and to another gifts of healing by the one Spirit, and to another the effecting of miracles, and to another prophecy, and to another the distinguishing of spirits, to another various kinds of tongues, and to another the interpretation of tongues.

---

[20] Craig S. Keener, *Spirit Hermeneutics: Reading Scripture in Light of Pentecost* (Michigan: Eerdmans Publishing, 2016); Robert P. Menzies, *Empowered for Witness: The Spirit in Luke-Acts* (London: T&T Clark, 2004); Roger Stronstad, *Prophet-hood of All Believers: A Study in Luke's Charismatic Theology* (Sheffield: Sheffield Academic Press, 2003).

[21] Wayne Grudem in his Systematic Theology outlines all the gifts of the Spirit. The numbers with a bracket are to denote repeated gifts in different references: 1 Corinthians 12:28 (1. Apostle 2. Prophet 3. Teacher 4. Miracles 5. Kinds of healings 6. Helps 7. Administration 8. Tongues); 1 Corinthians 12:8–10 (9. Word of wisdom 10. Word of knowledge 11. Faith (5). Gifts of healing (4). Miracles (2). Prophecy 12. Distinguishing between spirits (8). Tongues 13. Interpretation of tongues); Ephesians 4:11 ((1). Apostle (2). Prophet 14. Evangelist 15. Pastor-teacher); Romans 12:6–8 ((2). Prophecy 16. Serving (3). Teaching 17. Encouraging 18. Contributing 19. Leadership 20. Mercy); 1 Corinthians 7:7 (21. marriage 22. Celibacy); 1 Peter 4:11 (whoever speaks (covering several gifts), whoever renders service (covering several gifts)). Wayne Grudem, *Systematic Theology* (Michigan: Zondervan Publishing House, 1994), 895-897.

After listing these nine gifts Paul adds, "But one and the same Spirit works all these things, distributing to each one individually just as He wills" (v. 11). The spiritual gifts, accordingly, are distributions of the Holy Spirit. In Romans 12:6, Paul writes about having "gifts (*charismata*) that differ according to the grace given to us", and then he briefly describes seven of the gifts (vv. 6-9).[22]

It is important to emphasize that the context for the gifts of the Spirit was the experience of the Spirit's outpouring. Without this there would not have been vitality and power sufficient for the gifts to be manifested and multiplied. The Corinthians were "not lacking in any spiritual gift" because the testimony to Christ had been "confirmed" among them; they had been "saturated with" the Spirit. Whatever may have been their faults -and they were manifold-they knew the fullness of the Spirit and His multiple gifts.[23] William Rodman compares the Corinthian situation with today's Pentecostal and Charismatic renewals:

> The charismatic renewal of our day is in basic accord with the Corinthian situation. The background for the believers' claims to the operation of the gifts of the Holy Spirit is their experience of the outpouring of the Spirit. At some time, in some situation, there has been a distinctive -even "saturating"- experience of the Holy Spirit's presence and power. This has been, it is claimed, the dynamic source of all the spiritual gifts that have followed.[24]

And then he succinctly delineates the dynamic nature of spiritual gifts and their significance, he continues,

> What is of particular significance about the spiritual gifts is that through their expression there is *dynamic manifestation.* By the gift of the Holy Spirit there is entrance into the dynamic dimension; by the gifts of the Spirit there is the occurrence of dynamic manifestation. Hence, when we are dealing with the spiritual gifts, their importance is neither little nor secondary, but fundamental. For through the gifts the Holy Spirit Himself is "on the scene" in dynamic self-manifestation.[25]

Moreover, basic to the understanding of a "spiritual gift" is the idea that it is an ability which is given to someone by God. He is its source. It is not at the disposal of human beings, but rather it comes into play when God chooses. We must also understand that spiritual gifts seem to be tailored to particular

---

[22] J. Rodman Williams, *Renewal Theology: Salvation, The Holy Spirit, and Christian Living,* vol. 2, (Michigan: Academie Press, 1990), 323.

[23] Williams, *Renewal Theology*, 324.

[24] Williams, *Renewal Theology*, 326.

[25] Williams, *Renewal Theology*, 331.

situations. The main thrust of Paul's teaching on this point is his insistence that the gifts are to build up the Christians among whom they appear.[26]

If the baptism in the Spirit empowers the believers for the liberative mission, the gifts of the Spirit act as means of liberation. The Pentecostals believe that being filled with the Spirit means to equip the individual in such a way that he becomes an instrument for the ongoing process of the Spirit in the church and in the world.[27] Here the gifts of the Spirit play unique roles. Pentecostals view all gifts of Spirit as eschatological and prophetic signs of a kingdom of joy.[28] It is these gifts that make it possible for women and men today, to receive the healing and resources for living offered by Jesus as he is the supreme charismata, the concrete expression of new life. Moreover, they enable the believers to act in the world as Jesus acted. "Social values embedded in 'the fruits of the Spirit and the gifts of the Spirit' have implications for the way in which the church functions in the society", says Young-Gi Hong.[29] The *charismata* equip believers to move beyond their ability in this world of spiritual as well as physical bondages, rescuing people through healing their body and mind and bringing them to the kingdom of God. Though all the gifts are equally important, here we cannot deal with all but only those with an immediate relevance to the liberative mission.

The Gift of Speaking in Tongues

In Pentecostal teaching and practice, speaking in tongue is distinguished in two categories. First, speaking in tongue as the initial evidence of the baptism in the Holy Spit and second as one of the gifts of the Spirit.[30] The book of Acts, chapter 2 describes the descent of the Holy Spirit on the Day of Pentecost upon the disciples gathered there and "all of them filled with the Holy Spirit and began to speak in other languages, as the Spirit gave them ability" (v. 4). Then Luke records the reaction of the people who gathered there hearing the great sound and commotion; "We hear them declaring the wonders of God in our own languages" (v.11). Certainly the listeners had understood the message conveyed through the tongue speaking since the disciples spoke in their languages. As Luke narrates, at least fifteen language groups were present. Apostle Peter explains the phenomenon as the fulfilment of prophet Joel's prediction of granting gift of prophecy, visions

---

[26] Kydd, *Charismatic Gifts in the Early Church*, 2.

[27] Hendrikus Berkhof though not a Pentecostal, says that there are the gifts of the Spirit for us which are the instruments by which we partake in the wider ecclesiastical and cosmic dimensions of the Spirit's work. See Hendrikus Berkhof, *The Doctrine of the Holy Spirit* (London: Epworth Press, 1964), 89.

[28] Young-Gi Hong, "Church and Mission: A Pentecostal Perspective", *IRM* XC/358 (July, 2001), 301.

[29] Hong, "Church and Mission", 300.

[30] Russel P. Spittler, "Glossolalia", in *NIDPCM*, edited by Stanley M. Burgess (Michigan: Zondervan, 2002), 673.

and dreams upon all (v.17). Therefore, we can confidently say that coming of the Holy Spirit brings his gifts and the disciples were actually exercising speaking in tongues as one of the gifts of the spirit.

Later, in the city of Caesarea, in the household of Cornelius, the outpouring of the Spirit was accompanied with tongue speaking (Acts 10). The story Luke narrated tells us that Apostle Peter was sent by the Spirit. The preaching of apostle Peter was interrupted when the Spirit fell on the foreign group. Peter's fellow Jews who travelled with him "were astonished that the gift of the Holy Spirit had been poured out even on the Gentiles. For they heard them speaking in tongues and praising God" (10:45–46). Similarly, another occurrence of speaking in tongues appeared. In Ephesus, Paul met a group of people who knew only of John's baptism. After re-baptising them in the name of Jesus, Paul laid hands on them, then "the Holy Spirit came on them, and they spoke in tongues and prophesied" (19:6). Here we can assume that along with the gift of prophecy, speaking in tongues appeared as gift as well as a sign of Spirit outpouring.

However, when Paul explains the gift of speaking in tongues, he insisted that public speaking in tongues in worship services must always be interpreted (I Cor.14:27). The personal speaking in tongues, as Hollenweger put it, can be described as a non-intellectual prayer and praise too deep for words (Rom. 8.26). It happens in Pentecostal services in which the worshippers were caught up in an ecstatic volume of united worship. Speaking in tongues which occurs at such a time is not for the edification of others, but is devoted to the worship of the Most High God.[31]

Praying in tongues is something that brings personal edification and empowerment. It has been shown repeatedly, by psychologists, sociologists, and other scientists, that praying in tongues leads to greater personal happiness and a greater sense of personal empowerment. It relieves stress, helps to deal with negative emotions, builds community, and brings about positive transformational change both personally and in society.[32] A philosopher, James K. A. Smith, who exercises tongue speaking says that privately praying in tongues is "deeply cathartic and represents a kind of spiritual discipline". He continues, "And this spiritual discipline — a practice by which we learn to be friends with God and others — is also deeply therapeutic. Praying in tongues often brings healing and helps maintain spiritual and emotional health."[33]

---

[31] Walter J. Hollenweger, *The Pentecostals: The Charismatic Movement in the Churches* (Minnesota: Agsburg Publishing House, 1972), 342.

[32] Alexander, *Signs & Wonders*, 48; Margaret M. Poloma, "Glossolalia, Liminality, and Empowered Kingdom Building: A Sociological Perspective", *Speaking in Tongues: Multi - Disciplinary Perspectives,* edited by Mark J. Cartledge (Milton Keynes, England: Paternoster, 2006), 157, 167, 171.

[33] Alexander, *Signs & Wonders*, 55; James K. A. Smith, "Tongues as 'Resistance Discourse': A Philosophical Perspective", *Speaking in Tongues,* 93.

Studies of tongues speakers have consistently shown that they are *not* psychologically abnormal, and it is generally agreed by non-Pentecostal researchers that people who pray in tongues are not in a trance, and that they are in control of the experience. There is a growing consensus that praying in tongues has a lot in common with the altered states of consciousness experienced while listening to music. Studies have shown that Pentecostals in neighbourhoods and cities with higher rates of poverty, crime, and addiction pray in tongues "frequently each day as they are walking, driving, shopping, and going about other daily tasks and chores" which give them a sense of empowerment.[34]

The Anglican priest Morton T. Kelsey, makes an attempt to understand the phenomenon of speaking in tongues against the background of Jungian psychology. He sees speaking in tongues as an expression of the collective psyche. Kelsey regards speaking in tongues as an extremely effective therapeutic instrument. This is not only for primitive or uneducated people but also for modern and educated. Therefore, tongue speaking should not be despised as a pathological phenomenon, "hollow imitations of the first springtime of the Spirit", or as the work of demons.[35] Hollenweger, explains the tongue speaking phenomenon in a more amenable daily experience:

> Ultimately, one can give a medical explanation of why man needs food and sleep. In the same way, man needs the possibility of meditation and the relaxation of tension, and these are not limited to intellectual forms. For some people art fulfils this function, for others, speaking in tongues; and those who can unload their mental burdens in both ways are not so rare as commonly supposed.[36]

Along with the speaking of tongue for personal edification, it has been widely exercised as others directed, especially in Pentecostal evangelistic and mission endeavours. Walter Hollenweger narrates the story of a Jew who became a Pentecostal, highlighting its missional value.[37] After narrating the story,

---

[34] Alexander, *Signs & Wonders*, 56. Smith, "Tongues as 'Resistance Discourse'", 161.

[35] Hollenweger, *The Pentecostals*, 343.

[36] Hollenweger, *The Pentecostals*, 344.

[37] Rabbi Jacob Rabinowitz belonged to an old rabbinic family. In the summer of 1960 a friend invited him to a service of the Assemblies of God in Pasadena, Texas. When the pastor of the congregation invited for prayer for personal problem, Jacob Rabinowitz also knelt down with others in front of the altar. Then all congregation began to pray together, some in English, others in tongues. Suddenly Rabinowitz stood up and asked with tears in his eyes, "Which one of you is Jewish?" No one answered. "Which one of you knows me?" "It came from right here, behind me", the rabbi pointed out. "Just exactly where you're standing", he said to one of the men. However the man said that he was an Irish, named John Gruver. "That's the voice", said Rabinowitz, "but tell me where you learned to speak Hebrew so well. And how did you know my name and the name of my father? You said in perfect Hebrew, 'I have dreamed a dream that you will go into the big populated places and there you will preach. The ones who have not heard will understand you because you, Jacob, son of Rabbi Ezekiel, come in the fullness of the blessing of the Gospel of Jesus Christ'"; Quoted in Hollenweger, *The Pentecostals*, 3-4.

Hollenweger comments that speaking in tongues is a revival of the phenomenon of which Paul says, "Thus, tongues are a sign not for believers but for unbelievers" (I Cor. 14:22). There are numerous such incidents which helped pastors and missionaries in their mission activities.

Let me narrate an incident that underlines the value of speaking in tongue. In a private conversation among my colleagues, a faculty member narrated an incident happened few years before in which he was an eye witness. A Pentecostal church in Kerala, was just established and growing day by day. There was opposition of anti-Christian elements who were also waiting for opportunity to foment troubles against the church and the pastor. On a Sunday worship service, a young man came and showed his interest to participate in the prayer. During the worship, many were speaking in tongues. The pastor had the gift of interpreting the tongue and he interpreted the message spoken by a believer. It was about the young man; he was sent by a fanatic group to get the information of the activities of the church. Seeing the supernatural power of the Holy Spirit working in the Pentecostal congregation, the man repented of his evil intention with a loud cry and submitted his life to Christ.

Christy Wilson, the famous missionary to Afghanistan and later professor at Gordon-Conwell seminary narrated a true incident in the book, *More To Be Desired Than Gold,* that shows the significance of speaking in tongues for evangelism and bringing people to churches:

> Another Afghan Christian I knew, a student, attended a church service while he was visiting in California. During that service the pastor gave a message in tongues. After the service the Afghan went up to speak to the pastor. "When were you in Afghanistan?" he asked. "I've never been out of the United States", the pastor replied. "What do you mean?" "You were talking in Pashtu, my mother tongue", said the Afghan. "You told how Jesus died for my sins and how He rose again from the dead". "That was the Holy Spirit speaking to you through me", said the pastor. "I have never been to Afghanistan". The Afghan student recognized this as a miracle. As a result, he has accepted the Lord.[38]

The stories above give a taste of what the tongue speaking is meant for. It is obvious that the manifestation of the gifts of tongues, interpretation of tongues and prophecy convicts and convinces the unbeliever. Paul says that tongues "are a sign, not for believers but for unbelievers" (1 Cor 14: 22). He declares further: But if an unbeliever or someone who does not understand comes in while everybody is prophesying, he will be convinced by all that he is a sinner and will be judged by

---

[38] J. Christy Wilson Jr., *More To Be Desired Than Gold* (South Hamilton, MA: Gordon-Conwell Seminary, 2002), 145.

all, and the secrets of his heart will be laid bare. So he will fall down and worship God, exclaiming, "God is really among you!" (24,25).

The Gift of Prophecy

The gift of prophecy can be termed as one of the most important spiritual gifts that has been in use among Pentecostals and also been mostly abused. This gift is the most sought-after and highly appreciated gift. This is also used as a powerful tool in the mission endeavours and instrumental in bringing many people into the church. Along with the gift of prophecy, we shall also include the gifts of word of wisdom and word of knowledge and vision here since all of these can be categorised as gifts that declare God's counsel to the people. Pentecostals firmly believe that all these gifts are of supernatural origin and God speaks to human beings directly, not just through scripture. Whether it comes as a direct thought from God in our own head, through an event or another person, or in a direct vision or dream, God is speaking. Alexander quotes a Pentecostal who tries to help others understand prophecy: "When the Holy Spirit puts an idea in your mind and you share it with one or more people. God puts the idea in your mind and you put it in your own words."[39]

Prophecy, accordingly, is an immediate communication from God in the common language. It is a "speaking for" God by which a person's tongue is completely at the disposal of the Holy Spirit. The concepts and words do not derive from the speaker - but from a divine source. So, God communicates in a given situation a special message to his people.[40] Moreover, Pentecostals believe that anyone, of any age, gender, experience, or educational level can be used by God to speak the prophetic word. This democratizing move of God in Pentecost, where sons, daughters, slaves, free, young, and old can all prophesy, dream, and have visions, is empowering women and other traditionally excluded groups around the globe. It is a clear indicator of why the Pentecostal movement is so appealing and growing so fast. That is democracy of the Holy Spirit — everybody has a voice.[41]

As we turn to the New Testament, gift of prophecy has a prominent place. The Gospels of Matthew and Luke present the birth, life and ministry of Jesus in the context of Old Testament prophecies and Jesus himself predicts his mission as suffering messiah. His ministry was prophetic and he was rejected and died as a prophet (Lk. 3:22; 4:1,14,18).[42] Stronstad affirms that Jesus' reception of the Spirit at Jordan and the pouring of the Spirit on the day of Pentecost, everything which he said and did was the work and word of a Spirit-anointed, Spirit-filled,

---

[39] Alexander, *Signs & Wonders*, 118-119.

[40] Williams, *Renewal Theology*, 383.

[41] Alexander, *Signs & Wonders*, 121-122.

[42] Lk. 24:19 says, "The things about Jesus of Nazareth, who was *a prophet mighty in deed and word* before God and all people...".

Spirit-led and Spirit-empowered prophet.[43] Besides, Jesus himself was standing in the line of prophetic heritage.[44]

In the book of Acts we see gift of prophecy working in full force through the bestowal of the gifts upon the disciples along with the outpouring of the Holy Spirit. On the Day of Pentecost, when the 120 spoke in tongues, Peter declared that the prophecy of Joel had been fulfilled (Acts 2:16–18; Joel 2:28–29). In Joel chapter 2, however, there is no reference to speaking in tongues. What we find there is, a reference to the ability to prophesy. Evidently, the ability to speak in tongues and the ecstatic activity were the manifestation of the prophecy. Such a powerful manifestation of the prophecy led some in the multitude to charge the 120 with public drunkenness. However, Peter and many in the multitude understood the manifestation to be a form of "prophetic" speech (v. 11). This allowed Peter to explain the phenomenon in terms of the fulfilment of Joel's prophecy. Here Luke, along with Peter, in particular convey the longstanding picture of the Old Testament, that prophecy at its most basic level is nothing less than inspired speech given by God through an individual.[45] Moreover, as Oss explains, in Acts 2:18, Peter emphasizes universal nature of the outpouring by reiterating the prophecy theme with the addition of "and they will prophesy" which is not found in Joel. In so doing, Peter expands the prophetic gift to an even greater variety of persons such as male and female servants, than we find in Joel's original text. In the new age the gift of prophecy is no longer restricted to particular groups, such as institutional prophets, priests, and kings; rather, it is poured out on all of God's people, giving them the prophetic enduement.[46]

Throughout the book of Acts, Luke meticulously provides examples of prophecy and he records two striking incidents of genuine prophecy. There were two occurrences of prophecy through prophet Agabus, though the incidents were separated by some 12 intervening years. The first took place in Antioch. Prophet Agabus stood up and foretold by the Spirit that a famine was coming over all the earth (Acts 11:27–30) and it was fulfilled when Claudius was Caesar (11:28). The second one took place in Caesarea (Acts 21:10–14). In this case, Agabus took Paul's belt and bound his own hands and feet with it. Then he proclaimed: "The Holy Spirit says, 'In this way the Jews of Jerusalem will bind the owner of this belt and will hand him over to the Gentiles'" (Acts 21:11). It is clear that this particular oracle was given in a form that is similar to many found in the OT. By

---

[43] Roger Stronstad, "Affirming Diversity: God's People as a Community of Prophets", *Pneuma* 17/2 (Fall, 1995): 148.

[44] "The Spirit of the Lord is upon me, because he has anointed me…to let the oppressed go free, to proclaim the year of the Lord's favour", Lk. 4:18-19.

[45] C.M. Robeck Jr., "Gift of Prophecy", *NIDPCM*, 1005-06.

[46] Oss, "A Pentecostal / Charismatic View", *Are Miraculous Gifts for Today?*, 267.

using concrete examples from everyday life, Luke has provided a series of pictures that reveal much about the gift of prophecy.[47]

Now in the first epistle of Corinthians, apostle Paul elaborates the methodological exercise and purpose of the gift of prophecy. According to Paul, it is for up-building, exhortation, and consolation: "One who prophesies speaks to men for edification and exhortation and consolation" (l Cor. 14:3). Prophecy is for the purpose of building up and strengthening people, exhorting and encouraging certain actions, and bringing consolation and comfort. Hence prophecy, as a direct word from the Lord, serves first to build up people. Second, prophecy may be a word of exhortation. In that sense prophecy may contain an admonition about certain activities and an urging to move ahead in a proper manner. Third, prophecy may serve for consolation and comfort, where there is hurt and suffering or need for a sympathetic word, a prophecy may speak an inspired message that brings comfort and consolation.[48] Therefore, it is clear that prophecy is primarily for believers. So Paul later wrote, "Prophecy is not for unbelievers but for believers" (l Cor. 14:22).

However, a secondary function of prophecy is to convict unbelievers of sin so that they turn to God. Paul continues, "If all prophesy and an unbeliever or outsider enters, he is convicted by all, he is called to account by all, the secrets of his heart are disclosed; and so, falling on his face, he will worship God and declare that God is really among you" (vv. 24-25). This extraordinary change occurs not through the proclamation of one person (as in preaching) but through the prophesying of many. That many believers are channels for God to speak directly brings such overwhelming conviction, judgment, and heart searching that the unbeliever or outsider can only fall on his face and worship God. Moreover, he will know for a certainty that God is truly present among his people.[49]

However, a glimpse into the history of the church confirms that the subsequent generations ceased to function as prophets, either individually or corporately; only among some individuals and renewal or pietistic groups did prophecy sporadically reappear.[50] But, in the twentieth century, the gift of prophecy has been permanently, though only partially restored. Stronstad says, "This restoration began on January 1, 1901 when Agnes Ozman, a student at

[47] Cecil M. Robeck Jr., "Gift of Prophecy", 1006.

[48] Williams, *Renewal Theology*, 383-384.

[49] Williams, *Renewal Theology*, 384-385.

[50] Stronstad, "Affirming Diversity, 155. In the history of the church we can see some movements and individuals with the power of Spirit witnessed Christ with great vigour. They were great servants of God such as St. Agustine, Martin Luther, John Calvin, and John Wesley so on. However, the outpouring of the Spirit in the beginning of the Pentecostal movement was a mass phenomenon which included all sorts of people – black and white, men and women, rich and poor, educated and illiterate – and it was worldwide.

Bethel Bible School in Topeka, Kansas began to speak in other tongues. This fresh outpouring of the Spirit spread like prairie wild fire…to the end of the earth."[51]

Prophecy in Pentecostal Movement

From the days of the Azusa Street revival, Pentecostals have understood the modern outpouring of the Holy Spirit as a fulfilment of prophecy. "Early Pentecostals understood the outpouring of the Spirit in the first century at Pentecost and at the inception of the twentieth-century Pentecostal movement as the fulfilment of divine promises, especially Joel's prophecy concerning the last days", says Land.[52] According to him, this outpouring of the Spirit constituted the church as an eschatological community of prophets and provided an "apocalyptic vision" in the Last Days. This pouring forth of the Spirit of prophecy in the contemporary Pentecostal/Charismatic renewal restores important New Testament realities. For example, baptising with the Holy Spirit restores the immediacy of God's presence to his people. And the baptism in the Spirit and gifts of the Spirit restored the Spirit's empowering in witness. Hence, the Pentecostals witness as prophets by works which are empowered by the Spirit and by words which are inspired by the Spirit.[53]

Pentecostals are convinced that divine revelations occur through prophecy, dreams, and visions. According to Alexander, the statistics show that throughout the world, Pentecostals are two to five times more likely than the average Christian to report that they have "received a direct revelation from God". Pentecostals firmly believe that God can and will still speak to them individually.[54] Consequently, the gift of prophecy is exercised in most Pentecostal assemblies. Those who have the gift of prophecy, possessed by the Spirit speak biblically reminiscent sentences or phrases in the vernacular. The prophetic exhortation takes place most often with an eschatological and sometimes visional context and content. Moreover, prophecy occurs most often in an ecstatic or para-ecstatic condition and it differs from tongues-speaking only in that it is spoken in understandable speech.[55]

Such an understanding is fully realised in Pentecostal congregations and as a result, people are being healed, liberated and transformed. For instance, Pastor Paul Yonggi Cho, founder of the world's largest church, in Seoul, South Korea, realised that he was receiving strange impulses as he preached from his pulpit. He would 'see' twisted ankles, tiff joints, internal organs of the human body, apparently burning or decaying. He thought these must be from Satan or he was

---

[51] Stronstad, "Affirming Diversity", 156.

[52] Stephen J. Land, *Pentecostal Spirituality: A Passion for the Kingdom* (Sheffield: Sheffield Academic Press, 1993), 58.

[53] Murray W. Dempster, "Pentecostal Social Concern and the Biblical Mandate for Social Justice", *Pneuma* 9/2 (Fall, 1987): 147.

[54] Alexander, *Signs & Wonders*, 117.

[55] Bruner, *A Theology of the Holy Spirit,* 142.

going mad. He discovered soon after that they were message of the Spirit, 'words of knowledge', when he passed on a 'crazy' thought to a crippled woman in a wheelchair— "God wants me to tell you that you can walk. He has touched your body and commands you to stand up and walk". Not daring to wait and see what happened, Cho turned and walked away. But, the crowd started shouting. The woman was standing up and walking to and fro in front of the platform. It was God who had been speaking to him after all.[56]

Through the gifts such as prophecy and 'word of knowledge', troubles and infirmities of the people are revealed and they are being liberated from their agonies. David Pytches shares a similar story. Some two years ago a lady from Wales came to kneel at the communion rails after the service at St. Andrew's, Chorleywood, England. She was suffering from rheumatoid arthritis in the hands. As she was being prayed for, nothing seemed to be happening. After a while one of the team members offered the suggestion through the 'word of knowledge' that it was due to something which happened in her teens. The leader of the group, asked her if she could recall any trauma or problem to do with her teens. She looked quite blank. Then members asked her consent to pray for her past life. She readily consented and the Lord was asked to heal whatever it was. As this was done the sufferer suddenly began to weep profusely. The tears fell on her hands. Suddenly the fingers loosened up and she was healed.[57]

There are thousands of such miraculous stories happen all over the world every day. Through such events outsiders are convinced of the power of God, join the Pentecostal congregations and being liberated from their sinful lives and downtrodden situation. For instance, John Wimber testifies an incident happened through him:

> We've had numerous occasions where God has revealed sins of people either through a word of knowledge or a combination of that and a word of wisdom and prophecy. For example, I was once on an airplane when I turned and looked at a passenger across the aisle to see the word 'adultery' written across his face in big letters. The letters, of course, were only perceptible to spiritual eyes. He caught me looking at him and said, 'What do you want?' As he asked that, a woman's name clearly came into my mind. I leaned over the aisle and asked if the name meant anything to him. His face turned pale and he asked if he could talk to me. It was a large plane with a bar so we went there to talk. On the way the Lord spoke to me again, saying, 'Tell him to turn from this adulterous affair or I am going to take him'. When we got to

---

[56] Lars Wilhelmsson, *The Gifts of Holy Spirit: God's Provision for Effective Ministry*, 140; https://www. pdfdrive.com/the-gifts-of-the-holy-spirit-d23955742.html (accessed 10/08/2019).

[57] David Pytches, *Spiritual Gifts in the Local Church* (Michigan: Bethany Publishing House, 1987), 95.

> the bar I told him that God had told me he was committing adultery with the woman whose name God had revealed to me and that God would take him if he did not repent. He melted on the spot, and asked what he should do. I led him through a prayer for repentance and he received Christ. This was in front of a stewardess and two other passengers, who were shocked, but then also began to cry. Then he said that his wife was downstairs in the seat next to his. I told him to go and tell her the entire story which he did. He led her to Christ.[58]

Alexander narrates the story of a young man who received a prophetic revelation that resulted in the massive growth of the church in Uganda. Simeon Kayiwa was a philosophy major at Makerere University in Kampala the year President Idi Amin, the brutal dictator of Uganda, assassinated the Anglican bishop Jana Luwum. Simeon says that Jesus appeared directly in front of him while he was in bed and said, "Wake up! Read Isaiah 60. Go and bring my people back to me. Tell them I am the greatest power in all heaven and earth. Tell them to leave witchcraft and come back to Me. I will be with you to perform miracles and wonders by which people will know that I sent you". Kayiwa told other young people of his vision, and they organized an illegal church that emphasized prophecy, healings, exorcisms, and miracles in the midst of Idi Amin's reign of terror. His ministry received foreign media attention from the British Broadcasting Company and the London newspaper Daily Mail. It is also claimed that he has raised up to eighteen people from the dead. Kayiwa's work, which he began as a twenty year old college student, is credited with birthing, sustaining, and growing 90 percent of the thirty five thousand churches in Uganda. Simeon Kayiwa's youthful vision has led to six million more Pentecostal Christians.[59]

Thus, gifts of prophecy, the word of wisdom, word of knowledge, visions and dreams act as consolation, encouragement and building up of the members of the church. On the other hand, they act as tools of liberation and transformation for outsiders and bring them into the Kingdom of God and enable the growth of the church.

The Gift of Healing

Compared to the gifts of speaking in tongues, prophecy and other spiritual gifts, the gift of healing is more popular and a significant element in the Pentecostal movement for its proliferation and consolidation all over the world. This gift, though exercised in the Pentecostal congregations to bring healing to its adherents, it is most powerfully manifested as a tool for evangelism and mission. Experiencing

---

[58] Pytches, *Spiritual Gifts in the Local Church*, 101-102.

[59] Alexander, *Signs & Wonders*, 123; Ogbu Kalu, *African Pentecostalism: An Introduction* (Oxford: Oxford University Press, 2008), 96.

divine healing and resultant transformation, thousands join the Pentecostal movement all over the world, especially in third world countries. In the Asian and Indian context, the exercise of the gift of healing has unleashed mass movement among the poor and suffering populace that propelled the Pentecostal movement into a liberative movement. Pentecostal missionaries endowed with the healing gift, ushered new lease of life into the struggle-some circumstances of people who do not have adequate medical facilities and financial resources in Indian context. The gift of healing acts as the most potent weapon to alleviate the pain, suffering and poverty of the poor. Moreover, this gift liberate them from their menacing circumstance that consume their vitality and life.[60]

The gift of healing has enabled the Pentecostal message to penetrate into the poor masses of the third world. For instance, Gunther tersely draws a grim picture of the third world where Pentecostal movement is fast growing. She says that majority of people living in the two-thirds world, especially in growing urban areas where high population densities and unsanitary living conditions results in the spread of disease, poverty and poverty-related infirmities. Such a situation make daily survival uncertain. Although, globalization has touted as a panacea for most of the problems through the availability of new technologies, resources, and cures for diseases, poverty, hunger, and social strife, in actuality fetch opposite result. Despite advances in scientific medicines and globally disseminated reports of medical miracles, even basic medical care remains unavailable or prohibitively expensive for as much as 80 percent of the world's population. It is precisely in those regions of the world where poverty and sickness seem most overwhelming and where traditional religions and biomedicine alike have seemed insufficient in meeting practical, everyday needs that Pentecostalism has grown the most rapidly.[61]

For Pentecostals, healing practices are part and parcel of their life and it is an essential marker of Pentecostal and Charismatic Christianity as a global phenomenon. Gunther presents a statistics from the Pew research on Pentecostal healing practices. The Pew survey singles out divine healing as distinguishing Pentecostals and Charismatics from other Christians. In every country surveyed, large majorities (more than 70% in 8 of 10 countries) of Pentecostals reported having personally experienced or witnessed the divine healing of an illness or injury. In the Latin American, Asian, and African countries where Pentecostal growth is occurring most rapidly, as many as 80–90% of first-generation Christians attribute their conversions *primarily* to having received divine healing for themselves or a family member.[62]

---

[60] Shaibu Abraham, *Pentecostal Christology: Empirical Approach in Indian Context* (New Delhi: Christian World Imprints, 2019), 87-93.

[61] Candy Gunther Brown, *Global Pentecostal and Charismatic Healing*, edited by Candy Gunther Brown (New York: Oxford University Press, 2011), 7.

[62] Brown, *Global Pentecostal and Charismatic Healing*, 3

Pentecostal belief in healing is often based on testimonies of people who have themselves experienced healing, and they see this as a direct intervening act of God. The case for healing is built paradigmatically upon the ministry of Jesus, and theologically is rooted not in the doctrine of the Holy Spirit but in the doctrine of the atonement.[63] Pentecostals firmly believe that the healing ministry is based on the apostolic commission given to the disciples during Jesus' lifetime: "He called his twelve disciples to him and gave them authority to drive out evil spirits and to heal every disease and sickness...As you go, preach this message: 'The kingdom of heaven is near'. Heal the sick, raise the dead, cleanse those who have leprosy, drive out demons" (Matt. 10:1, 7–8; Mark 6:7–12; Luke 9:1–6).[64] Moreover, practice of healing within Pentecostalism also have been based on the charismatic gifts of healings referred to by Paul (1 Cor. 14:9) and the guidelines in Jas. 5:13-18. These, as well as the other healing references in the book of Acts, have formed the basis for the belief that supernatural healing may still occur today.[65]

In the New Testament, the Gospels present healing as the most significant component of Jesus' ministry. Jesus frequently heals people throughout his ministry. In addition, Jesus' acts of healing, announce and characterise the in-breaking of the kingdom of God, underscoring that in the ultimate consummation of the kingdom all sickness will be eliminated. Nearly all the statements in the synoptic Gospels that summarize the activity of Jesus, healing is mentioned. Matthew notice that "he went throughout Galilee, teaching in their synagogues, preaching the good news of the kingdom, and healing every disease and sickness among the people" (Matt. 4:23; 9:35).[66] Jesus, by his preaching, and his association with marginalized people (Matt. 9:12–13; Luke 15:1–2), and by his healings and exorcisms manifested the fact that "the kingdom of God is near" (Mark 1:14).

Moreover, the Old Testament prophecy that a servant, anointed by Yahweh, who would come and preach the good news to the poor, bind up the broken-hearted, open the eyes of those who had no vision, and comfort those who mourn (Isa. 61:1–2) is fulfilled in Jesus. In applying this promise to himself, Jesus was announcing that in his person the kingdom of God was breaking in (Luke 4:17–21). By healing from disease and casting out demons, Jesus inaugurated the kingdom and embodied it (Matt. 12:28; Luke 11:20).[67] Through healing, Jesus was evidencing the power and compassion of God to free human beings from all aspects of the power of evil. He himself made this explicit at times (Luke 13:16), and this is intensified by the fact that the Gospels may describe someone "demon-

---

[63] Bruner, *A Theology of the Holy Spirit*, 140-141.

[64] F. Martin, "Gift of Healing", in *NIDPCM*, 696

[65] Warrington, *Pentecostal Theology*, 268.

[66] This same type of statement is repeated frequently. Some examples are Matt. 4:24–5:2; 8:16–17; 12:15–16; 15:29–31; Mark 1:32–34; 3:7– 13; Luke 4:40–41; 6:17–19; et al.

[67] Martin, "Gift of Healing", 1693-1694.

possessed" as "healed" by the word of Jesus (Matt. 15:22–28; Mark 7:25–30; Luke 9:42).[68]

In the New Testament, healing miracles encouraged unbelievers to place their faith in Jesus. Healing is a dynamic demonstration of the supremacy of Jesus and a sign that the kingdom of God has been established. The relationship between healing and evangelism has always been prominent in Pentecostalism. Pentecostal theologians have asserted that healings have their true sphere in evangelism rather than among the believers. It is obvious that healing and deliverance from demonic power are integral parts of evangelization. It can become the avenue for the proclamation of salvation in Jesus Christ.[69] For instance, Stanley Frodsham had well documented the ministry of missionary Douglas Scott who went from England to Le Havre in 1930. After nine years of ministry in healings and miracles, Scott reported that "Every new work is opened on the ministry of divine healing, for without the supernatural it would be impossible to get any interest created in the gospel message."[70] Consequently, for Pentecostals, every healing and miracle, every spiritual manifestation, is a witness and testimony to the power of God. Healing leads to conversion and liberation of the person who received the healing. Signs and wonders become evangelistic means whereby the message of the kingdom is actualized in "person-centered" deliverance.[71]

The contemporary healing practices of the Pentecostal and Charismatic movements did not originate in early Pentecostalism.[72] The doctrines of 'divine healing' and 'healing in the atonement' were already existed in early Methodism and widespread in the North American Holiness movement in the nineteenth century. Holiness leaders like Charles Cullis, A.B. Simpson and Asa Mahan were staunch proponents of divine healing through faith. When Pentecostal movement formed out of these movements, the divine healing practice was wholeheartedly took over by the new movement.[73]

In Indian context, the gift of healing is extensively used for the growth of Pentecostal churches. As we already have explained, healthcare facilities are scant, as well as in disarray in remote villages and a large majority suffer from various illnesses while hundreds die every year. Besides, lack of financial resources, widespread poverty and inadequate transportation facilities have adversely

---

[68] Martin, "Gift of Healing", 1695.

[69] Warrington, *Pentecostal Theology*, 281.

[70] Stanley H. Frodsham, *With Signs Following: The Story of the Latter-Day Pentecostal Revival* (Gospel Publishing House, 1946), 91-92; Grant McClung, "Spontaneous Strategy of the Spirit", in *Azuza Street & Beyond,* edited by Grant McClung, 2nd edition (Florida: Bridge-Logos, 2012),146.

[71] Grant McClung, "Spontaneous Strategy of the Spirit", 146.

[72] See the chapter on The Full Gospel.

[73] Allan Anderson, "Pentecostal Approaches to Faith and Healing as Signs of the Kingdom", https://www.academia.edu/6068841/Pentecostal_Approaches_to_Faith_and_Healing?auto=download (accessed on 12/08/2019).

affected the chances of healing even ordinary diseases. We need to remember that even when they seek medical help from physicians available in villages, in many cases, this results in the draining of their hard-earned resources. In practice, they may not even get the results they desire. In some cases even if a medical doctor is appointed to a Public Health Centre, either the doctor may not be available or the centre may not have any medicines to dispense to these poor people. There are private practitioners, but several of them are either 'quacks' or extort money from the poor villagers.[74]

There are numerous examples divine healing and as a result poor people joined in Pentecostal congregations. Here is a story from the mission field of the state of Orissa reported by *Cross & Crown* magazine:

> Evangelist Elias Digal from Lakoti church informed of the healing testimony of a lady who was suffering from a blood condition for a long time. She was fed up with medications and tried traditional religious practices, which in turn also proved futile. She spent lot of money and was totally disappointed. Three months back, one of her neighbours who is a believer guided her to church and there she came to know Jesus the healer. She requested prayer from the pastor and believers of the church for her healing. On that day the saints prayed earnestly for that expectant lady that she could receive her miraculous healing. Now she is the happiest one to attend the church with all her dear ones in her family as they all repented, believed and were baptised in the water to join the body of Christ.[75]

Moreover, even as believers, people come to depend on divine healing. There are several testimonies in this regard. A woman who has experienced the miraculous healing of a cyst in her ovary testifies:

> I had developed a cyst in my stomach [later it was known from her husband that it was an ovarian cyst]. It caused intense pain and I could not work or sleep. I was taken to hospital and doctors recommended surgery. However, I needed a big sum of money. It was difficult for us to raise such an amount. I was not able to work and the wages earned by my husband were only enough for daily expenses of the family. It was beyond our capacity. Therefore, we began to pray. The matter was put before the congregation and the pastor earnestly prayed for me. To

---

[74] Abraham, *Pentecostal Christology*, 87.

[75] Editor, "From our Mission Field: Report from Orissa", *Cross & Crown* (September-October 2001): 13.

> our surprise within two weeks the cyst disappeared completely. I know that God loves me and heals his children.[76]

For ordinary people, who experience such healing miracles, the healing episode is not merely physical recovery or being healthy. Instead, the divine healing affects the totality of their life: physical, social, economic and spiritual. It is apparent that when a person is sick, it affects the net income of the family as one is not able to work. Therefore being healthy or being delivered from sickness is all-round well-being and peace of mind. The divine healing is a definite proof that God loves them and takes care of them. This understanding inculcates a new confidence in them: that they are someone special in the mind of God. This confidence, in turn, enables them to take 'a giant leap of faith' in the spiritual sphere and a renewed perception of themselves in society. When a person is convinced of the love and constant presence of God, he/she is able to overcome many of the nagging problems and obstacles which stand in the way of their progress whether it is financial, social, cultural, spiritual or personal. This new outlook situates a person in a higher pedestal and brings an attitudinal as well as a character change, which in turn results in a positive self-image and better perception of the realities surrounding the person. Thus, healing of the body contributes the wholistic development of a person and the family.[77]

See another healing experience that led to the dramatic growth of a Pentecostal church. The incident was narrated by Michael Bergunder who had carried out extensive research in south India to bring out the history of south Indian Pentecostalism:

> Similarly, a leading Pentecostal pastor from Madras gave a striking description of the role played by healing in founding his independent church. For months, he had no one attending his services except his own family. Then, on New Year's Eve at the midnight service, a family of three living in the same quarter attended the service because they could not get an auto-rickshaw to go to their non-Pentecostal, but Protestant, home congregation. The pastor—despite his apprehensions about how the gesture would be perceived—felt led to lay hands on the man and prophesy: "The Lord is doing a new thing in your life . . . . Receive it now!" Nothing obvious to the pastor occurred at the time, and he felt disappointed when the family slipped out while his eyes were shut for the closing prayer—before he could get their address. But the following day, the family returned, reporting that the man had received healing of a nervous breakdown that had kept him

[76] Abraham, *Pentecostal Christology*, 91; For more testimonies of miraculous healing in Indian Context, see Sarbeswar Sahoo, *Pentecostalism and Politics of Conversion in India* (New Delhi: Cambridge University Press, 2018), 99-105.

[77] Abraham, *Pentecostal Christology*, 92-93.

from working for four and a half years. During the prayer, he had experienced heat and his constant shaking had stopped, and the next day his doctor cleared him to return to work. When friends asked what had happened, the man answered, according to the pastor: "'This church.' That's all he said. So, that Sunday morning, we had about thirty-five people for the first time". The only thing that had changed since the previous week was this one man's healing testimony.[78]

In Indian context, the gift of healing acts a tool of substantial church growth and thousands of people are joining the Pentecostal churches.

Divine healing, the vital theme of Pentecostalism has been recently elucidated by Pentecostal theologians to capture its significance and develop a theology of healing in Pentecostal theology. Land explains divine healings as "sign of the eschatological breaking in of the kingdom of God and last days restoration for the proclamation of the gospel of the kingdom in all the earth."[79] For Pentecostals, healing is a means whereby the gospel is proclaimed in both the physical and spiritual dimension of life's reality. There is no dichotomising of spirit and body as in the western dualism but both are seen as integral parts of whole human person. Thus, healing restores an individual's sense of wholeness.[80] According to Martin, this understanding is congruent with the biblical understanding of anthropology.[81] Healing is a symbolic foreshadowing of the full life to which humankind is called, "our adoptive sonship, the redemption of our bodies" (Rom. 8:23). When unbelievers experience healing at the hands of Christians, they are being given a presentation of the Good News, "not simply with words, but also with power, with the Holy Spirit, and with deep conviction" (1 Thess. 1:5). Charismatic gifts of healing are qualities given to certain members of the body in and through which God demonstrates

---

[78] Michael Bergunder, "Miracle Healing and Exorcism in South Indian Pentecostalism", in *Global Pentecostalism and Charismatic Healing,* edited by Candy Brown Gunther (New York: Oxford University Press, 2011), 289.

[79] Land, *Pentecostal Spirituality,* 95.

[80] Cheryl Bridges Johns, "Healing and Deliverance: A Pentecostal Perspective", *Concilium* 3 (1996): 45-50.

[81] He says that in Hebrew, the state of being "healthy" is expressed in terms that indicate vigour, life, "being fat" (*br'*) or shalom. On the other hand, sickness is described as "weakness", "exhaustion", "lack of vitality", etc. That is, to recover health is to receive life once again. Moreover, healing is always the work of Yahweh. The Lord's act of rescuing his people from bondage is termed as "healing" in Exodus 15:27 and Hosea 11: 3. Jesus in his earthly ministry performed many healings and he termed them as the advent of the kingdom of God (Matt. 4:23; 9:35). Through healing, Jesus was evidencing the power and the compassion of God to free human beings from all aspects of the power of the evil. His command to the disciples to "heal the sick, raise the dead, cleanse the leaper, caste out demons..." shows that healing and deliverance from demonic power are integral parts of mission. Many of the needy people whom Jesus met were both spiritually put right with God and physically healed. F. Martin, "Gift of Healing", in *DPCM,* 350-351.

his saving power so that the response of faith will rest "not on men's wisdom, but on God's power" (1 Cor. 2:5).[82] Bridges Johns also explains the Pentecostal understanding of divine healing:

> In the ministry of healing there is the expression of the belief that salvation and healing are for the whole person. The laying on of hands and anointing with oil are means whereby Pentecostals give expression to this belief. As recorded in the gospels, Jesus comes as the great Physician, healing both sin-sick souls and physical sickness. His touch is one which brings *shalom*, restoring wholeness.[83]

"The divine touch upon human body reveals the good news that even the most weak and despised are worthy to become tabernacle of God's glory. Thus, the outcasts become vessels of honour through which God makes known the mysteries of his kingdom."[84] Today Pentecostal theology envisions divine healing as an overall liberative activity of God in the life of a disadvantaged person. Further, Pentecostals understand divine healing as "a means of achieving deeper solidarity with the oppressed and the suffering creation as well as with the Spirit of redemption at work in healing."[85]

However, Pentecostal theologian Frank Macchia cautions us that one should think critically about sickness in terms of social injustice and poverty. He contends that, "The problem with much of the popular teaching of Pentecostal evangelists on healing is its implicit isolation of sickness from the broader plight of human injustice and suffering. Also involved in this emphasis is the isolation of healing from the work of the Spirit of God in all of the creation to bring redemption and liberation. As a consequence, this popular teaching on healing also tends to be isolated from the final eschatological redemption of the body and renewal of that will occur when the kingdom of God comes in fullness."[86] This is an important critique of popular Pentecostalism. Nonetheless, within a fuller theological framework, Pentecostals understand divine healing "a means of achieving deeper solidarity with the oppressed and the suffering creation as well as with the Spirit of redemption at work in healing,"[87] and "more than any other aspect of Pentecostal spirituality and belief this provides a potential corrective to

[82] Martin, "Gift of Healing", in *NIDPCM*, 697.

[83] Bridges Johns, "Healing and Deliverance", 49.

[84] Bridges Johns, "Healing and Deliverance", 49.

[85] Frank D. Macchia, "The Struggle for Global Witness: Shifting Paradigms in Pentecostal Theology", in *The Globalization of Pentecostalism*, edited by M.W. Dempster, B.D. Klaus, & D. Petersen (Carlisle: Regnum, 1999), 22.

[86] Macchia, "The Struggle for Global Witness", 21.

[87] Macchia, "The Struggle for Global Witness", 22.

a one-sided emphasis on inwardness and otherworldliness that tends to dominate Pentecostalism."[88]

Martin delineates the significance and effects of divine healing in a suffering world. For him the miraculous healing reverses the structural injustice as well as rectifies physical and mental disorders:

> To heal a poor person of the effects of malnutrition is to reverse a process created by the structures of sin of which the person may be an innocent victim. To heal a person of AIDS is to claim the victory of the cross of Christ not only over physical disorder, but also over the very forces of death that lead to eternal ruin. To heal an angry or anxious person of heart disease or cancer is to initiate a process of reconciliation and restoration that derives from the power of the cross. To free someone from Satan's domination, gained through a life exposed to alienation and violence, is to liberate a human memory from the power of evil so that it can generate thoughts and attitudes that correspond to the truth of the gospel and become a temple in which the Father is adored in spirit and truth. In brief, healing is an essential part of preaching the gospel and of bearing witness to the reality and majesty of Jesus Christ.[89]

Today the gift of healing operates through the believing community for the community and for the needy in the world as in the days of Jesus. When we are being filled with love and compassion as Jesus had, the Holy Spirit will make use of us as channels of liberation to the society. However, Young-Gi Hong cautions us that we need to integrate God's faithfulness (i.e., faithfulness to God's healing promises) and God's freedom (i.e., the choice of how and when to heal) in our theology.[90]

Exorcism

Along with the gift of healing, exorcism is another important spiritual element that acts as an instrument of liberation among the ordinary people and impacts large-scale church growth in Pentecostal movement. The history of Pentecostal growth in majority world is full of stories of casting out of evil spirits and testimonies of people who have been liberated. Pentecostals strongly believe the personal and malevolent existence of the devil whose major role is to undermine the mission of Jesus as it is expressed through the Church and to combat the work of the Spirit which is to lead people into truth.[91] Pentecostals have always been very aware of spiritual warfare, with casting out of demons and "praying

[88] Macchia, "The Struggle for Global Witness", 20.

[89] Martin, "Gift of Healing", 1698-1699.

[90] Hong, "Church and Mission", 301.

[91] Warrington, *Pentecostal Theology,* 293.

through" to victory over the powers of darkness. According to McClung, a review of the literature, history, and oral "stories" of Pentecostalism reveals the centrality of the practice of exorcism in the expansion of the Pentecostal and Charismatic movements.[92]

Pentecostals believe that Satan and his hosts work against the wellbeing of humanity, oppress and attack to destroy their lives. Moreover, Pentecostals attribute many of the misfortunes and violence that take place in the world to the work of devil. They also believe that there is a spiritual battle between the powers of darkness and the believers and in this battle the victory belongs to believers because Christ has defeated the devil. Christ has all authority and power on the earth and heaven and his dominion is over all things, including demons and the devil. They also believe that the victory of Jesus over satanic forces is to be experienced in the present, both personally and globally by resisting him through prayer, obedience, self discipline and other strategies of spiritual warfare.[93] Moreover, through the gift of the Spirit, they are able to cast out demons and bring liberation to the people who are under the clutches of satanic forces.

The act of exorcism is one of the mission strategies adopted by the Pentecostals all over the world. Paul Pomerville affirms that the power encounter involved in exorcism has been an intentional church growth strategy among Pentecostals. Church growth proponents have noted that seriously dealing with demonic opposition has been one of the distinctive marks of Pentecostal growth. McGavran underlines that the act of exorcism is what makes Pentecostal churches grow. He says that Pentecostals accept the fact that demons and evil spirits invade men and women, bind them, and rule over them. Pentecostals believe that the mighty name of Jesus drives out evil spirits and heals all manner of sickness. Wagner concludes that exorcism was a key factor in the exploding growth among Latin American Pentecostals, and De Wet believes that it is the only way to successfully deal with the worldview of animists and the unseen spiritual resistance in the Muslim world.[94]

For Pentecostals, casting out demons and delivering people from satanic bondage is not an option but paramount in their mission practices. It is commanded by Christ and therefore, it should be carried out as an objective of the Great Commission. They recognize the act of exorcisms by Jesus and the apostles in the Gospels and the books of Acts as literal and emulate today. The Pentecostal theology and practices of exorcisms are drawn out of the New Testament practices, especially exorcism stories of the Gospels and Acts. The Synoptic Gospels are replete with stories and references to demon possession and exorcisms. The Gospel of Mark, dedicates nearly one-third of his Gospel to the

[92] L. Grant McClung Jr., "Exorcism", in *NIDPCM*, 625.

[93] Warrington, *Pentecostal Theology*, 293.

[94] McClung Jr., "Exorcism", 1540.

conflict between Christ and the demonic powers of darkness. The first recorded miracle of Jesus in Mark's Gospel is the exorcism of a man with an unclean spirit in the synagogue of Capernaum (Mark 1:21–28). The dramatic deliverance of the Gerasene demoniac (Mark 5:1-20) and healing of spirit possession of the daughter of the Syrophoenician woman from a distance are instances of spiritual and social liberation and generate faith in the readers (Mark 7:24-30). We also find healing of the epileptic boy (Mark 9:14-29), the mute demoniac (Matthew 9:31-34), and the blind and mute demoniac (Matthew 12:22f) as illustrations of Jesus' power and authority over the satanic forces. Luke 8:2 tell us that Jesus cast out seven demons from Mary Magdalene.

In Mark, Jesus called to him the twelve men who would become his apostles, "He appointed twelve, to be with him, and to be sent out to preach, and to have authority to cast out demons" (3:13-19). When Jesus sent them out on their first mission "they cast out many demons and anointed with oil many that were sick and healed them" (Mark 6:13). Throughout first three Gospels sickness and demons are closely associated. A number of reasons can be given for the emphasis on liberation from demon possession in the ministry of Christ. First of all, it is to highlight the climax in the confrontation between the Kingdom of God and the Satanic powers of darkness. Secondly, to demonstrate the loving compassion of Christ for suffering and sin-oppressed humanity. Finally, to validate his message by the demonstration of his power over the agents of Satan.[95]

According to Twelftree, exorcism stories are the bedrock of reliable data about the historical Jesus and the most compelling evidence of Jesus being an exorcist.[96] The Beelzebul passages clearly depict the power of Jesus over demons as the evidence that God's kingdom had broken into the present world order ruled by Satan.[97] Moreover, Jesus declared that "If it is by the Spirit of God that I cast out demons, then the kingdom of God has come upon you" (Matt. 12:28), thus declaring that the plundering of the house of Satan is a sign of the in-breaking of the reign of God by the coming of Jesus. Jesus' exorcisms were an eschatological sign. Jesus' authority over the power of Satan was conveyed to his disciples as well.[98] Reese comments: "In fact, the only activity that runs consistently from the

---

[95] Reddin, *Power Encounter,* 66.

[96] Graham H. Twelftree, *Jesus the Exorcist* (Peabody, Mass: Hendrickson Publishers, 1993); Graham H. Twelftree, *Jesus the Miracle Worker: a Historical & Theological study* (Illinois: IVP, 1999); Graham H. Twelftree, "Demon, Devil, Satan", in *DJG,* edited by Joel B. Green & Scot McKnight (Leicester: IVP, 1992).

[97] The Beelzebul passages deal with the charge that Jesus cast out demons by Beelzebul; see, Matt 12:25–29; Mark 3:23–27; Luke 11:17–22; Mk 3:22 [par. Mt 9:34 and 12:24; Lk 11:15].

[98] For example, Matt 10:8; Mark 3:13–19; 6:7–13; Luke 9:1–2; Graham H. Twelftree, *In the Name of Jesus: Exorcism among Early Christians* (Michigan: Baker Academic, 2007).

opening summary of Jesus' ministry through the accounts of his miracles and into the commission given to his disciples is the casting out of demons."[99]

The apostles continued to have the authority to cast out demons after ascension of Christ. Each time the church advanced into a new geographical region, the book of Acts shows confrontation with the evil spirits as the first stage of ministry in the evangelistic spread of the gospel.[100] In the ministry of apostles, people brought "the sick and those afflicted with unclean spirits, and they were all healed" (Acts 5:12–16). In Ephesus, when handkerchiefs or aprons that touched the body of apostle Paul brought to the affected people, the evil spirits would come out of them (Acts 19:11–12). Having seen such a miraculous happenings, some Jewish exorcists, the seven sons of Sceva, sought to do exorcism using the name of "Jesus whom Paul preaches" as a magic formula, but the demoniac man leaped on them and injured them (vv. 13–16).

The Gospels and Acts definitely convey the idea that the power to cast out demons was from God, not in the words used. One clear difference between Jesus' exorcisms and those of pagans and Jews is that Jesus did not use incantations and magic. Jesus cast out demons with a word, "Come out!" (Matt 8:16). Disciples expelled the demons in the name of Jesus (Luke 9:17). What was important was not the words used, but the spiritual state of the exorcist. When the disciples were not able to cast out the demon from an epileptic boy and asked Jesus why they had suffered such a humiliating failure, he replied, "This kind cannot be driven out by anything except prayer and fasting" (Mark 9:29).[101]

The transference of power and authority to the disciples was appropriated by Pentecostals by their Spirit endowment. In Pentecostal movement, missionaries, pastors and even ordinary believers are empowered to cast out demons. In a study conducted among the Pentecostals in India to understand their popular Christology, people confessed Jesus as the exorcist.[102] There are thousands of stories that are documented and which resulted in adding new members to Pentecostal congregations and bringing people into liberation in Indian context. Hear the story of a married woman, narrated by her husband:

> My wife was troubled by evil spirits from her childhood. Even after the marriage they used to torment her, make her fall down and wound her and sometimes make her unconscious. Later she was paralysed in one of her legs and became bed-ridden. We spent lot of money for traditional religious practices. All of my income would go towards

[99] David George Reese, "Demons (New Testament)", in *ABD*, edited by David Noel Freedman (New York: Doubleday, 1997), CD Rom.

[100] Alexander, *Signs & Wonders*, 106.

[101] Robert M. Johnston, "Demon Possession and Exorcism In the New Testament", https:// digitalcommons. andrews.edu/jams/vol11/iss2/4 (accessed on 12/08/19).

[102] Abraham, *Pentecostal Christology*, 94-99.

> traditional religious practices and treatment but without any results. However, somebody introduced me to the pastor of this church and he prayed for her; she got relief from her trouble. Then we continued to attend the church and now she is totally healed.[103]

People not only suffer from the direct attack of evil spirits, but there are many instances of the use of wicked spirits by witch-doctors to extract money and torment gullible people. The *Cross & Crown* magazine published a story narrated by Merchand Masih, an evangelist:

> A certain witch-doctor cast a spell on a simple villager and in the process, took nine hundred rupees from him. The man came seeking salvation in the church... When the people of God pray, something in the spirit realm happens. The villager got healed and the witch-doctor came and returned the money to him. This was an instant answer to prayer. This was enough to convince the man and several others to accept the Lord as their saviour.[104]

In Indian context, especially in interior villages people go through untold miseries because of attack of malevolent spirits as well as devious attack of witch-doctors. However, through the works of Pentecostal missionaries and pastors many have been rescued and they live a better life. Look at another story Bergunder recorded which was narrated by a pastor in the city of Bangalore:

> One lady's husband had spent ten thousand rupees to kill her by witchcraft. This was revealed to me [by the Lord]. I said: "Who is that lady here? Your husband has spent ten thousand rupees to kill you. Come forward". So, nobody came. I called three times and then I left it. Then, this lady got up and she came. [She said:] "I am the one . . . .". From that distance I looked at her and said: "In the name of Jesus!" She fell flat by the power of God . . . . And, then, she got up. She was having this demon and evil spirits. Three times, she had planned to kill herself. From all those powers of the enemy, she was released completely, with the anointing of God. And her husband was totally shocked. Three months [and] she was still alive. So, again he went to that witchcraft fellow, because he had promised that she would die. When the man came back to him, he said: "I am chanting the maximum evil on her, but something powerful is stopping it."[105]

---

[103] Abraham, *Pentecostal Christology*, 96-97.

[104] No Author, "Field News", *Cross & Crown* 26/6 (August-September 1996): 20.

[105] Quoted in Bergunder, "Miracle Healing and Exorcism in South Indian Pentecostalism", 294.

There is another remarkable incident that had occurred in today's Bangladesh which resulted in a breakthrough in church planting in a village in the ministry of Assemblies of God missionary Maynard Ketcham (1905-1993). He arrived in Purulia, India, in 1926 as the first Assemblies of God missionary to Bengal. He served in North India and the far east until his retirement in 1969. One of his missionary experiences he recounts in the opening pages of his book, *Tigers that Talk.* It was late afternoon, Maynard Ketcham and Indian Christian Abdul Munshie exhaustedly neared Abdul's village in the scorching heat. They were returning from a day of mission work, witnessing in the villages of one of the most militant Muslim districts.

On that particular day a few had listened, but just as it had been day after day for many weeks, there had been no result. Daily they had experienced curses, spittle, sticks and stones. On the worst days they were attacked with knives and were humiliated with barrages of animal manure or human excrement. Suddenly they found their path blocked by a women possessed by evil spirits. The villagers called her "pagli" (crazy woman). She was notorious for demonic manifestations in which, under the domination of evil spirits, she would crawl on the ground, writhe, foam at the mouth, and fall into trances. Even though she was illiterate, while in these states she could read the Koran fluently. She could also prescribe complicated medicinal formulas for the sick which only a doctor or pharmacist could understand. Her demonically generated prescriptions were amazingly effective. The people sought her advice as to the best times to plant seed, go fishing, take journeys, and get married. Charlatans took advantage of her to make money from her prescriptions and predictions.

The woman stood in the path with her naked, filthy body and hair smeared with cow dung. Her eyes were fixed in a burning demonic stare. She was gushing out filthy, harsh, blasphemous words. The Indian missionary Abdul rebuked her in the name of Jesus and then the missionaries began to pray, "Dear God, you have told us that we have authority over the devil and his angels. Today we are asking for a miracle. We take authority over every demon in this woman. We command them to release their hold on her and come out in Jesus' name". Suddenly, the woman fell to the ground, writhing in spiritual agony, as the demons left her. When the demons had gone she lay as still as death for a long time. Finally, she sat up and then stood to her feet. Instead of the demonic stare she now had a gentle, intelligent look in her eyes. In a soft voice she said, "Jesus has driven out the devil. Please get me a sari to cover my naked body". Then she ran through the rice paddies into the village rejoicing as she told all about Jesus! Within a few minutes word of the woman's deliverance had spread throughout the village of Kamarol, and within hours it had covered the region. From all over the area people came seeking prayer. Many were healed, converted, and baptized in the Holy Spirit.

Soon Muslim persecution came against the missionaries and new Christian converts. The Muslim leaders proposed a debate, but brothers Ketcham and Munshie were reluctant because they did not see how it could honour Christ or advance his cause. When they could not avoid the encounter, they refused to debate. Instead, Abdul just testified about how Jesus had given him peace and love. The Muslim leaders cursed them, called them "pigs", and taunted the Christians for losing the debate. However, these leaders were not able to sleep at night, their hearts burned, convicted by the Holy Spirit. Late that night eight Muslim leaders knocked on Abdul Munshie's door begging for prayer that they might know the peace and love about which the Christians had testified. They were converted, and one of them, Mukhtar Uddeen, the doctor who had led the Muslims, became a preacher and built a church on the site of the debate! The deliverance of the possessed woman resulted in one of the greatest breakthroughs ever accomplished in such a militant Muslim region.[106]

The above mentioned incidents of exorcism through prayer and power of the Spirit change the life of ordinary people. For them being freed from the fear of malevolent spirits as well as liberation from spirit possession is more than a life regained. The deliverance in the spirit realm positively affects the people's social, economic and spiritual domains; the spirit infestation breaks their financial security, their physical as well as their mental well-being. However, deliverance removes their fear of demonic activities and fear is turned into safety and joy. It is the peace of mind and body which rules in them after they receive deliverance in the name of Jesus.[107]

Further, in Indian context, the rituals and practices for casting out evil spirits are costly. The witch-doctors exploit the fear of the people and earn a lot. However, exorcism enacted in the name of Jesus is totally free of cost and it does not impinge their financial security. Pastors or members conduct exorcism without any rituals or chants. This raises a new consciousness: that satanic forces come to steal their financial resources (John 10:10). According to Dasan, the 'power encounter' with Christ, in which Tribals are healed, expelled the evil spirits that were blighting their lives, reformed their morals and ethics, broke the hold of the *bhagats*, and allowed them to stand up to the shopkeepers who exploited them.[108]

Moreover, the ordinary adherents come to know that through prayer and faith now they can counter the evil forces. David Hardiman of the University of Warwick, U.K. who conducted a study of healing among the Tribals of Gujarat agrees with it, "There is a strong emphasis on the healing of all maladies and

---

[106] Maynard Ketcham, *Tigers That Talk.* (Charlotte, NC: PTL Television Network, 1979), 2-7.

[107] Abraham, *Pentecostal Christology,* 98.

[108] Ebenezer D. Dasan, "Conversion and Persecution in South Gujarat", in *Conversion in a Pluralistic Context: Perspectives and Context,* edited by Krickwin C. Marak & Plamthodathil S. Jacob (Delhi: ISPCK, 2000), 161-164.

sicknesses through the power of faith alone. They consider that malign forces cause ill health, and that these forces can be countered through prayer and faith."[109] This brings spiritual empowerment and leads to what we call 'spiritual warfare' which is carried out as an everyday affair one where no specialists are needed. Even though, miracle healings and exorcisms are one of the main attractions of the Pentecostal movement, they are not the basis on which Pentecostal congregations are built. They just represent the contact point for winning church members and, through healing testimonies, they are understood to demonstrate God's power in the life of the congregation.[110] Besides, the casting out demons and deliverance of the affected result in church growth.

Pentecostal theologians have tried to explain the Pentecostal perspective on exorcism in a wider context. For Pentecostals, the act of exorcism is the establishment of God's supremacy over the evil powers and signals the in-breaking of the reign of God over the evil structures of this world. However, theology in general has taken a negative attitude towards this issue because twentieth century cosmology relates only to the physical universe and to the physical dimension of reality. Enlightenment thinking and western scientific worldview visualise reality as mechanistic and deterministic, and dichotomise the physical and spiritual, the body and spirit. According to Christenson, 20th century cosmology relates only to the physical universe and physical dimension of the reality. Modern people, by the influence of scientific advancement, reject any reality which they cannot touch or understand. In contrast, the New Testament gives a very clear picture of a spiritual world which includes God, the devil, angels, demons, good as well as evil and unclean spirits, principalities, thrones, powers, dominions, authorities, etc., (Eph. 6:12). Human beings are caught between these two worlds – physical and spiritual – and participate in both of them. Christenson sarcastically comments that the cosmology of some of our out-dated theologians "is still picnicking in Sir Isaac Newton's apple orchard."[111]

However, the Pentecostal world-view is holistic and trans-rational. "For Pentecostals, truth is not limited to reason. They view evil as a reality and know that there are epiphanies of darkness which surround all knowing. For them, the world is in a fallen state in which the powers of evil inhabit the created order. Pentecostals believe that evil spirits may inhabit human beings and use them for evil things."[112] Therefore, any act of liberation must give primary attention to this spiritual realm because many of the injustices are induced by satanic

[109] David Hardiman & Gauri Raje, "Practices of Healing in Tribal Gujarat", *EPW* (1 March 2008): 49.

[110] Bergunder, "Miracle Healing and Exorcism in South Indian Pentecostalism", in Brown, *Global Pentecostal and Charismatic Healing*, 298.

[111] Larry Christenson, *A Charismatic Approach to Social Action* (London: Lakeland, 1974), 42.

[112] Bridges Johns, "Healing and Deliverance", 48.

influence. Our protest marches or demonstrations cannot adequately deal with satanically instigated injustices but can achieve victory only by a spiritual encounter. Christenson underlines the point, "Any action in the social arena which is not sensitive to this dimension of struggle, *or is ignorant of the kind of strategy which one uses in the spiritual warfare*, will miss the real thrust and earnestness of New Testament social concern."[113] Bridges Johns describes the Pentecostal view,

> The devil, who is the 'prince of this world', is a personal spirit-being who controls the powers of darkness. Much like the ancient church, Pentecostals are engaged in a holy war against the kingdom of darkness. The war is fought in the spiritual realm and does not consist of violence in the physical world. It is fought through the weapons of prayer and often involves fasting... Exorcisms are open confrontations in which the evil ones are cast out and persons rescued for the kingdom of Christ.[114]

However, though believers are in a spiritual struggle with evil forces, they live in the realm of the Holy Spirit and achieve victory in everyday life. Shaull says, "They see the world and human life infested with demons. At the same time they firmly believe that their lives and their world are in the hands of God...With all the threats of demonic forces around them, they experience something even greater: the presence and the power of the Spirit."[115] In contexts where many are under crushing spell of evil spiritual forces and sickness, the healing of the spirit and the body has much relevance. This will surely change the outlook of the person and lead him/her in to a better life. What Wagner says is apt, "Praying for the sick and casting out demons are New Testament practices which should not hastily be pushed outside of the sphere of Christian experience. The influence of secularism and scientism has dulled the edge of Christian sensitivity to these matters, undoubtedly to Satan's advantage."[116]

However, it is significant to exercise these gifts with great care so that they are not be used in inappropriate ways. Oss cautions us some of the significant dangers that can creep into those who hold the Pentecostal view of spiritual gifts: Signs and wonders can sometimes become elevated over truth. False teachers, masquerading as apostles of Christ, often claim to perform signs and wonders to which they point in defense of their ministries. It is true that signs and wonders confirm the gospel when it is indeed preached. But, those of the Pentecostal

---

[113] Christenson, *A Charismatic Approach,* 56 (Italics his).

[114] Bridges Johns, "Healing and Deliverance", 48.

[115] Richard Shaull and Waldo Cesar, *Pentecostalism and the Future of the Christian Churches* (Michigan: Eerdmans, 2000), 162.

[116] C. Peter Wagner, *Look Out! The Pentecostals are Coming* (Illinois: Creation House, 1973), 136.

and charismatic movements must focus first on the truth of what is preached in order to discern if it is biblical. Moreover, we should pay close attention to Jesus' admonition to the seventy when they reported that even demons were subject to them, "Do not rejoice that the spirits submit to you, but rejoice that your names are written in heaven" (Luke 10:17-20).

Another concern in relation to the gift of healing and other signs and wonders in public is lack of loving concern for people coming for deliverance. It is sure that suffering people come with great expectation to be healed. However, sometimes healing evangelists create such an atmosphere that if the healing does not happen, the suffering person is counted as responsible as not have enough faith to be healed and that definitely negatively impact the psyche of the person. Here we need to cultivate more loving and humane attitude.[117] Charles Kraft raises a genuine concern in this regard:

> My point is that *we are called to minister to people, not simply to heal or to pass on information from God.* A healing or another manifestation of spiritual power is from God's point of view only a means of demonstrating his love to the person who receives it. We are dealing with persons—persons whom Jesus loves enough to give his very life. If he gave his life for them, we should be willing to spend enough time to really minister to them. We dare not treat them un-lovingly if we claim to be doing God's work in God's way. For the subject is people, not power. And the true mark of a disciple is not power or even spirituality, but love (John 13:34–35). It is possible to be spectacular in using God's power without being Christian about it. Let us be careful not to fall into that trap. Jesus treated people as persons. He wrapped his power in love.[118]

Furthermore, prophetic gifts can be used to manipulate and cajole rather than to encourage. All believers have the Spirit, who is perfectly capable of speaking directly to the believer's heart without any human intermediary, especially in the case of personal guidance. Finally, Pentecostals should not become pragmatists in which the miraculous ends justify any means, including high-tech manipulation.[119]

Let us bring the discussion into a conclusion; it is obvious that the spiritual gifts exercised in the Pentecostal congregational and mission settings bring dramatic changes in the lives of the people. The gift of tongues, prophecy, healing and exorcism enact immediate transformation in the lives of the poor and downtrodden and lead them into social and spiritual liberation. Besides, the use

---

[117] Charles H. Kraft, "A Third Wave Perspective on Pentecostal Missions", in *Called & Empowered: Global Mission in Pentecostal Perspective*, edited by Murray W. Dempster, Byron D. Klaus & Douglas Petersen (Michigan: Baker Academic, 1991), 226.

[118] Kraft, "A Third Wave Perspective on Pentecostal Missions", 227.

[119] Oss, "A Pentecostal / Charismatic View", *Are Miraculous Gifts for Today?*, 282-283.

of *charismata* greatly help in the dissemination of the message of the kingdom of God and attract more and more people to Pentecostal congregations. This is very true in the Indian context where many people suffer because of evil spiritual forces. However, gifts of the Holy Spirit are to be exercised in utmost care, in holiness and integrity so that Christ may be glorified.

Chapter 6

Evangelism and Mission Methods of Liberation

Evangelism and mission stand as the strongest pillars of Pentecostal spirituality from its beginning and continue to act as the major contributing factors in the large-scale growth and consolidation of Pentecostal movement worldwide, especially in the developing world. Most of the dramatic church growth in the twentieth century has taken place in Pentecostal and independent Pentecostal-like churches. Half the world's Christians today live in developing, poor countries. The reason behind such world-wide growth within few years can be attributed to its basic nature - Pentecostalism by its very nature is intrinsically missiological.[1] The phenomenal growth of the movement has generally attracted the attention of non-Pentecostal Christianity. Even those in disagreement with Pentecostal theology began to praise the Pentecostal movement's missionary success. In terms of numbers, growth, and influence, the Movement was recognized to be at the heart of the international missionary movement.[2] It was noted that "Pentecostalism and mission are almost synonymous."[3] David Hesselgrave, one of the most influential evangelical missiologists, asserts that "if anything is generally characteristic of Pentecostal churches world-wide, it is an ethos of growth. In a time of defeatism,

[1] Grant McClung Jr., "'Try To Get People Saved': Revisiting the Paradigm of an Urgent Pentecostal Missiology", in *The Globalization of Pentecostalism*, edited by M. W. Dempster, B. D. Klaus & D. Petersen (Carlisle: Regnum, 1999), 32.

[2] Paul A. Pomerville, *The Third Force in Mission: A Pentecostal Contribution to Contemporary Mission Theology* (Peabody, Massachusetts: Hendrickson Publishers, 1985), 20.

[3] Frederick Dale Bruner, *A Theology of the Holy Spirit: The Pentecostal Experience and the New Testament Witness* (Michigan: Eerdmans Publishing, 1970), 32.

stagnation, and retreat in many churches, a growth climate may prove to be one of the great bequests of Pentecostalism to the larger church of Christ."[4] Similarly, McClung concludes that the Pentecostal Movement has encouraged the Church Growth Movement and has been admired by its researchers.[5] Some might dare to say that if it were not for Pentecostal growth around the world, the Church Growth Movement might not have had much growth to study.[6] Pentecostal mission and evangelism are not merely engines of growth but they are actions for liberation. Millions of people are being transformed spiritually, socially and economically because of Pentecostal mission in the third world nations.

Pentecostal movement is growing fast world-wide. An estimated 35,000 people join the Pentecostal churches each day. Of the world's two billion Christians, a quarter are now Pentecostal—up from 6 percent in 1980.[7] It is in the majority world, 66% of Pentecostals of the world are found and Pentecostalism is reshaping the social, political and economic landscape of many countries in Latin America, Africa and Asia. Barrett provides a succinct description of the Pentecostal/Charismatic movement, including third wave believers: Some 29% of all members worldwide are white, 71% non-white. Members are more urban than rural, more female than male, more children (under eighteen) than adults, more third world (66%) than Western World (32%), more living in poverty (87%) than affluent (13%), more family related than individualist.[8] Similarly, writing specifically about the growth of the Pentecostal/Charismatic movement in the non-Western world, Peter Wagner, the church growth expert cites Barrett's statistics and states that, "if Barrett's statistics are accurate, it represents what would undoubtedly prove to be one of the highest if not *the* highest recorded rate of growth of a non-political, non-militaristic human movement across history."[9] Pentecostal historian Vinson Synan observes that one fourth of all full-time Christian workers in the world are Pentecostal/charismatic and these workers are active in 80% of the world's 3300 largest metropolitan areas.[10]

---

[4] David J. Hesselgrave, *Today's Choices for Tomorrow's Mission: An Evangelical Perspective on Trends and Issues in Missions* (Grand Rapids, MI: Zondervan Publishing House, 1988), 126.

[5] The Church Growth Movement is a movement within the Evangelical Christianity which aims to grow churches based on research, sociology, analysis, etc. Donald McGavran is universally considered the father of the Church Growth Movement. He was a missiologist and third generation missionary born in India. Other names that shaped the early thinking of the church growth movement included Win Arn and C. Peter Wagner.

[6] Grant McClung, "From BRIDGES (MCGavran 1955) to WAVES (Wagner 1983): Pentecostals and the Church Growth Movement", *Pneuma* 7/1 (1985): 12.

[7] Atlas of Pentecostalism; http://www.atlasofpentecostalism.net/ (accessed on 01/09/19).

[8] Larry D. Pate, "Pentecostal Mission from the Two-Thirds World", in *Called & Empowered: Global Mission in Pentecostal Perspective,* edited by Murray W. Dempster, Byron D. Klaus & Douglas Petersen (Michigan: Baker Academic, 1991), 178.

[9] Pate, "Pentecostal Mission from the Two-Thirds World", 178.

[10] Byron D. Klaus & Loren O. Triplett, "National Leadership in Pentecostal Missions", in *Called & Empowered*, 166.

It is not only the Pentecostal movement but other "Spirit movements" are also active in the mission endeavours in today's world. The editors of *The World Christian Encyclopaedia* define the entire Spirit movement (Pentecostal type) as consisting of three distinct "waves", or sub-movements. The "first wave" is the label given to classical Pentecostals and the "second wave" represents the charismatic movement which includes all 150 traditional non-Pentecostal ecclesiastical confessions, families and traditions. Over 300 million people in the world are considered charismatic Christians. Until the 1950s, the experiences and teachings of the Pentecostal movement were not generally accepted in traditional churches. In 1960, Dennis Bennett, an Episcopal priest received the baptism of the Holy Spirit and embraced Pentecostal teachings in the Episcopal Church. Many consider this event as the beginning of the charismatic movement (as separate from the more specific Pentecostal movement). This trend expanded to many other churches in mainline denominations in the 1960s. The "third wave" is the appellation given to those in non-Pentecostal, or even anti-Pentecostal traditions who are experiencing spiritual renewal and emphasizing the practice of spiritual gifts (which may or may not include tongues). Sometimes they are also called "neo-charismatics" or "quasi-charismatics". This third group does not identify with either Pentecostal or charismatic movement, but the group does actively participate in the practice of the *charismata*.[11] The "third wave" began early in the decade of the 1980s and finds its adherents primarily among evangelicals who did not want to identify with either the Pentecostal or charismatic movements. Distinctive features of the third wave include an affirmation of signs and wonders, particularly healing and deliverance from demonic forces and activities. The baptism of the Holy Spirit and speaking in tongues do not tend to be a focal point for third wave participants, who view themselves as neither Pentecostal nor charismatic, but simply open to the moving of the Holy Spirit.[12]

The Pentecostal revival at the beginning of the twentieth century brought a renewal of the power and gifts of the Holy Spirit. Pentecostals placed primary emphasis on being "sent by the Spirit" and depended more on the Spirit's leading than on formal structures. They often went for mission through some spiritual revelation like a prophecy, a dream or a vision. The single most important contribution that Pentecostalism has made to world mission is to draw attention to the role of the Holy Spirit in the Christian mission. Even though Protestant mission has a well developed missiology, the role of the Holy Spirit in mission is unwittingly marginalised. Pomerville states that there was a an inordinate "silence on the Holy Spirit" in part of the Protestant mission heritage. Contemporary theologies of mission neglect the role of the Holy Spirit. Max Warren terms Pentecostalism and the Charismatic Movement as "protest" movements, against

[11] Pate, "Pentecostal Mission from the Two-Thirds World", 178.

[12] Murray W. Dempster, Byron D. Klaus & Douglas Petersen (eds.), *Called & Empowered* (Michigan: Baker Academic, 1991), 192.

the neglect of the Spirit. He argues that the movements protest the neglect of the role of the Holy Spirit and that they are a healthy correction to the torpidity of church life.[13] Michael Green also speaks of the neglect as a "domestication" of the Spirit in the West and William Menzies speaks of a "practical subordinationism" of the Spirit in Christian theology.[14]

Peter Wagner affirms that the Pentecostal movement has brought the person of the Holy Spirit out of virtual hiding. According to him, for non-Pentecostals, the Holy Spirit had truly become a "Holy Ghost"—some vague background figure we were taught not to talk about too much. Many of non-Pentecostals had been so strongly influenced by the rationalism and secular humanism that had developed into a worldview with what Paul Hiebert calls "the excluded middle". The excluded middle refers to the world of spirits and angels and demons with which so much of the non-Western world is in constant touch. A major reason for the success of Pentecostal missions is that their missionaries were also in touch with this important dimension of reality. The phenomena of tongues, prophecies, faith healings, words of knowledge, deliverances, falling under the power, angelic visitations, visions, dreams, and other direct manifestations of the Holy Spirit have been common enough to keep Pentecostals very much aware of varieties of spiritual power. When Pentecostal missionaries entered the cultures of the non-Western world to "preach the gospel to every creature" they fully expected that "these signs will follow those who believe: In My name they will cast out demons; they will speak with new tongues; they will take up serpents; and if they drink anything deadly, it will by no means hurt them; they will lay hands on the sick, and they will recover" (Mark 16:17–18). Without arguing the canonicity of the longer ending of Mark's Gospel, the simple but powerful belief that the Holy Spirit would accompany the preaching of the word with supernatural signs and wonders provided the missionaries with a direct entrance into the middle zone. In contrast to many non-Pentecostal missionaries, they had the ability to recognize and deal with satanic and demonic forces through spiritual warfare.[15]

This vibrant element of mission is amply illustrated in the words of David du Plessis when he was asked the difference between mission theologies of Protestant mission and Pentecostal mission:

> Gentlemen, comparisons are odious, and I do not wish to injure anyone's feelings or hurt your pride. But, the truth as I see it is this: You have the truth on ice, and I have it on fire.[16]

[13] Max Warren, *I Believe in the Great Commission* (Grand Rapids, MI: Wm. B. Eerdmans, 1976), 126.

[14] Pomerville, *The Third Force in Mission*, 3.

[15] C. Peter Wagner, "A Church Growth Perspective on Pentecostal Mission", in *Called & Empowered*, 199.

[16] Quoted in *Grant McClung*, "Truth on Fire: Pentecostals and an Urgent Missiology", in *Azuza Street & Beyond*, 2nd edition, edited by Grant McClung (Florida: Bridge-Logos, 2012), 78.

This "on fire" Pentecostal mission theology has tended to be a theology on the move. Its character has been more experiential than cognitive, more activist than reflective. Pentecostals have often acted now and theologized later.[17] This Spirit emphasis on the mission activities was a hallmark of the Pentecostal movement from its inception.[18]

However, the Spirit experience is not the only factor that makes the Pentecostal mission activities unique. There are various other factors that impel the missionary endeavours to the end of the earth. Pentecostal Missiologist Grant McClung points out seven characteristics of Pentecostal missions: Mission is experiential and relational; Mission is expressly biblical and theological; Mission is extremely urgent; Mission is focused, yet diversified (prioritise evangelism but not to the exclusion of social concern); Mission is aggressive and bold; Mission is interdependent (among various Pentecostal and charismatic groups); and Mission is unpredictable.[19] Similar kinds of characterizations have also been proposed by others.[20]

However, more than all these aspects, the most significant aspect of Pentecostal mission is its liberative nature. The liberative potential of the Pentecostal movement is achieved through the Pentecostal mission activities, especially in the third-world context. The question of liberation and transformation is a burning issue in the contemporary majority world scenario. The common masses suffer rampant poverty, oppression, injustice, enormous disparities, discrimination, and other maladies. It is often a result of deliberate

---

[17] *McClung*, "Truth on Fire: Pentecostals and an Urgent Missiology", 78.

[18] For instance, J. Roswell Flower, initially the foreign editor and later the associate editor of a monthly magazine known as *The Pentecost,* published during the years 1908-1910, tersely explained the relationship of the baptism in the Holy Spirit to world evangelization: The baptism of the Holy Ghost does not consist in simply speaking in tongues. No. It has a much more grand and deeper meaning than that. It fills our souls with the love of God for lost humanity, and makes us much more willing to leave home, friends, and all to work in His vineyard...When the Holy Spirit comes into our hearts, the missionary spirit comes in with it; Carrying the gospel to hungry souls in this and other lands is but a natural result of receiving the baptism of the Holy Ghost. J. Roswell Flower, "Editorial", *The Pentecost* (August 1908), 4; McClung Jr., "'Try To Get People Saved'", 36-37.

[19] Grant McClung, "Pentecostal/Charismatic Perspective on a Missiology for the Twenty-First Century", *Pneuma* 16/1 (Spring, 1994): 11-21.

[20] For instance, Pomerville outlines some of the characteristics of Pentecostal mission strategy: 1) the planting of indigenous churches; 2) the evangelization of the humble, responsive masses; 3) the mobilization of the laity in witness; 4) spiritual gifts; 5) the spiritual dynamic of supernatural power in the power-encounter of mission; and 6) the development of spiritual leadership. Similarly, Van der Laan and Kärkkäinen, have suggested these factors: naïve biblicism and eschatology, individualism, total commitment, pragmatism, flexibility, a place for emotions, personal testimonies, establishment of indigenous churches as a goal of missions, demonstration of the power of the Spirit, and participation of all believers. See Pomerville, *The Third Force in Mission,* 109; Veli-Matti Karkkainen, "Missiology: Pentecostal and Charismatic", in *NIDPCM*, Stanley M. Burgess (ed.) (Michigan: Zondervan, 2002), 877-885.

policies, which result in the constantly increasing accumulation of wealth and power in the hands of a few. These oppressive mechanisms, which were legitimised by social, and religious hierarchies and justified in the name of sacred religious duties. Moreover, nations like India, people not only suffer poverty and oppression, many of them face illness due to lack of medical facilities, evil inspirit infestations, caste oppression and religious persecution.[21]

However, in such conditions, the Pentecostal missions have been able to bring considerable changes among the suffering masses. Many of the religious observers, theologians and missiologists testify this fact.[22] For example, Richard Shaull, while explaining the liberative nature of Pentecostal movement in Latin American nations says, "Our engagement with Pentecostals has convinced us that they not only have richness and depth of experience but that many individuals and communities are becoming increasingly involved in a variety of forms of social action as a direct result of this faith experience."[23] He continues, "We found massive evidence of the power of these movements to touch the lives of the poorest and most excluded, to help them reorganise their lives, and to give them a new sense of identity and hope for the future. In a society in which all forms of life in community are in crisis, they are creating new human relations in community at the most basic level of the society."[24] Then he describes his own realisation as he entered into the real world of the poor and experienced their religious life,

> *The more aware I became of the nature of their search, the more I realised that Pentecostals are the ones who are now present among the poor and are responding to them. According to the testimonies of those we interviewed, this is where they have found new life. As I listened to them, I could not escape the conclusion that Pentecostals were offering them something I and my communities of faith did not have and thus could not offer.*[25]

This is true in Indian situation too. Lot of people are being liberated from poverty, healed of their illness, delivered of attacks of malevolent spirits and witch-crafts.[26] Thus, the Pentecostal movement in general and the Pentecostal mission in particular making a deep impact among the poor and suffering population of the third-world nations.

---

[21] Shaibu Abraham, *Pentecostal Christology: Empirical Approach in Indian Context* (New Delhi: Christian World Imprints, 2019), 34-58.

[22] See Harvey Cox, *Fire from Heaven* (Cambridge, MA: Da Capo Press, 1995); Donald E. Miller & Tetsunao Yamamori, *Global Pentecostalism: The New Face of Christian Social Engagement* (Berkeley: University of California Press, 2007).

[23] Richard Shaull & Waldo Cesar, *Pentecostalism and the Future of the Christian Churches* (Michigan: W. B. Eerdmans, 2000), 211.

[24] Shaull and Cesar, *Pentecostalism and the Future,* 212.

[25] Shaull and Cesar, *Pentecostalism and the Future,* 118 (Italics original).

[26] Abraham, *Pentecostal Christology,* 87-106.

In the following pages we shall briefly explore various factors that empower Pentecostal missions and evangelism which lead people to liberation. Besides, we shall look into some of the mission strategies employed, particularly, social mission activities carried out by the Pentecostal missionaries, which actually lead masses to liberation. In the context of religious pluralism and violence against Christians, especially against Pentecostals, we try to propose a mission theology that will help missionaries and evangelists to deal with the difficult situations.

Pneumatological Factors

As we have already explored, the very heartbeat of Pentecostal missions is its experience with the person and power of the Holy Spirit. This profound experience was integrated with an eschatological urgency and a passion for souls. According to McClung, the mission fervour of Pentecostal movement is a combination of eschatology, experience and evangelism. Apparently, the movement's earliest understandings of the experience that came from the 'Baptism in The Holy Spirit' and this experience produced a missiological fervour and ministry and provided the empowerment for the same.[27] This is the beginning point in understanding the Pentecostal methodology for church growth. Whereas for most other Christians, the presence of the Spirit is just that, *presence,* for Pentecostals the presence of the Spirit in their midst implies *empowerment.* While this empowerment often manifests itself in spiritual gifts such as speaking in tongues, prophesy, or healings and so on.[28] The emphasis on the Spirit and supernatural phenomena has also meant that Pentecostals have been better aware of the emphasis on the spirit world in the many societies in which they have ministered. Because Pentecostals are aware of the phenomena of supernatural healing, revelation, blessings, curses and the spirit world, they are better placed to engage with people who have similar worldviews concerning these features.[29] For Pentecostals, God is not an idea but a presence and a power. God saves; He has the power to save, and even more concretely the power to cure, whether it be from the effects of sin or of illness.[30] Hence, Pentecostal movement provides direction for contemporary

---

[27] McClung Jr., "'Try To Get People Saved'", 36.

[28] Veli-Matti Kärkkäinen, "The Pentecostal Understanding of Mission", in *Pentecostal Mission and Global Christianity,* edited by Wonsuk Ma, Veli-Matti Kärkkäinen & J. Kwabena Asamoah-Gyadu (Oxford, UK: Regnum Books International, 2012), 36.

[29] Keith Warrington, *Pentecostal Theology: A Theology of Encounter* (London: T&T Clark, 2008), 253; McClung also says that Pentecostals strongly believe that through the baptism of the Holy Spirit they can experience the "God who is there—now". Moreover, the biblical portrayal of divine omnipotence and omnipresence are more than mere abstract theological formulation; it is an incarnational truth available and experienced by faith through the baptism of the Spirit. The Pentecostal "theology of immediacy" has seen the kingdom that is coming but has also lived in the kingdom that is now. *McClung*, "Truth on Fire: Pentecostals and an Urgent Missiology", 78-79.

[30] Christian Lalive d'Epinay, *Haven of the Masses: A Study of The Pentecostal Movement in Chile* (London: Lutterworth Press, 1969), 204.

missions based on its emphasis on experiential dimension of the Christian faith, the dynamic experience of the Spirit.[31]

Moreover, Pentecostals assert that the direct power of God is poured out upon all Christians and can be experienced personally to be empowered for mission. Each Pentecostal, therefore a potential missionary irrespective of one's ability or educational qualification. They testify their own conversion stories and the story of Jesus to their neighbours and co-workers. Pentecostals see aggressive evangelism in the pages of the New Testament and feel that they must respond accordingly.[32] Evangelism is a matter of obedience and they believe that they will be called to account for indolence on their part. There is always the fear that people may have come to faith if they had been faithful in speaking to them. Pentecostals also believe that unbelievers will blame them on the day of Judgement.[33] Most of them believe in a literal hell and desire to rescue as many fellow human beings from it as possible. Many of them make considerable sacrifices of time, energy, and money to see that the good news of Jesus Christ gets to unbelievers while there is yet time either before they die or before Jesus returns.[34]

Moreover, the availability of the power of the Spirit for ministry has enabled them to see the future through eyes filled with extraordinary hope that people will be saved by their mission effort.[35] McClung describes the social psychology of Pentecostals as: "God has chosen us! We are a people of divine destiny for this hour!" He goes on to assert that this has been a powerful motivating force thrusting the movement around the world in the face of any opposition. McClung call this "Mordecai-Esther factor" ("Thou art come to the kingdom for such a

---

[31] David J. du Plessis, made this very clear: "I have held from the beginning that the Baptism in the Holy Spirit has really no place, no need in the church unless it is to equip the church for ministry, and the tragedy to me is that there are millions today who have received the baptism of the Holy Spirit but were never taught what really is the responsibility they've taken upon themselves by accepting the baptism. I say there is no reason for the baptism but to minister, for the ministry of Christ began after his enduement on the bank of Jordan". Quoted in *McClung*, "Truth on Fire: Pentecostals and an Urgent Missiology", 82.

[32] Grant McClung, "Spontaneous Strategy of the Spirit", in *Azuza Street & Beyond, 147.*

[33] Warrington, *Pentecostal Theology*, 249.

[34] Wagner, "A Church Growth Perspective on Pentecostal Mission", 197.

[35] Wagner narrates his own realisation of this fact by looking into the massive growth achieved by Paul Yonggi Cho's church in south Korea. He elaborates: I began to learn this secret of Pentecostal growth when I first met Pastor Paul Yonggi Cho in 1976. I was greatly impressed by the pastor of a church which at that time counted over 50,000 members. But, I was unprepared for what he told me in the living room of the home of a mutual friend. He said that he was believing God for a church of 500,000 members by 1985, the 100th anniversary of Protestant Christianity in Korea. To be honest I thought he must have a screw loose, but I kept in touch with him through the years. Was this faith or foolishness? Now that the goal has not only been accomplished, but surpassed in the Yoido Full Gospel Church of Seoul, Korea, it is clear that Cho knows something about setting goals as an exercise of faith that other Christian leaders need to learn. Wagner, "A Church Growth Perspective on Pentecostal Mission", 199.

time as this" Esther 4:14) and has been a powerfully motivating force thrusting the movement around the world into the face of any opposition. It has been central to Pentecostal ideology.[36]

Pentecostal literature is full of instances in which a person was recruited into cross-cultural ministry through supernatural means such as dreams, visions, prophecies, tongues and interpretation, and other signs and wonders.[37] Allan Anderson explains that based on the experience of the baptism of the Spirit, early Pentecostal missionaries scattered themselves most of the nations of the world within a remarkably short space of time to spread the 'fires' and these fires were somewhat unpredictable and out of control. He also points to the fact that, although mostly untrained and inexperienced in the art and science of mission, early Pentecostal missionaries simply thought of mission as foreign mission. Their only qualification was the baptism in the Spirit and a divine call.[38]

Along with the power of the Holy Spirit among Pentecostals, the gifts of the Spirit accompanied with the signs and wonders significantly enhance the evangelistic and mission activities. Pentecostals believe that the coming of the Spirit brings an ability to do "signs and wonders" in the name of Jesus Christ to accompany and authenticate the gospel message. The role of "signs and wonders", particularly that of healing and miracles, is prominent in Pentecostal mission praxis. Pentecostals see the role of healing as good news for the poor and afflicted.[39] When the gospel is presented with supernatural phenomena, the message is readily accepted by the listeners. Moreover, the gifts of the Spirit such as healing, exorcism, prophecy and other miraculous elements acts as tools of liberation in mission endeavours.[40] Paul Yonggi Cho, the pastor of the largest church in the world affirms this aspect:

> ...I made the point that without signs and wonders, the church cannot grow...I do not believe I have received a special gift from God. I just read the Word of God diligently and apply the principles contained therein to my own ministry. As a result, the Holy Spirit works through my ministry. I have seen souls saved, broken hearts healed, physical diseases touched by the power of the Holy Spirit. In addition, I have seen many people become successful after the Holy Spirit came into their lives.[41]

---

[36] McClung, "Truth on Fire: Pentecostals and an Urgent Missiology", 85.

[37] McClung "Spontaneous Strategy of the Spirit", 143.

[38] Allan Anderson, *Spreading Fires: The Missionary Nature of Early Pentecostalism* (London: SCM, 2007), 5, 27.

[39] Anderson, "Towards a Pentecostal Missiology for the Majority World", *AJPS* 8/1 (2005): 33.

[40] See the chapter on Spiritual gifts.

[41] David Yonggi Cho, "The Secret Behind the World's Biggest Church", in *Azuza Street & Beyond,* 131.

Signs, wonders, and miracles do not merely describe categories of miraculous acts. Malik, who was a missionary practitioner among Muslims see them as mighty deeds that should be understood from three different aspects. First of all, in their ability to authenticate the message, they are signs. Secondly, they evoke awe and astonishment, therefore they are wonders. Thirdly, in their display of divine supernatural power, they are miracles. Apostle Paul states that these are the things that mark an apostle. Listeners needs may also be met through a message in tongues and interpretation or a prophetic message which exposes sin or unspoken thoughts. When people are sick, they can be ministered to through the gift of healing. Miracles can lead non-believers to soften their antagonism toward the gospel and consequently place their faith in Christ. When in the name of Jesus an evil spirit is exorcised, a taboo is broken, a miracle takes place, or when the sick are healed, the blind see, the deaf hear, and the lame walk and the Lord is exalted, people will be disposed to put their faith in him. According to Malik, signs and wonders greatly boost the mission among Muslims and the use of gifts marks a missionary as an apostle to Muslims.[42]

Another significant element in Pentecostal movement in relation to pneumatological factor is employing of "power encounter" for pioneering missions. This is true in Indian situation. Power encounters are found quite frequently in Pentecostal missionary literature and form a central part of Pentecostal missions strategy.[43] The power encounter is "a dynamic confrontation between two different and opposite religions in which the two are pitted against each other in open confrontation of power."[44] When gospel is preached in new mission fields, as Pentecostals believe, there is a possibility of mission is being opposed by evil forces and their agents.[45] However, the concept of "power encounter" is used by Pentecostal missionaries in such contexts, which breaks the strongholds of satanic forces and also the people control such powers. This is true in all mission fields especially in rural areas where people are uneducated and poor and in animistic societies or whose history has a marked tradition of spirit forces. Pentecostals are willing to tackle 'the dark side of the soul' and challenge the growing phenomenon of occultism, Satan worship, and demon possession. This head-on tackling of the enemy's power has brought relief to the suffering masses and lead them into spiritual liberation and all round transformation.

One of the reasons the Pentecostal movement making great strides in tribal areas is due to the power encounter. The Pentecostal use of exorcism and other miracles correspond with some of the tribal characteristics, thereby meeting the felt needs of the people. Moreover, the Pentecostal world-view is

---

[42] Sobhi W. Malek, "Islam Encountering Gospel Power", in *Called & Empowered*, 136-137.

[43] Grant McClung, "Spontaneous Strategy of the Spirit", in *Azuza Street & Beyond*, 146.

[44] McClung, "Spontaneous Strategy of the Spirit", 146.

[45] See the chapter on Spiritual gifts.

also somewhat similar to animistic world-view where spirit activities are greatly acknowledged. When an exorcism or miracle is performed, people readily accept the gospel message and surrender their lives. Accordingly, missions efforts normally are well received and result in church growth. The following aspects, according to Aigbe, are significant in animistic contexts: First, the most fundamental and revolutionary Pentecostal mission response to tribal animism is the distinctive teaching and practice of the doctrine of the Holy Spirit. Tribal animism is concerned with spirits and with a continual hunger for spiritual powers. Pentecostals respond by proclaiming and *demonstrating* the presence and power of the Holy Spirit who satisfies this inner hunger and provides power for living.[46]

The second aspect of the power encounter is, since the tribal people believe there are all kinds of spirits and that they have limited power. Therefore, there is constant competition among the gods and goddesses to win followers. Pentecostals respond to these assumptions by teaching and exercising the gifts of the Holy Spirit in and outside the church. They do this first by destroying the shrines of these gods, by initiating power encounters, and by the working of miracles, divine healings, and exorcisms. These signs and wonders demonstrate that indeed the Christian God is the only one true God who is greater than all other gods. Third, to the tribal belief of ancestral and spirit world, the Pentecostals respond with the proclamation of the kingdom of God and the eternal bliss of heaven. God the loving Father, and not the dreadful spirits, is in charge of their lives and destiny. The once and for all sacrifice of Jesus the Son of God not only reflects the love of the Father for his followers, but also ends the continuing sacrificial activity. More importantly, the Holy Spirit now dwells in their hearts with great power. The more they can pray, the more power they receive from the Holy Spirit to live daily with inner peace, to ward off evil spirits, and to work miracles.[47]

Christological Factors

Another significant element in Pentecostal mission emphasis is the Christological factors. Pentecostal movement is fundamentally Christological in nature and emphasised the importance of Christology from its inception in mission activities. Pentecostals proclaim Christ and salvation, healing and other benefits comes through his redemptive acts. Earlier it is misconceived that Pentecostals neglect Christology and the Movement has been accused of being pneumacentric at the cost of Christology. However, even cursory investigation will prove it be

---

[46] Matt. 28:18–20; Luke 24:49; Acts 1:8; 2:1–47; John 1:12; 14:14–26; 16:7–15; 1 Cor. 12, 14.

[47] Sunday Aigbe, "Pentecostal Mission and Tribal People Groups", in *Called & Empowered*, 129-130; Abraham, *Pentecostal Christology*, 54-58.

an overwhelmingly Christocentric movement.[48] Early Pentecostal leader Frank Bartlemann exemplifies the importance of Christology in Pentecostalism:

> We may not even hold a doctrine, or seek an experience except in Christ. . . .A true Pentecost will produce a mighty conviction for sin, a turning to God . . . Any work that exalts the holy or gifts above Jesus will finally land up in fanaticism. Whatever causes us to exalt and love Jesus is well and safe. The reverse will ruin all. The Holy Ghost is a great light, but focused on Jesus always for his revealing.[49]

Pentecostal mission activities reveal that it is in the name of Jesus that proclamation, healing, exorcism and so on are carried out. In fact, Christology stands prominent and Pneumatology always stands behind to power the mission activities. McClung rightly affirms that the Christocentric confession stands as the 'centre' of the Pentecostal missiology and Christ holds all things together.[50] Like the early church, Pentecostals exalt Christ in their proclamations and exercise all the miraculous signs in the name of Jesus. Seymour, and subsequent Pentecostal leaders since him, had a strong Christology, which centered more on the Giver than the gift.[51]

It is the "Four-fold Gospel" or "Full Gospel" that forms the basic message of Pentecostal mission; that is Jesus Christ is Saviour, Healer, Sanctifier, Spirit Baptizer, and Coming King.[52] Therefore, the Pentecostal proclamation in the evangelistic campaign is based on the themes of salvation, healing, the baptism of the Holy Spirit and second coming of Jesus. These themes are proclaimed everywhere and to everyone, irrespective of nationality, religion, colour or language. For ordinary Pentecostals, sharing the testimony of their salvation and the miracles they have experienced is a way of doing mission. This way of conveying the salvation message results in thousands of people joining Pentecostal churches. This is especially true in Indian context. They narrate their healing stories, exorcisms and peace and blessing received from Jesus Christ. This attract the people who go through such conditions and they join Pentecostal churches. In fact, for the Indian Pentecostals, mission and evangelism are a default life-style. It is not anything carried out by special agencies or highly trained experts. Rather, evangelism is deeply ingrained in the psyche and daily life of the believers and Jesus as the only saviour is proclaimed without any hesitation. Moreover, the ministry of healing and exorcisms are carried out in the name of Jesus and many

---

[48] Byron D. Klaus, "The Holy Spirit and Mission in Eschatological Perspective", *Pneuma* 27.2 (Fall 2005): 335.

[49] Quoted in Klaus, "The Holy Spirit and Mission in Eschatological Perspective", 335.

[50] McClung Jr., "'Try To Get People Saved'", 48.

[51] *McClung*, "Truth on Fire: Pentecostals and an Urgent Missiology", 83.

[52] See the chapter on Full Gospel.

are being liberated from their struggling situations in Indian context.[53] This way of communicating and sharing of life-experiences explains the rapid proliferation of the Pentecostal churches in the Indian context.

Moreover, Easter faith, the central element of the Christian faith, is proclaimed in Pentecostalism evangelism as the liberating and redemptive action of God in human history. Jesus' resurrection is the clear and overwhelming test of the saving power of God and of the hope of the believers faith in the new and eternal life. Pentecostal Christology and missiology underline the image of the glorified, victorious and powerful Christ who is able to heal diseases, liberate people from evil spiritual forces and lead them to prosperity and protect them from all perils of the world.[54] This liberative message is the core of Pentecostal evangelism and mission. Similarly, the imminent coming of the Kingdom of God in Jesus is proclaimed in the mission endeavours emphasising on the eschatological element of the *parousia*. For the believing Pentecostals, Jesus' return is imminent, and the events lived in our time (wars, hunger, epidemics, etc.) are the test that one is living in those 'last of times.'[55] Therefore, the message of the return of Christ who will come with power and glory to judge humanity should be conveyed to all. Paradoxically, those sufferings of the present life are identified as part of the commitment to the gospel, and with Christ's sufferings, but for the believer the most important thing is the prize that God will give him in the 'other world.'[56]

In Christological factors, another noteworthy aspect is, mission and evangelistic ventures follow the methods and activities of Jesus, portrayed in the gospel stories. For Pentecostals, Jesus is the paradigm; whatever he had done and the way he had done is imitated by Pentecostal missionaries. A cursory glance will reveal that Pentecostal missionary methods follow the missions in the gospels. Pentecostal mission emphasises salvation of all, especially targets the poor, despised, downtrodden and outcastes of the society. This we see uniquely in the Gospel of Luke. Luke, himself a Gentile, had come to recognize that the heart of the ministry of Jesus was "salvation for all". Moreover, for Luke, Jesus came to liberate the "poor", that are represented by every kind of first-century outcast—the traditional poor, sinners, Samaritans, Gentiles, and women.[57] In the book of Acts, by focusing on the Gentile mission, Luke demonstrated that it was God's intent through the Holy Spirit to take that salvation to the ends of the earth. Such an understanding was absolutely central to the ministry of Jesus himself.[58] This is

---

[53] Abraham, *Pentecostal Christology,* 94-99.

[54] Abraham, *Pentecostal Christology,* 87-113.

[55] Kärkkäinen, "The Pentecostal Understanding of Mission", 33.

[56] Kärkkäinen, "The Pentecostal Understanding of Mission", 33-34.

[57] Gordon Fee, "The Kingdom of God and the Church's Global Mission", in *Called & Empowered*, 23-24.

[58] Fee, "The Kingdom of God and the Church's Global Mission", 27.

the methodology followed by the Pentecostals from its beginning and even today it is true in the majority world. The people join Pentecostal churches are the least in the society.

Besides, signs and wonders are part and parcel of Pentecostal mission and evangelism. The poor, downtrodden and suffering masses join Pentecostalism by experiencing miracles in their life. Here also Pentecostal mission follow Jesus' method. For Jesus the demonstration of the love of God meant using the power of God as an integral part of his ministry. The "miracles" were a part of the message Jesus lived, not simply a part of the method he used. According to Kraft, if we properly honour the scriptural revelation, we cannot, regard his acts of healing and deliverance as secondary to the more intellectual aspects of Jesus' life and ministry. Probably because evangelicals have not experienced this part of our Christian heritage, we tend to see Jesus' miracles more as proofs of his deity than as essential to his message. Yet he himself urged his enemies to focus on his works as proof of his authenticity (John 10:36–38).[59]

Biblical Factors

Pentecostals take Bible as their rule book for life and mission. Early Pentecostals were marked by their exactness in following a literal interpretation of Scripture. What is said in the Bible is fully believed and practised in missions. Biblical mandate of proclamation of gospel and making disciples through teaching and baptism are fully followed. Therefore, church growth is an important element in Pentecostal mission. Moreover, the biblical mission pattern is accompanied by miracles of healing, exorcism and signs and wonders. Therefore, unlike Protestant mission, Pentecostals expect miracles and church growth in their mission. Pentecostals develop their mission strategies after the models found in the pages of the New Testament - the mission methodologies of Jesus and the apostles are closely followed. Following such patterns enable Pentecostal mission to be focused on a Bible based practice in mission. McClung comments, "Viewing mission strategy as biblical theologizing provides a constant reminder that such thinking is to be under Scripture's authority, even though it involves the use of extra-biblical knowledge and insights."[60]

In addition, Pentecostals see their movement as a fulfilment of Joel 2:28-32 and relates their experiences as normative from what they see in the Book of Acts. Pentecostal missiologist Paul Pomerville, refers Pentecostals as the "people of 'The Book:'"

> While some may question their *use* of the Book, their hermeneutics, nevertheless Pentecostals seek to be led by Scripture as by the Spirit in

[59] Charles H. Kraft, "A Third Wave Perspective on Pentecostal Missions", in *Called & Empowered*, 221.

[60] Pomerville, *The Third Force in Mission*, 112.

their missions efforts. Their textbook for missions strategy often boils down to the Book of Acts.[61]

Biblical Pragmatism is the hallmark of Pentecostal movement, particularly in mission and evangelism. It is the result of their literal interpretation of scripture and task-oriented approach to world missions. This leads them to examine Paul's strategy and observe him planting churches, training leaders, and trusting the Holy Spirit to equip and develop the church in its native setting. Therefore, it is this "biblical pragmatism" which characterizes Pentecostal missions strategy and leads Pentecostals to emphasize that which they find in Scripture in their missions approach.[62] This fact has been acknowledged by missiologists. For instance, Robert Niklaus, while reporting the mushrooming growth of Brazilian Pentecostalism, attributes Pentecostal growth to a literal interpretation of the Bible. Unlike the denominational clergy, the Pentecostals believed in a literal interpretation of the Bible and took a "strong stand on the scriptures", which "found immediate acceptance among the people, if not among the church leaders."[63]

Eschatological Factors

Another significant motivational element in the Pentecostal theology of mission has been an intense premillennial eschatology. Premillennialism, dispensationalism, and the belief in the imminent return of Christ forged the evangelistic fervour of the movement in its infancy. The churches and individuals set mission as their urgent priority. The Azusa Street Mission, for example, became a missionary deployment centre from the very beginning. Missionaries as well as the supporting churches were united in their eschatological urgency. This resulted in many heroic works, which went beyond their expected coming of the Lord.[64] Early Pentecostal J. Roswell Flower typified this urgency by testifying, "Over and over messages were given in the Spirit that the time would not be long and what was done must be done quickly. We were impressed that the time was so short that the heathen in the neglected parts of the earth would scarcely have time to hear before Jesus should come."[65]

Pentecostals believe that they have been called by God in the 'last days' (Acts 2:17) to be Christ-like witnesses in the power of the Spirit. The hope in the imminent coming of the Lord has energized Pentecostal churches and movements into a world-wide missionary enthusiasm and activity. Pentecostals

[61] Paul A. Pomerville, *Pentecostalism and Missions: Distortion or Correction?* (Pasadena, California: Fuller School of Intercultural Studies, 1982), 352.

[62] Pomerville, *Pentecostalism and Missions: Distortion or Correction*? , 353.

[63] *McClung*, "Truth on Fire: Pentecostals and an Urgent Missiology", 80.

[64] Julie C. Ma, "Pentecostal Evangelism, Church Planting, and Church Growth", in *Pentecostal Mission and Global Christianity*, 91.

[65] Klaus, "The Holy Spirit and Mission in Eschatological Perspective", 335.

have consistently taught that the church must be ready for the coming of the Lord by means of faithful witness and holy living.[66] Vinson Synan writes about the missionary endeavours of the early Pentecostals as they were looking for His soon return; "But many were still reached, and around the world the message shouted from the housetops was "Jesus is coming". Listeners were warned to be sure they were among the bride-hood saints who were sanctified and filled with the Holy Spirit.[67] Their motivation was to evangelize the world before the imminent coming of Christ – and so evangelism was more important than education or civilization.[68] Moreover, the fact that they saw Jesus return as imminent, led them to desire to live a deeper walk with Christ and to call for it in the lives of others as well. In fact, this view led them urgency in fulfilling the Great Commission of Christ and taking this 'Full Gospel message' to not only their neighbours, but to the ends of the earth.[69] Their mission fervour and urgency were such that a large number of evangelists and missionaries went out with little or no institutional or financial support, often with only a one-way ticket to their destination. Vinson Synan calls them as the "missionaries of the one-way ticket."[70] This led to the exponential growth that the movement experienced which was also amplified by the fact that this movement started with very little distinction between clergy and laity.[71]

Mission Strategies

Pentecostals have tended to be very practical and literal in their missions strategy. Their attitude has been: "If it is working, fine. If not, let's try something else". Pentecostals are flexible in their approach that they follow the method of "Reaching the receptive". McClung calls it a biblical pragmatism, which has caused Pentecostals to concentrate on the winnable, going where the harvest is ripe. Following Jesus' example, Pentecostals have "looked on the fields" and have responded where there has been "the immediate possibility of a harvest". Pentecostals have located where growth is happening, either by the leading of the Holy Spirit or by observing social and demographic trends.[72] Such a strategy has resulted in reaching the lower classes—masses of suffering, deprived, and

---

[66] Kärkkäinen, "The Pentecostal Understanding of Mission", 27.

[67] Vinson Synan, "The 'Second Comers'", *Christian History* 61 (1999): 38.

[68] Allan Anderson, *Spreading Fires*, 5, 27.

[69] Dale Sanger, "Early Pentecostal Eschatologies and Their Effect on Shaping the Worldwide Pentecostal Movement", https://www.academia.edu/27187458/EARLY_PENTECOSTAL_ESCHATOLOGIES_AND_THEIR_EFFECT_ON_SHAPING_THE_WORLDWIDE_PENTECOSTAL_MOVEMENT_PENTECOSTAL_SPIRITUALITY_PENT0504 (accessed on 10/09/19).

[70] Vinson Synan, "Missionaries of the One-Way Ticket", in *Azuza Street & Beyond*, 41.

[71] Sanger, "Early Pentecostal Eschatologies".

[72] *McClung* "Spontaneous Strategy of the Spirit", 148.

oppressed humanity. In third world context this fact is all the more true as Pentecostal missions have transformed the lives of millions of suffering people. In India, the Pentecostal mission approach of reaching the poor has resulted in considerable church growth among tribal groups, Dalits and ordinary people. Moreover, these groups who are suffering due to poverty, illness, evil spirit attacks, caste-system and other anomalies have been liberated.

Pentecostal missiologist, Melvin Hodges explains various ways in which Pentecostals deals with mission activities. In one place, an evangelistic campaign may be the means for opening the area to the gospel. Elsewhere the beginning will be made by opening a small outstation in a home, following up with literature saturation. Again, the healing of a paralytic, or the restoring of sight to a blind person through the prayer of faith may be the means of stirring interest and founding the church. Pentecostal believers pray for their sick neighbours and lead them to Christ. The deliverance of an alcoholic or a narcotic addict may open the door in a community. Admittedly, all this may seem foreign to those who are accustomed to an institutional approach to the mission of the Church, but to Pentecostals such happenings are to be expected and are entirely in accord with the New Testament concept of the Church's mission.[73] Even though Pentecostals follow flexible mission strategies, they carry out systematic propagation of gospel message to the targeted audiences. Pentecostals are characterized by a "spontaneous strategy of the Spirit", nevertheless, they have not been without a plan. Their master plan has included numerous elements, methods and strategies for the systematic propagation of the movement. Among them are: indigenous churches, church planting, urban strategies, literature distribution, and missions stewardship.[74]

Another important strategy is leadership training. Even though most of the Pentecostal leaders come from the lower strata of society, Pentecostal leaders have tended to be loyal to the movement which has made them. They have responded faithfully to apprentice-style training because they were not accustomed to the elite practice of seminary level education. One of the earliest items on the Pentecostal missions agenda was the establishment of Bible schools around the world. In many areas, Pentecostals are actually the leaders in the number of Bible schools and even higher level training institutes.[75]

One of the significant factors in the growth of Pentecostalism is lay participation in mission which results in minimizing of the clergy/laity barrier present in mainline Christianity. This minimization grew from a belief that Pentecostal baptism equipped every believer for Christian witness. Pentecostals do not have a tradition of formal theological training for "the ministry" as a class

---

[73] Melvin L. Hodges, "A Pentecostal's View of Mission Strategy", in *Azuza Street & Beyond,* 163.

[74] McClung, "Spontaneous Strategy of the Spirit", 151.

[75] McClung, "Spontaneous Strategy of the Spirit", 149.

set apart. The emphasis has been on the whole body as ministers supernaturally recruited and deployed. Since the Holy Spirit speaks to all believers equally, regardless of education, training or worldly rank, each member is capable of carrying out the task. Believers know intuitively that they should replicate themselves by bringing others to a knowledge of Christ. Converts witness out of an overflow of zeal, thus necessitating teaching and guidance so that the resulting witness will be effective.[76]

Along with effective lay participation, employing women in mission is a strategy that brought significant results in Pentecostal missions. A large part of the dynamic growth of the Pentecostal Movement is due to its ability since its inception to mobilize and effectively deploy women into missionary service. Many Pentecostal organizations have provisions for "Lady Ministers" or "Lady Evangelists" and will allow for their licensing. The Pentecostal experience on the day of Pentecost broke the last barrier of separation between humanity. On the day of Pentecost, Jesus "baptized the women exactly like the men, for the exact same purpose as the men are baptized so the women are baptized."[77] The empowerment of lay people, in particular, women have enabled Pentecostal growth in third world situation. Ordinary women share their stories of liberation and transformation to their neighbours in casual talks, thus attracting people to churches to pray for their troubles. Such personal exchange empowers both the person who shares testimony and the listener to face troublesome situation in their life.

For Pentecostals, all the mission strategies, evangelism and charity endeavours boil down to church planting. Pentecostals have believed that church planting is the abiding fruit of world evangelism and have measured their progress by the development of mature congregations and the buildings which they erect. Evangelism has been understood not only as proclamation but in persuading men and women to commit their lives to Christ and become members of a local church and that these churches should multiply.[78] Here Pentecostals apply 'indigenous church principle'. When a considerable number of missionaries went overseas without any pledged support in the beginning of Pentecostal mission, this principle helped missionaries. The 'faith missions' was enthusiastically adopted by many pioneers both because of the biblical idea of miraculous provisions and an intensive expectation of the Second Coming, but it soon gave way to a more traditional mission praxis.[79] Nevertheless, it is to be noted that the 'faith mission' principle is a universal idea among Pentecostal missionaries. The Indian Pentecostal mission history shows stories of early Pentecostal missionaries, going to north of India from south India and carrying

---

[76] Byron D. Klaus & Loren O. Triplett, "National Leadership in Pentecostal Mission", in *Called & Empowered*, 166-167.

[77] McClung, "Spontaneous Strategy of the Spirit", 150.

[78] McClung, "Spontaneous Strategy of the Spirit", 152.

[79] Kärkkäinen, "The Pentecostal Understanding of Mission", 28-29.

out 'faith missions.'[80] Even today, this is true in many of the mission activities. This has resulted in tremendous growth of indigenous independent churches all over India, outstripping the denominational churches. Pentecostal emphasis on indigenous principles of self-propagation, self-government and self-support has considerably helped church growth in the majority world.

Another noteworthy aspect of Pentecostal mission is their focus on urban centres of the world. Pentecostals and Charismatics of all nations have focused their preaching and church-planting efforts on the world's teeming cities. Christian and non-Christian scholars alike have documented that both missionary and independently sponsored indigenous urban Pentecostal and charismatic churches and fellowships have been multiplying rapidly, especially in the fast-growing cities of the poorer third world nations.[81] Donald McGavran, founder of the Church Growth movement, claimed that in India Pentecostals were "buying up urban opportunities."[82] Today Indian cities are experiencing magnificent growth of Pentecostal and charismatic churches. Moreover, Indian cities are seeing mushrooming of mega churches where thousands of people worship in multi-lingual services. Pentecostals also employ mass evangelism, where thousands gather to listen to gospel and receiving healing and other blessings. They also use literature, television, radio, internet and social media to disseminate the gospel message.

Furthermore, significantly, Pentecostals generously contribute to the cause of missions. Though not generally people of means, Pentecostals have given sacrificially because there was a cause. Pentecostals have been doing the job because they have put their money where their heart is and God has blessed their missions stewardship.[83] Last but not least, Pentecostal mission and evangelism totally depend on prayer for forward movement. Even though Pentecostals employ all the available resources and methods, it is strongly asserted that without prayer and intercession all other aspects are in vain. According to Yonggi Cho, it is utterly impossible for a pastor to expect his church to grow without prayer. Many ministers today think the motivating power of church growth is in a particular system, or in a particular organizational structure. This is a wrong opinion. The motivating power behind church growth is fervent prayer. Signs and wonders can never take place without prayer.[84]

---

[80] Shaibu Abraham, *The History of the Pentecostal Movement in North India: Unfolding its Social and Theological Contexts* (New Delhi: Christian world Imprints, 2017).

[81] Kärkkäinen, "The Pentecostal Understanding of Mission", 38.

[82] Augustus Cerillo, Jr., "Pentecostals and the City", in *Azuza Street & Beyond*, 193.

[83] *McClung* "Spontaneous Strategy of the Spirit", 155.

[84] David Yonggi Cho, "The Secret Behind the World's Biggest Church", 130.

Social Missions

Social programs designed to care for the welfare of the poor and the oppressed as well as to change unjust social conditions are fast becoming a hallmark of Pentecostal church ministry at home and abroad.[85] There are those who contend that the Pentecostals' view of Christian mission is too narrow, that only personal conversion emphasised, physical and economic needs are not addressed. However, Pentecostals have different take on this issue. Hodges comments that there is nothing as important as getting people's hearts right with God. The center must be put right before the periphery can be corrected. To try to remedy peripheral conditions leaving the heart unchanged is useless and deceiving. When a person is truly converted, he seeks a better life for himself and for his family.[86]

Pentecostals, However, do not Neglect Social Work. The Observation by Some Non-Pentecostal leaders that Pentecostals are on a "social strike" has been proven by further research to be misguided. Wherever Pentecostal churches have flourished, the social conditions of the working class converts have improved. Loving your neighbour as yourself has been a way of life for Pentecostals. Quoting Dean Kelley, Wagner argues that churches high on the strictness scale such as Pentecostals end up with more social strength than others.[87] Peterson also toes the same line; "In modern times, despite complaints that Pentecostals have neglected the "here and now" for the "sweet by and by", the fact is that the explosive growth of Pentecostalism among destitute and vulnerable peoples has made the movement a force in addressing the contemporary situation facing millions of third world adherents". For example, many of the larger Pentecostal churches establish day schools. Orphanages, old-age homes, assistance to poor students etc. All is carried on in an unassuming way, without fanfare, and with a minimum of outside help.[88] As Pentecostal missionaries went out around the world, not many of them with university degrees, they naturally began their work among the poor and oppressed, finding that God had prepared many of them to hear and receive the gospel. Wagner's research into Latin American Pentecostalism reveals that targeting the working class is a key factor in its growth.[89] This sense of God's special love for the oppressed has enabled Pentecostals to rescue many from their predicament and lead them into transformation.[90]

---

[85] Murray W. Dempster, "Evangelism, Social Concern and the Kingdom of God", in *Called & Empowered*, 30.

[86] Hodges, "A Pentecostal's View of Mission Strategy", 165.

[87] Wagner, "A Church Growth Perspective on Pentecostal Mission", 198.

[88] Hodges, "A Pentecostal's View of Mission Strategy", 165.

[89] Wagner, "A Church Growth Perspective on Pentecostal Mission", 201.

[90] Douglas Peterson, "The Kingdom of God and the Hermeneutical Circle: Pentecostal Praxis in the Third World", in *Called & Empowered*, 48.

Moreover, it is established that the Pentecostal movement spared better in liberating downtrodden masses than the Liberation Theology movement.[91] In an important essay, Miroslav Volf, compares both Pentecostalism and the Liberation Theology and argues that both Pentecostalism and Liberation Theology with all their differences, share a vision of salvation in this-worldly, physical, material, embodied terms. While neither of the movements leaves behind the eschatological, future-oriented hope, relegating salvation merely to the future will not do either. Liberationists focus their efforts on socio-political (including gender) liberation, while for Pentecostals it is more about the individual's release from sicknesses and ailments, physical or emotional.[92] There is resistance to excluding the bodily this-worldly reality from the vision of salvation. Alongside the idea of the materiality of salvation and search for holism goes the continuing work for social, political, and economic justice and righteousness. With all its problems with 'other-worldliness', Pentecostalism is also characterized by a commitment to social justice, empowerment of the powerless, and a 'preferential option for the marginalized' tracing back to its roots at Azusa Street as a kind of paradigm of marginalization – a revival in an abandoned stable, led by an African American preacher.[93]

Pentecostals carry out social ministries in the Kingdom perspective. Dempster underlines that the Kingdom perspective in Pentecostal mission generates its own particular brand of interpretation of the church's *diakonic* ministry. Therefore, programs and deeds of social service are understood as theological activity that express God's love for all people everywhere and God's desire that justice rule in the whole creation. Moral deeds that without discrimination express love for the hurting and promote justice for the needy are theologically motivated. In so serving the world, the church desires that hurting and needy people experience meaningful expressions of God's great compassion and of God's verdict to right the wrongs and establish justice.[94] Another example of Pentecostal social ministries in relation to the heavily professionalized drug rehabilitation field with a cure labelled conversion and

---

[91] For instance, Richard Shaull observes, "In Latin America, the Christian base communities became the incarnation of this faith that created a new life in community among those dedicated to the struggle for liberation and that grew rapidly across the continent. Today the vitality and impact of these communities in society are much less evident, and they seem to have largely lost their former capacity to reproduce themselves". Shaull and Cesar, *Pentecostalism and the Future*, 210. See Shaibu Abraham, *Pentecostal Theology of Liberation: Holy Spirit and Holiness in the Society* (New Delhi: Christian World Imprints, 2014).

[92] Miroslav Volf, "Materiality of Salvation: An Investigation in the Soteriologies of Liberation and Pentecostal Theologies", *JES* 26 (1989): 447- 467.

[93] Veli-Matti Kärkkäinen, "'The Leaning Tower of Mission in a Postmodern Land': Ecumenical Reflections on Pentecostal Mission in the After-Edinburgh World", *JEPTA* 10/2 (2010): 82-93, 86; Kärkkäinen, "The Pentecostal Understanding of Mission", 38.

[94] Dempster, "Evangelism, Social Concern and the Kingdom of God", 37.

baptism in the Holy Spirit. Cerillo says that Pentecostals have not hesitated to enter into untutored field. He continues, "The great success over the years of the Teen Challenge ministry, started by David Wilkerson in the late 1950s, and of countless similar programs sponsored by Pentecostals and Charismatics exemplify the "brash side" of Pentecostalism at its best. Impatient with social scientific theory, oblivious to odds against success, and sure of possessing God's own solutions, Pentecostals have ministered among the city's alcoholics, drug addicts, prostitutes, pornographers, and youth gangs."[95]

In relation to social ministries, Douglas Peterson suggests Pentecostal to be more determined and involve in social ministries rather than dogmatic. He strongly advocates that, to be relevant, Pentecostal theology simply must respond to the questions that the poor are asking. The marginalized are not interested in the traditionally articulated scientific/theological ideas; rather, they want to know how God could abandon them so totally in the physical realm. Unless the church is a participant in this quest, it has no reason for being.[96] Pentecostals must come to terms with God's designs to reach out to the non-persons of society—to those that have no one to plead their cause, to those who have been left on the roadside of life, consistently ignored and abandoned with little hope—those non-persons are also created in God's image. If Pentecostal theology adequately conveys the gospel message of the kingdom, the Spirit-filled person must move from the theoretical to the practical in realizing God's purposes.[97]

Pentecostal Mission and Religious Pluralism

Another vital aspect that needs to be discussed in relation to the Pentecostal mission and evangelism is the religious pluralism and the violent persecution faced by Pentecostal missionaries, particularly in Indian context. Although, Pentecostal movement grows in rapid pace, Pentecostals have been target of frequent attack from violent communal forces in Indian context. Any mission or evangelistic endeavours attract the ire of religious fundamentalists and leads to violent attacks on Pentecostals. The Pentecostal practices of divine healing, exorcism or use of other charismatic gifts for people who are in dire needs are considered as influencing people for forcible conversion. Even without slightest provocation, pastors and missionaries are attacked, churches are vandalised, Bibles are burned and believers are terrorised and brutalised. When such incidents take place, very often the political authorities and police either look away or abet the perpetrators of violence and register court cases against the Pentecostals in the name of forcible conversions. This sort of attacks not only come from the *Hindutva* ideology, but also from other religious groups when a person is joined from their flocks to Pentecostal churches.

---

[95] Cerillo, Jr., "Pentecostals and the City", 197.

[96] Peterson, "The Kingdom of God and the Hermeneutical Circle", 46.

[97] Peterson, "The Kingdom of God and the Hermeneutical Circle", 47.

Such a context warrants a mission strategy which avoids violence and also nurtures a harmonious relationships in society. At the same time, who are in dire need of healing or deliverance from evil spiritual forces or looking for salvation through Christ are to be reached out. This is a need of the hour and perceiving the significance of this situation, Anderson recommends that there is an urgent need to ponder the relationship between the Christian Gospel and the ancient pre-Christian religions that continue to give meaning to people's understanding of their lives.[98] Therefore, it is significant to have a valid, vibrant Pentecostal theology of religions or what I want to call "community-centric mission theology for pluralistic context that does not compromise biblical, historic Christianity or act condescendingly or contemptuously toward other world religions, that is also desirable for Pentecostals and for our friends of other faith."[99]

Although, Pentecostals are generally hesitant to discuss the issue of religious pluralism and related questions, recently Pentecostal scholars are beginning to appreciate the need for dialogue with other religions and have developed a theology of religions. Now more pastors and evangelists encounter people of other faiths. Taking this reality into consideration, Kärkkäinen argues that it is vital to include theology of religions in the Christian educational curriculum.[100] Similarly Richie contends that it is not appropriate to relegate all religious experience beyond the border of the institutional church to the demonic realm. Although, there is no salvation outside Christ, that does not mean that there is no possibility of salvation outside the church.[101]

Amos Yong argues that the stress of Charismatic-Pentecostal Pneumatology on the universality of experience of God through the Spirit may contribute to a contemporary Christian theology of religions.[102] He sees the presence of the Spirit active in creation and in all cultures, which includes religions because the Spirit has been poured out on all flesh.[103] The emphasis of pneumatic elements enables Pentecostals to be open to other religious traditions. According to him, a Pentecostal-Charismatic theology of religions should free human beings for

---

[98] Anderson, "Towards a Pentecostal Missiology for the Majority World", 38.

[99] Tony Richie, "Neither Naïve nor Narrow: A Balanced Pentecostal Approach to Christian Theology of Religions", *Presented to the Annual Meeting of the American Academy of Religion* (Philadelphia, PA: November 19-22, 2005): 2, http://www.ncccusa.org/pdfs/naive.pdf (accessed 2 November 2010).

[100] Veli-Matti Kärkkäinen, *An Introduction to the Theology of Religions: Biblical, Historical, & Contemporary Perspectives* (Illinois: IVP, 2003), 20; Veli-Matti Kärkkäinen, *Trinity and Religious Pluralism: The Doctrine of the Trinity in Christian Theology of Religions* (Hants: Ashgate, 2004).

[101] Tony Richie, "'The Unity of Spirit': Are Pentecostals Inherently Ecumenists and Inclusivists?", *JEPTA* 26/1 (2006): 31-33.

[102] Amos Yong, *Discerning the Spirit(s): A Pentecostal-Charismatic Theology of Religions, Journal of Pentecostal Theology Supplement Series* (Sheffield: Sheffield Academic Press, 2000), 29-30.

[103] Amos Yong, *The Spirit Poured Out on All Flesh: Pentecostalism and the Possibility of Global Theology* (Michigan: Baker Academic, 2005).

participation in interreligious dialogue. The goal of such dialogue is not merely to agree on similarities, rather even the "activity of apologetics needs to be included in acknowledging such conversations to be in the service of the righteousness, peace and truth that characterise the Kingdom of God."[104] He articulates "pneumatological imagination", as an experience of and orientation to the Holy Spirit through which one may determine the presence of the Holy Spirit. He also stresses that it is vital to discern the absence of the divine or presence of the demonic in other religious traditions.[105]

Yong proposes a theological framework for interfaith encounter. First, God is universally present by his Spirit; therefore, he sustains religions for his divine purposes. Second, the Spirit ushers in the Kingdom of God and hence, the signs of the Kingdom are made manifest through the Spirit's presence. Third, when there are signs of resistance to and activity against the Kingdom of God, the Spirit can be said to be absent from religions.[106] Nonetheless, he emphasises that the possibility of the presence of the Spirit in other religions should not de-emphasise the centrality of Christ to salvation, nor should it undermine the importance of evangelism.[107]

Similarly, Richie, draws on the narrative of Acts 2 and the day of Pentecost, offers a Pentecostal perspective of dialogue.[108] The outpouring of the Spirit enabled a diversity of tongues; the many tongues retain their particularity even as they point to the unity of the one Spirit. These tongues represent, at least potentially, many religions, which in turn point to the redemption of religions (eschatologically), as well as of languages and cultures. The tongues or testimonies of the religious other must first be heard in their own terms, before a theology of religion can be constructed. This will involve a critical analysis of religious beliefs and practices, using a "hermeneutic of charity."[109] With this background, Richie proposes a model of Pentecostal engagement based on the notion of testimony; telling others of what God has done in one's life in order to encourage them. It can be transformative for the testifier and hearer alike. It contains significant autobiographical elements and doxological content. Use of testimony as a way

---

[104] Yong, *Discerning the Spirit(s),* 313.

[105] Amos Yong, "'Not Knowing Where the Wind Blows ...': On Envisioning a Pentecostal-Charismatic Theology of Religions", *JPT* 14 (1999): 81-83.

[106] Yong, *The Spirit Poured Out on All Flesh,* 250–253.

[107] Amos Yong, *Beyond the Impasse: Toward a Pneumatological Theology of Religion* (Michigan: Eerdmans, 2003), 52-53.

[108] Richie, "Speaking by the Spirit", 89-90.

[109] Richie, "Speaking by the Spirit", 113-115; Tony Richie, "God's Fairness to People of All Faiths: A Respectful Proposal to Pentecostals for Discussion Regarding World Religions", *Pneuma* 28/1 (Spring 2006): 105-119.

of interreligious dialogue benefits Pentecostals, since it is integral to Pentecostal spirituality and helps Pentecostals to retain their original energy and vitality.[110]

Hollenweger, however, develops a theology of "dialogical evangelism" that is less rigid and more respectful regarding mutual sharing between religious others that decry too a sharp demarcation between Christian mission and interfaith dialogue. This is based on the encounter of Peter and Cornelius (Acts 10), and is used as a biblical model for contemporary Pentecostals. Significantly, both participants learn from each other as the Holy Spirit is poured out afresh.[111] It seems that emphasis on pneumatological elements in Pentecostal spirituality make it possible to interact with other religious traditions. Added to that, for Indian Pentecostals the centrality of Christ is a point of contact with other religionists. This point of contact is actualised through their testimonies and activities of signs and wonders which happen through the agency of the Spirit. Richie rightly endorses a typical Pentecostal position: "Inclusivism by no means necessitates even a nascent compromise of Christian integrity or of Pentecostal theology and spirituality; rather, it enables Pentecostals to witness with respect to everyone of the limitless love of God in his Son by the power of the Spirit."[112] Since ordinary Pentecostals constantly interact with people of other faiths and also come under the attack of extremist elements, this notion can be useful for context.

Having seen the significant factors of Pentecostal missions that bring liberation to masses who are affected by various anomalies of our society, it is important to look into some of the areas where Pentecostal mission endeavours need correction and further development. Pages below we look into some of the issues.

It is true that the Pentecostal movement has enjoyed unprecedented growth during the twentieth century. However, all over the world where Pentecostal movement becomes old, the growth has fallen considerably or almost nil. This is true in the twenty-first century. Wagner diagnosis the trend and says, "If history repeats itself, the life cycle of human organizations might catch up with the Pentecostal movement and result in stagnation and decline. Some warning signs are appearing on the horizon". He presents the example of the world's largest national Pentecostal fellowship, the Assemblies of God in Brazil, which has slowed in its mode of growth and has started to plateau. The Church of God (Cleveland, Tenn.) has recently lost the place it held for years as one of the two or three fastest growing denominations in the United States. Neither is declining, but they are

---

[110] Richie, "Speaking by the Spirit", 165-166.

[111] Walter J. Hollenweger, "Critical Issues for Pentecostals", in *Pentecostals after a Century: Global Perspectives on a Movement in Transition,* edited by Allan H. Anderson & Walter J. Hollenweger (Sheffield: Sheffield Academic Press, 1999), 176-191; Walter J. Hollenweger, "Evangelism: A Non-Colonial Model", *JPT* 7 (1995): 116-121.

[112] Richie, "'The Unity of Spirit'", 34.

not growing nearly as rapidly as they have in the past.[113] Similarly, Pentecostal movement in Kerala state of India which had impacted Pentecostal missions in north India is in a stagnant state. However, neo-Pentecostal movement is attracting lot of people from denominational churches as well as from Pentecostalism.

There are many reasons behind such stagnation among Pentecostals. What is proposed by Donald McGavran seems to explain this trend. One of his foundational concepts for the Church Growth Movement is what he calls "redemption and lift". He points out that the gospel is usually introduced into a new people group through the lower socio-economic strata of population. But, the blessings of God ordinarily lift Christian families out of poverty, some to the middle class. The newly lifted Christians then frequently neglect the poor and at times even distance themselves from their roots.[114] It seems that this principle has affected many of the Pentecostal denominations. Alongside the issue above, fading of eschatological fervour is another factor that retards the Pentecostal missions. Wonsuk Ma, for instance, traced the changes that took place in Asian Pentecostal theology. As the eschatological urgency that was identified with the first generation missionaries began to wane; it was gradually replaced by a here-and-now prosperity gospel that was imported from the Charismatic movement and a this-worldly organizational orientation that was imported by Pentecostals that emphasized church growth.[115] This is true all over the world.

Another issue that retards the growth of Pentecostal movement is the lack of denominational structures that enhance the missions. In Pentecostal churches there is a historic tension between those who have vision for cross-cultural ministry and those who are in control of the churches and can potentially send missionaries. Visionary, outward looking, missionary leaders motivate the church to reach other peoples. However, denominational leaders tend to be more concerned with growth and development among their own people. When control is centralized, there is often little opportunity for visionary missionary leaders to get a start within their own denominations. Even when something is started, such mission leaders are often frustrated from insufficient autonomy to carry out their mandate. This tendency of church leaders to control missionary activity often leads visionary missions leaders to start their own independent organizations. This way many independent mission agencies have begun in many places, especially in India. However, such a state of affair negatively affected denominational Pentecostal missions and it has often served to short-circuit the denominations from developing their own mission programs.[116]

---

[113] Wagner, "A Church Growth Perspective on Pentecostal Mission", 205.

[114] Wagner, "A Church Growth Perspective on Pentecostal Mission", 205.

[115] Wonsuk Ma, "Pentecostal Eschatology: What Happened When the Wave Hit the West End of the Ocean", *AJPS* 12/1 (2009).

[116] Pate, "Pentecostal Mission from the Two-Thirds World", 184.

Another reason for stagnation is, the creeping nominality in Pentecostal churches. Desiring for the power of the Holy Spirit and exercising of the spiritual gifts are waning away in the churches. Wagner rightly points out the problem. The church which the apostle Paul planted in Ephesus looked very much like a Pentecostal church. The believers spoke in tongues and prophesied; Paul did signs and wonders; evil spirits were cast out; healing cloths were being passed around; occult practitioners burned piles of valuable books (Acts 19:1–20). Ephesus then became an evangelistic centre from which the gospel spread throughout Asia Minor. But, forty years later, St. John wrote in the book of Revelation that they had lost their first love (Rev. 2:4). Nominality had set in. They had succumbed to the disease that Wagner calls, "St. John's Syndrome."[117] This is exactly what happened with Pentecostals today, thus, loosing their liberative thrust.

Bureaucratization is another issue that stops the growth of Pentecostal movement. During the first generation the leaders have so much power and authority that not much structure was needed. Later, however, a process called "routinization of charisma" sets in. Leadership tends to become more legal-rational, and a bureaucracy is set up to keep the ship afloat. In tracing the history of Assemblies of God missions, Gary McGee points out that there exists tension between bureaucracy in denomination and "the 'private vision' of some missionaries preferring to be led solely by the Spirit. As long as tensions persist, growth may continue. However, if bureaucrats have their way and finally remove the annoyance of charismatic leadership, the growth dynamic of the past may be history.[118]

Lastly, another possible area of concern that negatively impact Pentecostal mission is the ecumenical tendencies shown in the Pentecostal denominations. Cordial relationship and co-operation among the churches are warranted, nonetheless, when the Pentecostal spirituality and distinctives are diluted for ecumenical concerns, surely that is going to affect Pentecostal growth by reducing its liberative potentials. According to Wagner, memories of scorn, ridicule, and persecution at the hands of denominational churches are not easily erased from the Pentecostal consciousness. This has caused some second and third generation Pentecostal leaders to develop a deep desire for gaining the love and respect of other Christians. They are increasingly uncomfortable with some of the theology and practices of their parents and grandparents. Historically, one of the prices to be paid for interdenominational cooperation and ecumenism is watering down Pentecostal distinctives, a known deterrent to church growth.[119]

Let me conclude here. Mission and evangelism form the lifeline of Pentecostal movement and its core spirituality. The reason behind its significant growth is its emphasis on the work of Holy Spirit and the use of spiritual gifts

---

[117] Wagner, "A Church Growth Perspective on Pentecostal Mission", 206.

[118] Wagner, "A Church Growth Perspective on Pentecostal Mission", 206.

[119] Wagner, "A Church Growth Perspective on Pentecostal Mission", 206.

in mission fields. The Gospel message accompanied with healing, exorcism and other signs and wonders have attracted suffering masses to Pentecostal fold. This has not only resulted in Pentecostal growth but have liberated masses from their troubles and the predicament that pulls them down in the majority world. There are various factors that impel Pentecostal mission endeavours which we have discussed and they act as liberative factors in missions. However, after a century, many denominations are losing their original spiritual fervour that has affected their spiritual and numerical growth. Pentecostals ought to regain their original liberative spirituality.

Chapter 7

Worship
Cradle of Liberation

Worship holds a unique place in Pentecostal movement. It is in the context of worship, Pentecostal spirituality is formed and exercised. Pentecostal worship is unique in its form and content as well as its spontaneity and vibrancy. Exuberant singing, clapping and dancing along with shout of praises stand as the hallmark of Pentecostal worship. These elements make worship a place of heavenly foretaste, as Pentecostals claim, though for outsiders it may seem chaotic and confusing. The worship plays a significant role in the spiritual and character formation among Pentecostals. Moreover, all the other unique Pentecostal traits such as the Spirit baptism, tongue speaking, exercise of spiritual gifts, energy for mission are being continuously manifested and internalised in worship context. For Pentecostals, worship is a community affair and here they intimately experience the presence of God. It is in the worship, participants literally experience the liberative presence of the Holy Spirit by receiving bodily healing, emotional release and spiritual edification. Hence, the Pentecostal worship can be termed as the birth place of Pentecostal theology and spirituality and thus, termed as the cradle of liberative spirituality.

The Pentecostal worship is a key growth factor and this fact is acknowledged by both insiders and outside observers of the movement. More and more young people are attracted to the movement as the worship is live, vibrant and involving. Pentecostal worship allows the participant to be involved in a personal and direct way with the manifestation of God.[1] The personal God-experience through the

[1] Grant McClung, "Spontaneous Strategy of the Spirit", in *Azuza Street & Beyond,* edited by Grant McClung, 2nd edition (Florida: Bridge-Logos, 2012), 144.

work of the Holy Spirit is available for everyone, and the involvement of the laity became the most important feature of Pentecostal worship in contrast to the dominant role played by the priest or minister in older churches. Pentecostalism's emphasis on "freedom in the Spirit" rendered it inherently flexible in different cultural and social contexts and this trait enabled the movement to grow in all cultures, especially in the Two-Thirds World context.[2] In Indian context, the youths, the poor and the disenfranchised are more attracted to the Pentecostal churches as Pentecostal spirituality, particularly the worship is dynamic and energetic. Here, the participants are able to release their emotional burdens, anxiety and fears. Besides, in Pentecostal worship many receive healing for their sickness and deliverance from spirit-possession. Such a profound spirituality attracts people of every walk of life, especially the poor and the movement is growing fast in the Indian sub-continent.

Pentecostals have always taken strenuous efforts to keep the spontaneity of their services and at times feeling somewhat superior to other church traditions that use a written liturgical format. Spittler comments: "Spontaneity is prized in Pentecostal piety. The Holy Spirit guides worship and leads each believer and he moves unpredictably. All the members expect anyone of the local assembly to follow the Spirit's leading and to do so at once."[3] Pointing out his own experience, Hudson rightly affirms that what attracted him and others who joined Pentecostal churches from other Christian traditions was the vibrancy and immediacy of the worship, which subsequently fashioned their view and understanding of God. He continues,

> Worship was no longer simply a rational, cognitive assent to certain articles of the creedal statements of the church. It was a time when we were encouraged to experience the presence of God in our midst. We no longer had to merely sing about and commemorate the experiences of believers who had met with the living God in days gone by; this was now open to us all, male or female, young or old, rich or poor. The liberation found was not to be analysed but simply enjoyed. The freedom of knowing that God loved us, not because we had been told this, but because we felt his touch in our lives, was exhilarating.[4]

Similarly, Albrecht describes Pentecostal worship as an occasion when "God is the audience and the congregation performs the drama of praise."[5] This drama

---

[2] Grant McClung, "Spontaneous Strategy of the Spirit", 73; Allan Anderson, "Towards a Pentecostal Missiology for the Majority World", *AJPS* 8/1 (2005): 43.

[3] D. Neil Hudson, "Worship: Singing a New Song in a Strange Land", in *Pentecostal Perspectives*, edited by Keith Warrington (Carlisle, Cumbria: Paternoster Press, 1998), 187.

[4] Hudson, "Worship: Singing a New Song", 177.

[5] Daniel E. Albrecht, "An Anatomy of Worship: A Pentecostal Analysis", in *The Spirit and Spirituality: Essays in Honor of Russell Spittler*, edited by Wonsuk Ma & Robert Menzies (New York: T & T Clark International, 2004), 72.

is often accompanied by physical movements such as clapping, hands raised, dancing, ejaculatory expressions of praise in the forms of words or phrases which may be pronounced aloud, and emotional responses of joy and laughter or tears and sorrow. The praise to God is often accompanied with prayer for and ministry to others present and on behalf of those who may be absent.[6] What Miller affirms in his study of Pentecostal movement is not an exaggeration, as he portrays the dynamic worship:

> A sociologist we interviewed in Latin America said that Pentecostalism is a "warm" religion, whereas Roman Catholicism, in his view, is a "cold religion". Inherent in this distinction is the idea that Catholic liturgy is served up to people through a hierarchical structure, whereas Pentecostalism is highly participative. While there is order and structure to Pentecostal worship, the people are full participants in creating a sacred drama.[7]

Harvey Cox observes that "the great strength of the Pentecostal impulse" lies in "its power to combine, its aptitude for the language, the music, the cultural artefacts, the religious tropes... of the setting in which it lives."[8] Many older missionary churches arose in western historical contexts, with set liturgies, theologies, well-educated clergy, and patterns of church and leadership with strongly centralized control. This often contributed to the feeling that these churches were "foreign" and that one first had to become a westerner before becoming a Christian. In contrast, Pentecostalism emphasised an immediate personal experience of God's power by his Spirit, it was more intuitive and emotional, and it recognized charismatic leadership and national church patterns wherever they arose.[9] Warrington points to the two pertinent aspects of Pentecostal spirituality; expectancy and encounter. Pentecostals expect to encounter God and this happens in the worship context. Besides, God-encounter defines their worship and theology and may even be identified as another way of defining worship. Pentecostals expect to experience an intimate relationship with God in which God is felt and they are moved emotionally.[10] Du Plessis, a Pentecostal statesman, identifies the elements of "a good Pentecostal

---

[6] F. Bixler, "Dancing in the Spirit", in *NIDPCM*, edited by Stanley M. Burgess (Michigan: Zondervan, 2002), 570-71.

[7] Donald E. Miller & Tetsunao Yamamori, *Global Pentecostalism: The New Face of Christian Social Engagement* (Berkeley: University of California Press, 2007), 143.

[8] Harvey Cox, *Fire from Heaven: The Rise of Pentecostal Spirituality and the Reshaping of Religion in the Twenty-first Century* (Cambridge, MA: Da Capo Press, 1995), 259.

[9] Anderson, "Towards a Pentecostal Missiology", 44.

[10] Keith Warrington, *Pentecostal Theology: A Theology of Encounter* (London: T&T Clark, 2008), 219.

meeting" as "there is atmosphere. Everyone knows something is happening."[11] For Pentecostals, the worship has always been the vehicle for their theology, bringing it to life and giving it validity. The framework for an individual believer's commitment to Christ is created and sustained by the language and concepts used in corporate worship.[12] Thus, the worship form the very cornerstone of Pentecostal spirituality, theology and mission and acts as the birthplace of liberative credentials of Pentecostalism. In the following pages we shall delve into various aspects of Pentecostal worship to understand their unique nature. Moreover, we shall see how these elements lead participants into spiritual and social transformation to create a new identity and social standing in the life of the poor and the ordinary.

Biblical Pattern of Worship

Pentecostals always claimed and prided that their worship is based on biblical principles and they see parallel with the New Testament pattern of worship, particularly of the Book of Acts. The outpouring of the Holy Spirit, violent sound, fiery signs are anticipated and the phenomena of speaking in tongues, prophecy and other manifestations are still exercised in the worship services (Acts 2). Similar to we see in the Acts of Apostles, Pentecostals look forward to miraculous demonstrations such as shaking of the place, signs and wonders in their prayer meetings (4:23-31). In worship services, it is expected new believers to receive the baptism of the Holy Spirit and speak in tongues as happened in the household of Cornelius (Acts 10:44). Moreover, they strongly believe that through their praise and worship, chains and bondages of life will be broken asunder to make people free, just as happened to apostles Paul and Silas in the Philippi Jail (Acts 16:25-26). By receiving prophecies, visions and illuminations in the worship sessions, Pentecostals go out for missions as we see in the case of Paul and Barnabas (Acts 13:2-3).

Pentecostals theologians have asserted the biblical nature of Pentecostal worship. They see literal and direct connections with Pentecostal worship and biblical examples of worship. For instance, Alexander explains that there is plenty of biblical support for expressive, emotional, physical worship, and Pentecostals have gone to great lengths to show it. King David danced so crazily "with all his might" in public in honour of God that he embarrassed his wife because she thought he acted like a lower-class person (2 Samuel 6:1-22). Alexander exclaims, "Happy feet, rejoicing in a relationship with Spirit, that's Pentecostalism."[13] Another Pentecostal, Telford Work, feels that Pentecostals "shout back to the Lord what the Spirit has written in our hearts. *Shouting* means not holding back either

[11] Warrington, *Pentecostal Theology*, 220.

[12] Hudson, "Worship: Singing a New Song", 195.

[13] Paul Alexander, *Signs & Wonders: Why Pentecostalism is the World's Fastest Growing Faith* (San Francisco: Jossey Bass, 2009), 23.

our joy or our tears. It means not letting either pride or shame tell us how to act. It means giving God our love as outwardly as God gave us his."[14] Similarly, Alexander explains apostle Paul's exhortation to Ephesian believers in Eph. 5:18;

> "Be not drunk with wine for this leads to debauchery, but be filled [get drunk?] with the Spirit! Speak to one another with psalms, hymns, and spiritual songs. Sing and make music to the Lord". Paul the Apostle's play on spirits and Spirit also helps us think about the ways different Christians worship. Without being judgmental, we can observe that some churches seem not to drink of the Spirit too deeply; others sip daintily from fancy glasses and talk quietly. Pentecostals drink a lot and let loose. They are the ones who claim to drink the most and claim to experience the Spirit most thoroughly. They dance, hug, and tell one another how much they love each other. For them, the church is like a fiesta celebrating what God is doing in the world to redeem it. Worship is partying together.[15]

Worship in the Pentecostal church is a prophetic experience. When sinners are present, the Holy Spirit "convicts" or "confronts" with a call to repentance. Worshipers experiencing the presence of God identify with the prophet Isaiah, who cried, "Woe is me, for I am ruined! Because I am a man of unclean lips, and I live among a people of unclean lips; for my eyes have seen the King, the Lord of hosts" (Isa. 6:5). The apostle Paul experienced a sense of the same as he wrote, "But if all prophesy, and an unbeliever or an ungifted man enters, he is convicted by all, he is called to account by all; the secrets of his heart are disclosed; and so he will fall on his face and worship God, declaring that God is certainly among you" (1 Cor. 14:24-25). The presence of God in worship is a prophetic call whereby sins are disclosed, sinners are convicted, and God is exalted.[16]

Pentecostals very well understand that worship is, as Wayne Grudem explains, something we do especially when we come into God's presence, when we are conscious of adoration of him in our hearts, and when we praise him with our voices and speak about him so others may hear. Paul encourages the Christians in Colossae, "Let the word of Christ dwell in you richly, teach and admonish one another in all wisdom, and sing psalms and hymns and spiritual songs with thankfulness in your hearts to God" (Col. 3:16).[17] The elements of worship that are mentioned here, singing spiritual songs, singing in tongues,

---

[14] Alexander, *Signs & Wonders*, 23.

[15] Alexander, *Signs & Wonders*, 21.

[16] Dan Tomberlin, "Pentecostal Worship: The Spirit in the Sacraments", in *Issues in Contemporary Pentecostalism*, edited by R. Keith Whitt & French L. Arrington (Cleveland, Tennessee: Pathway Press, 2012), 246-247.

[17] Wayne Grudem, *Systematic Theology: An Introduction to Bible Doctrine* (Leicester: IVP, 1994), 880.

teaching, admonitions take place in the Pentecostal worship. Hence, Pentecostals believe that their worship is based on the practice of the early Church and they have attempted to adopt principles of worship that they have identified in the NT, especially where these relate to opportunities for all to participate, in ways that are meaningful, edifying and honouring of the group (1 Cor. 14:26). The Spirit is identified as the one who facilitates worship.[18]

God Encounter in Worship

Another crucial characteristic of Pentecostal worship is, it creates a context for God encounter. Albrecht claims that Pentecostal worship is "designed to provide a context for a mystical encounter, an experience with the divine. This encounter is mediated by the sense of the immediate divine presence."[19] This claim would readily be agreed by Pentecostal believers as in each aspect of Pentecostal services, whether it is singing of songs, testimonies, messages or the Lord's Supper, they anticipate divine encounter. Ask a Pentecostal believer about the ultimate purpose of participating a worship; s/he would emphasis the desire to experience God. A service, which does not yield this Godly experience, whether it is singing, message or any other activities be counted as "lifeless" and mere "human". Albrecht says, "Pentecostals believe that God "desires to meet with His people"...God will encounter God's people. This understanding moulds the style and structure of the ritual and informs the symbol of worship as a type of encounter with hierophany (manifestation of the sacred)."[20] Therefore, every worship is a festival, a joyous celebration. In this encounter, Pentecostals receive new vitality and new perspective about life and answer for their nagging troubles. Quoting a former drug addict in Honk Kong, Miller says that in Pentecostal worship one doesn't simply sing about God and Jesus, but "touch" God. Pentecostal worship is not a matter of mere cognitive assent to theological propositions. It is an experience of allowing oneself to feel the presence of God, and for this reason worship is a full-bodied expression.[21]

For Pentecostals, "worship" is another way of saying "presence of God", says Albrecht. "Worship" functions as a code term. For many, it refers to the encounter with the divine as mediated by a sense of the divine presence or power. Pentecostals believe strongly in the manifest presence of God. Their experience of the holy presence shapes them spiritually. Forms of musical expressions, including powerfully suggestive symbolic worship choruses and verbal and kinesthetic praise

---

[18] Warrington, *Pentecostal Theology*, 220.

[19] Daniel E. Albrecht, "Pentecostal Spirituality: Looking Through the Lens of Ritual", *Pneuma* 14 (1992): 121.

[20] Daniel E. Albrecht, "Pentecostal Spirituality: Ecumenical Potential and Challenge", *Cyber Journal for Pentecostal Charismatic Research,* http://www.pctii.org/cyberj/cyberj2/albrecht.html (accessed 12/10/19).

[21] Miller & Yamamori, *Global Pentecostalism*, 138.

practices serve to "trigger" a sense of close presence, a hierophany. Within the milieu of hierophany, the Pentecostals encounter and experience the divine.[22] As the New Testament underlines, this God encounter happens through the agency of the Spirit and brings transformation in the lives of the worshippers - "Now the Lord is the Spirit, and where the Spirit of the Lord is, there is freedom. And we all, who with unveiled faces contemplate the Lord's glory, are being transformed into his image with ever-increasing glory, which comes from the Lord, who is the Spirit" (2 Cor. 3:17-18). Moreover, for Pentecostals, God is the audience and the congregation is to perform the drama of praise. For as they say, "God inhabits the praises of His people". This "performance" for the ritualists represents a way of attending to God, a way of focusing on the divine, a "ministry to God."[23] Miller also points to the same understanding, "The assumption was that God was present, enabling direct communication with the transcendent. God was not a concept or a being who dwells somewhere in the stratosphere. He was there in the midst of these people."[24]

For Pentecostals the church building or setting comes as secondary but the encounter experience is the significant part in the worship. In the early part of the movement, Pentecostals did not have proper structures to gather for worship. They usually hired small houses, or even conducted worship in *veranda* of some believers. Even today this is the case in many parts of India. As apostle John foresees the New Testament worship, it was not the place or the structure but "the true worshipers will worship the Father in the Spirit and in truth, for they are the kind of worshipers the Father seeks. God is Spirit, and his worshipers must worship in the Spirit and in truth" (Jn. 4:23-24).

For the poor and the downtrodden, struggling with life's predicament, the assurance of the presence of God and the immediate experience make a huge difference. For them it is a life changing moment, a transformative time that produces a range of responses. Robeck describes a worship that he witnessed and its liberative effects:

> There were those who ... broke into dance. Others jumped, or stood with hands outstretched, or sang or shouted with all the gusto they could muster. Others were so full of awe when they encountered God that their knees fell on the floor, "slain in the Spirit". Some spoke, rapid-fire, in a tongue they did not know, while others were struck entirely..... The ecstatic ritual practices were generally seen

---

[22] Albrecht, "Pentecostal Spirituality: Ecumenical Potential and Challenge".

[23] Albrecht, "Pentecostal Spirituality: Ecumenical Potential and Challenge".

[24] Miller & Yamamori, *Global Pentecostalism*, 131.

as "a symbolic rebellion on the part of socially disenfranchised Pentecostals."[25]

Having observed Pentecostal churches world over, Miller shows the liberative nature of encounter experience in the Pentecostal worship. According to him, deep within all of us is undoubtedly a desire to be free, unguarded, and open with our emotions, since the responsibilities of ordinary life tend to require a certain degree of restraint. However, worship for Pentecostals creates these moments on a regular basis, where they can step outside the boundaries of the usual polarities. The lid can be taken off our repressive tendencies; public worship is a safe place to realize the unity of mind, body, and spirit. Emotions can flow, and in fact tears of joy, tears of sorrow, and tears of healing often intermingle in Pentecostal worship. In this blending, there is a momentary forgetfulness about the body, so that it is no wonder that people dance, fall down prostrate before God, and lift their hands high in celebration.[26] Furthermore, the energy released during worship is closely akin to what psychiatrists refer to as the libidinal force of life. It is a resource that can be channelled for good. The joy and exuberance that Pentecostal worship sometimes generates may also have a renewing and energizing effect on individuals that potentially translates into compassionate service to others.[27]

Spirit Experience in Worship

Another unique nature of Pentecostal worship is its emphasis on the work of the Spirit. Pentecostalism is a Spirit movement; therefore, Pentecostals favour a worship in which the Spirit moves. For Pentecostals, worship means experiencing the Holy Spirit in the fellowship of the Church.[28] The Pentecostal churches that were organized during the first decades of the 20th century place emphasis on the work of the Holy Spirit in worship. The central focus of the service is not the sermon or the music, but the moving of the Holy Spirit. There is the expectation that God will minister in love to the worshiper through the agency of the Holy Spirit.[29] Pentecostals consider their worship as Spirit-filled. People expect every aspect of the worship to be led by the Spirit. The very basic expressions of Spirit-filled worship are Spirit movement, passionate praise, emotional release, and spiritual gifts in operation, make its expression a transformative, vibrant,

---

[25] Wolfgang Vondey, *Beyond Pentecostalism: The Crisis of Global Christianity and the Renewal of the Theological Agenda* (Michigan: Eerdmans, 2010), 148-149.

[26] Miller & Yamamori, *Global Pentecostalism*, 141-142.

[27] Miller & Yamamori, *Global Pentecostalism*, 142.

[28] Dan Tomberlin, *Encountering God at the Altar: The Sacraments in Pentecostal Worship* (Cleveland, TN: Center for Pentecostal Leadership and Care, 2006), 13.

[29] J. W. Shepperd, "Worship", in *NIDPCM*, edited by Stanley M. Burgess (Michigan: Zondervan, 2002). 1219.

and moving encounter with the divine.[30] Moreover, the Spirit-filled worship is dualistic in nature which is portrayed by the Scriptures. It recognizes and affirms the 'in-breaking' of the consummated kingdom into the immediate space-time reality in which the church lives. Spirit-filled worship is marked and characterized by a vivid awareness of the presence of God and the activity of the Holy Spirit within the lives of the saints and within the context of the worship experience.[31]

What distinguishes Pentecostal worship from that of other traditional denominations is this atmosphere in which the Holy Spirit is expected to move in visible and sometimes even 'violent' ways. Asamoah-Gyadu beautifully depicts 'signs of the Spirit' within early renewal movements in Africa:

> [Rhythmic] swaying of the body, usually with stamping, to repetitious music (both vocal and instrumental, particularly percussion), hand-clapping, ejaculations, poignant cries and prayers, dancing, leaping and various motor reactions expressive of intense religious emotion; prophesying, speaking in tongues, falling into trances, relating dreams and visions, and witnessing, i.e., recounting publicly one's own experience of miraculous redemption.[32]

Pentecostal gatherings, as evidenced in the description above, can be characterized by emotional cries and sobbing, moans, spontaneous prayers and sober and reflective moments. In those reflective moments people stand still to hear the voice of the Spirit relayed in prophetic messages, revelations and words of knowledge. Sometimes in the quietness of Pentecostal worship, the Spirit suddenly feels like a blowing wind knocking people off their feet and throwing them on to the floor. Such catharsis empowerment are considered to be signs of the presence of the Spirit of God.[33]

Another significant aspect in Spirit experience in worship is the use of spiritual gifts, such as tongue speaking, prophecy, vision, healing, exorcism and so on. Occasionally, someone would stand and give a prophecy during the middle of the service, typically in tongues, and then an interpretation would follow. A more common phenomenon is healing. The pastor would ask individuals to come forward for prayer. He would then inquire about their specific need and place his hands on them, asking God to cure their infirmity.[34] Speaking in tongues constitutes the most common supernatural event take place

---

[30] Johnathan E. Alvarado, "Worship in the Spirit: Pentecostal Perspectives on Liturgical Theology and Praxis", *JPT* 21 (2012): 139.

[31] Alvarado, "Worship in the Spirit", 143.

[32] J. Kwabena Asamoah-Gyadu, "'You Shall Receive Power': Empowerment in Pentecostal/Charismatic Christianity", in *Pentecostal Mission and Global Christianity*, edited by Wonsuk Ma, Veli-Matti Kärkkäinen & J. Kwabena Asamoah-Gyadu (Oxford, UK: Regnum Books International), 46.

[33] Asamoah-Gyadu, "'You Shall Receive Power'", 46.

[34] Miller & Yamamori, *Global Pentecostalism*, 149.

in Pentecostal worship services. Harvey Cox captures the relevance of *glossolalia* as a distinctive mode of religious expression for Pentecostal worship:

> Not only is the ultimate mystery indescribable and its ways unsearchable. Not only is the infinite God unapproachable in mere human language. The even deeper insight of ecstatic utterance is that, despite all this, human beings can nonetheless speak to God because God makes such speech possible. Prayer itself is an act of grace. We are unable to pray, but the Spirit 'maketh intercession'. Our corrupt and inadequate language is transformed by God's love into the tongues of angel...the 'excruciating pain' of linguistic atrophy, desiccation, and banality is transfigured, if only momentarily and episodically, into free flowing praise. No wonder the people one sees and hears 'praying in the Spirit' in Pentecostal congregations and elsewhere frequently appear so joyful.[35]

It is not only speaking in tongues but sometimes Pentecostal congregations break into "singing in tongues" or "singing in the Spirit". This is singing in tongues by a number of persons at the same time. Pentecostals repeatedly described the event as one of unearthly beauty. The "singing in tongues" can lift both the singer and the listeners to another level of spiritual experience. It is an overwhelming and edifying experience that makes the presence of God palpable. The phenomenon changes the atmosphere of worship to the extent that the very presence of the living God becomes real. The biblical justification for this practice has been the interpretation of Paul's statement in 1 Corinthians 14:15, "I will sing with my spirit, but I will also sing with my mind". Although, this may happen only infrequently and only last for a short time, in its purest form, the rising cadences of a gathered body of believers singing unlearnt songs in a 'heavenly language' is genuinely moving and impressive. It has been at these times that people have been able to sense God's presence.[36] Smail explains the transformative potentials of singing in the Spirit:

> Singing in the Spirit by-passes the rational faculties; it reminds us that alongside the praise of the renewed mind there is the praise of the renewed heart that, when it is being evoked by the Spirit, expresses not simply our superficial feelings, but engages the deep primal emotions at the hidden centre of our being in our self-offering to the living God. Such praise is direct, spontaneous and simple. It escapes from a complicated conceptuality and a second-hand dependence on such liturgical resources as prayer-books and hymn-books, and responds in

[35] Cox, *Fire from Heaven*, 96.

[36] Hudson, "Worship: Singing a New Song in a Strange Land", 190; Grant Wacker, *Heaven Below: Early Pentecostals and American Culture* (London: Harvard University Press, 2001), 110.

> immediacy and freedom to the contact with the loving Lord that the Spirit makes possible and, in joyous serenity, rejoices in and meditates upon his poured out grace and his revealed glory.[37]

Another phenomena that happens in Pentecostal worship, especially in neo-Pentecostal churches is known as 'slain in the Spirit'. From the earliest days, some believers have on occasion fallen to the floor in a virtual faint while being prayed for. Various terminologies have been used such as 'slain in the Spirit,' 'resting in the Spirit', 'falling under the power'. Hudson explains that this occurrence brings release to the believers. For the individual concerned, it can best be described as a relaxing of all the muscles. While on the floor, the individual concerned may be conscious of what is happening around them, but they may also be receiving a sense of God ministering to them, imparting a sense of peace or power. In certain cases, this may be accompanied by shaking, laughter or crying. In each case, it is assumed that the Holy Spirit is doing a specific work of release in the believer's life.[38]

Music in Worship

Singing and music play significant role in Pentecostal worship and can be termed as the lifeline of the worship services. In the singing session, people not only praise God but unburden themselves of their troubles. The singing time is considered as the moment in which people freely enter into the act of worship, by singing in tongues, shouting praises and experience the touch of the Holy Spirit. It is the time Pentecostal believers declare their love towards Christ through openly expressing their feeling, and through their melodious voice and words. Music in Pentecostal worship is often very personal in terms of endearment and communication between the singer and God and songs are increasingly viewed as vehicles for people to communicate directly with God. The songs have increasingly taken the form of more directional expressions to God than doctrinal reflections on his character. They function as modern day psalms expressing a wide range of emotions, requests and statements of praise to God.[39]

Additionally, the Pentecostal singing is marked by wide participation. Singing is a community affair where believers in unison declare their allegiance to Christ and dedicate their self to his lordship. There is action from beginning to end and it is in large part a musical service. Throughout there is much singing and when people sing, they sing not only with their voices but with their hands, and their feet and their bodies. Bruner comment, "The songs and choruses

---

[37] T. Smail, A. Walker & N. Wright, *Charismatic Renewal: The Search for a Theology* (London: SPCK, 1993), 110; Hudson, "Worship: Singing a New Song", 190.

[38] Hudson, "Worship: Singing a New Song", 192.

[39] Warrington, *Pentecostal Theology*, 224.

usually constitute the liturgical element of the Pentecostal meeting."[40] Besides, as Alexander observes, "Pentecostal worship music often has drums, electric guitars, horns, pianos, tambourines, and any other instrument that somebody has and wants to play. People clap their hands and move to the music. There's sometimes dancing, there's almost always hugging, and it's OK to connect your head with your heart."[41] Pentecostal worship music is the kind of music that expresses the feelings that people have for God and for those around them. Pentecostal worship seems to affect people in deep and special ways; it touches them. It releases feelings and emotions that are perhaps suppressed or hidden or unacknowledged. Pentecostals create safe environments in which to worship where feelings are honoured and respected, where the struggles and ideas and sentiments of working-class folk are not discredited.[42]

Most Pentecostals around the world are working-class, not elites, and they come from the less privileged classes, who work physically hard in unrewarding jobs. Tex Sample, a theologian and sociologist, has shown that upper-class people evaluate and enjoy music differently than working-class people do. Their tastes and style are distant, detached, disinterested, and indifferent "to the emotional impact of music". They're cool, removed, and "objective"; art is thought to be an end in itself.[43] However, working-class music taste is rather different and comes at the opposite spectrum. Pentecostal worship, like working-class taste, is "rowdy and loud, celebrates in festivity or moans the hard times, revels in active participation and physical enjoyment or laments loss, that is plain speaking and expressed in hearty laughter or tears and despair, that will often mock and debase elitist expressions.[44]

Nel says that music is rhetoric and a viable language that has been used to embody theology for many centuries, enabling theological reflection to get away from argumentative controversy generated by doctrines. The reason is that music has the ability to carry emotional meanings where semantic parameters are less critical. And forms of musical expression including suggestive, symbolic worship, choruses and verbal praise practices serve to trigger a close sense of God's presence.[45]

As we know, a major portion of the Bible contains songs and singing. All the people, tribes, languages, and nations are exhorted to worship and serve the Lord through singing. The songs in the Bible present a theology of adoration

---

[40] Frederick Dale Bruner, *A Theology of the Holy Spirit: The Pentecostal Experience and the New Testament Witness* (Michigan: Eerdmans Publishing, 1970), 133,

[41] Alexander, *Signs & Wonders*, 21.

[42] Alexander, *Signs & Wonders*, 31-32.

[43] Alexander, *Signs & Wonders*, 26.

[44] Alexander, *Signs & Wonders*, 29.

[45] Marius Nel, "Attempting to develop a Pentecostal theology of worship", *Verbum et Ecclesia* 37(1), 2016, a1661. https://doi.org/10.4102/ve.v37i1.1661 (accessed 2/10/19).

and exaltation of God-head. They manifest his majesty and sovereignty over all the creations. As Pentecostals sing and worship, it not mere shouting or venting out their emotions rather they proclaim and establish the supremacy the Lord, thus forming a theology. In addition, the Scripture portrays that music can soothe mental disturbances caused by evil spirits (in the case King Saul, 1 Sam. 16:14-23). Prophet Elisha asked for a musician to play to receive a revelation (2 Kings 3: 15). Thus, music has close affinity with emotional and spiritual healing and illumination. This last aspect of music, healing and illumination are well established in the Pentecostal singing. "Singing in Pentecostal worship offers spiritual therapy", says Kgatle. Since, Pentecostal worship is Spirit worship, it connects to the spiritual well-being of the members. Through the agency of the Spirit, the singing becomes a means of grace, and in many instances of therapy. This is similar to preaching, the presence and working of the Spirit is the constituting factor changing a ritual into a life-transforming event and serving to instruct, exhort and model the life of faith.[46] Singing has the potential to heal physical ailments in a Pentecostal service; the more people sing, the more they attract the power of God to heal any physical ailment. Singing is the source of a strong positive experience. Positive experiences are very important in life; they provide the power and motivation to do something less pleasant.[47] Nonetheless, in Pentecostal worship, singing is more than a positive experience; it is a spiritual activity that is able to deal with physical, emotional and spiritual problems. Thus, in Pentecostal worship singing plays a key role in the experience of renewal and liberation.

Physical Expressions in Worship

Along with music, it is significant to have a look at physical expressions in Pentecostal worship. In Pentecostal worship, actions like dancing, clapping and raising of hands and shouting praises in top voices are usual sight. In other times, being moved by the Spirit believers have the experience of shaking of their bodies, jumping, speaking in tongues, ecstasy and so on. Pentecostal churches have the freedom to have physical expressions in the singing session and such experiences are highly priced. Such spontaneity in worship attract outsiders, especially youths. Pentecostal worship expresses the feeling and belief that God is alive, Jesus is here with us right now, and we can celebrate! Pentecostal worship does not feel like it's just an ancient faith, thousands of years old; it feels like a faith that is in touch with a living God who is accessible immediately. The vibrant singing and worship reflect this closeness and reality.[48] Additionally, the spontaneity of Pentecostal

---

[46] Nel, "Attempting to develop a Pentecostal theology of worship".

[47] Mookgo S. Kgatle, "Singing as a Therapeutic Agent in Pentecostal Worship", *Verbum Ecclesia* (Online) 40/1 Pretoria, 2019; http://www.scielo.org.za/scielo.php?script=sci_arttext&pid =S2074-77052019000100006 (accessed 2/10/19).

[48] Alexander, *Signs & Wonders*, 20.

worship with its emphasis on oral and narrative expressions of praise and dynamic preaching has resulted in Pentecostalism more easily being accommodated into a range of different settings than a more liturgically based spirituality might allow. The Pentecostal emphasis on freedom initiated by the Spirit which encourages all participants to engage with God personally has further enhanced the attractiveness of Pentecostal spirituality.[49]

Pentecostals carry out their worship not in their spirits only, the body is also employed in full force. 'Dancing in the Spirit' has a long tradition within Pentecostalism, always done for the Lord, never for effect; and if done 'in the Spirit', never viewed as provocative. The raising of hands is seen as a symbol of submission and receptivity. As Pentecostals raise their hands, the worshippers are able to express their need of the Spirit and receive him afresh into their lives.[50] A profound theology undergirds such worship expressions. The worshippers declare that their bodies are the temple of Holy Spirit and God has the total control of their spirits and physical bodies. Here through their bodies they glorify God. Alexander brings out further theological dimensions:

> Even though Pentecostalism should not be reduced to religious sensuality, its music and worship style show that God is OK with the human body. In fact, God is so OK with the human body that God "incarnated" — God became flesh, meat, human. Incarnation is an important idea when it comes to worship because God became a body, not just a brain.[51]

Alexander continues, "Moving your body is getting closer to incarnation, for the Spirit has all of you, your whole body—you are *filled* with the Spirit, and all of you, even your emotions and meat, is worshiping God. We are physical and emotional beings, not just thinking brains. Pentecostalism creates space for a full human experience, even for people to dance. Pentecostals' 'exuberant, expressive worship' is about praising with our whole selves."[52]

The feature of spontaneity has sometimes resulted in Pentecostal worship being informal and on rare occasions, disorderly. Nevertheless, Pentecostals would rather run the risk of making mistakes in worship in their exuberance than restrict the Spirit from doing that which he wants on account of a desire for propriety. Although, they aim for balance, they recognize that when a sovereign God interacts with flawed humanity, the result may not be that which the believers anticipated.[53] Harvey Cox views spontaneity in Pentecostal worship as a cure for the maladies of crushing poverty and bewildering chaos of globalised world, thus

---

[49] Warrington, *Pentecostal Theology*, 255.

[50] Hudson, "Worship: Singing a New Song", 189.

[51] Alexander, *Signs & Wonders*, 23.

[52] Alexander, *Signs & Wonders*, 24.

[53] Warrington, *Pentecostal Theology*, 223.

leading them to liberation and transformation. For the poor, "Pentecostal worship with its ear-splitting noise and tumultuous prayer is something of a homeopathic cure. It invites people to plunge into the chaos in order to overcome it, by the power of the Holy Spirit."[54] It offers the possibility of an experience with God that will touch the emotions of people and respond to their aspirations while also promising an eternal dimension that will rescue them from all that imprisons and oppresses them in the present. It is in this regard that Pentecostals may be offering something primal with regard to spirituality in its ecstatic form, a dimension that is dynamically present in Pentecostal worship.[55]

Prayer in Worship

Prayer is one of the most vital elements of Pentecostal worship. Communal prayer in the form of praise, petition and intercession stays as the backbone of worship sessions. Every member in the congregation engages in prayer and special time is separated for intercession for personal and communal needs. Special prayers are offered for mission activities, persecuted Christians, affairs of the society, local government and the world. Miller rightly observes,

> Pentecostal churches are filled with sound at prayer. There is no lack of vital congregational participation in this important activity. The prayer, too, borders constantly on ecstasy; one or both hands are often raised in petition or praise, very often the entire congregation descends to its knees. The Pentecostal church is a house of prayer for all members.[56]

Unlike the beautifully scripted prayers of the Anglicans, Catholics, and others who have compiled prayers in books that are appropriate to every season of the calendar year as well as every moment of the liturgy, there is something primitive and personal about the prayers of Pentecostals. They tend to flow from the heart, expressing spontaneous feelings of praise as well as the deepest anguish of the heart.[57] This cathartic role of prayer is not simply an emotional outlet only. Prayer in Pentecostal churches have liberative and transformational effects. It has empowering quality. Miller explains the way prayer works for believers and lead them into transformation:

> By sharing their burdens with others, individuals often gain new strength and energy to deal with the problems of life. The shared burden is no longer their personal problem; their concerns have been offloaded to God and, less directly, to the community. For Pentecostals

---

[54] Harvey Cox, Quoted in Warrington, *Pentecostal Theology*, 252.

[55] Warrington, *Pentecostal Theology*, 256.

[56] Bruner, *A Theology of the Holy Spirit*, 134.

[57] Miller & Yamamori, *Global Pentecostalism*, 145.

> who believe that they are God's hands and feet in the world, clearly the body of believers is not off the hook; they must exercise their faith, which means that they pray for the sick, take them to the hospital, and act as responsible members of the body of believers.[58]

Community Formation in Worship

One of the far-reaching effects of Pentecostal worship is its inherent power of community forming. In Pentecostal churches all are welcomed, irrespective of caste, religion, nationality, language, the rich and the poor alike. Pentecostals expect new people to join their worship services; believers are overjoyed if non believers are turned up. In the formative years of Pentecostalism in India, people from every caste group joined Pentecostal movement. Higher castes and lower castes, the rich and the poor gathered together to experience the move of the Spirit. They became one family. It was not a planned social programme but the egalitarian impulses were formed in the worship context. It created a foretaste of kingdom fellowship which transcended human made social and cultural boundaries of caste prejudices and superiority complexes. It was like the early church where the barriers between the rich and poor, men and women, the slave and the free were broken down. However, these barriers were broken down not logically nor on the basis of a social theory, but in the actual event of worship.[59] Worship has the potential to energize and transform people. Rather than following their own self-interest, believers view themselves as agents of God, carrying out his will and desire for their lives. Worship is a communal activity. Fulfilling one's call does not depend on heroic individualism; one is part of a community—an organ within the collective "body" of Christ.[60]

Martin explains how the egalitarian ideals are created in a Pentecostal community. He views the Pentecostal community as a haven where liberative and transformative affections are created. He notes that these havens provide for the dispossessed 'a new cell taking over from scarred and broken tissue'. Within these new cells, a 'new faith is able to implant new disciplines, re-order priorities, counter corruption and destructive machismo, and reverse the indifferent and injurious hierarchies of the outside world'. Within these havens, a person may re-invent himself or herself in an atmosphere of fraternal support.[61] The fellowship and closer bond that created in the worship points to the future hope that God is going to establish at the return of Christ. Having already experienced a taste

[58] Miller & Yamamori, *Global Pentecostalism*, 146.

[59] Cheryl Bridges Johns, *Pentecostal Formation: A Pedagogy Among the Oppressed* (Eugene, OR: Wipf and Stock Publishers, 2010), 90.

[60] Miller & Yamamori, *Global Pentecostalism*, 133.

[61] Bridges Johns, *Pentecostal Formation,* 98; David Martin, *Tongues of Fire: The Explosion of Protestantism in Latin America* (New Jersey: Willey Blackwell, 1993), 284-88.

of the not yet eschatological future of God's reign, the Pentecostal community becomes both "a sign" of the presence of the kingdom and "a signpost" to the future consummation of the kingdom.[62]

Furthermore, the spiritual and community affections formed in the worship context impel Pentecostal believers to go out and serve the larger world. Worship creates an altered perception of realities around the worshippers. Often they dive into daring actions around them which may not be done in a natural course of action. Having received power for mission, many have involved in ministries among the poor and downtrodden. Miller affirms, "It is strongly believed that the root of Pentecostal social engagement is the experience of collective worship. It is the divine-human encounter that empowers people to help their immediate neighbour as well as engage in various community building activities. It is also this encounter that humbles people, enabling them to be, in the view of believers, the servant of others."[63] This social mission is capable of giving a new hope to a hopeless world. In the context of injustice, violence and hatred, Pentecostals can impart meaning to the life of many in a broken world with the warmth they receive from the worship.

Having seen the unique features of Pentecostal worship, now we shall look into some of the areas where Pentecostals need corrections. A keen observation of the worship would reveal some of the unhealthy trends that crept in among the Pentecostals. Outward expressions, emotionalism and high octane sound-bites are sometimes mistaken as the Spirit-move. Over emphasis on such human elements can spoil the original fervour and affection that are inherent in Pentecostal worship, which in turn may reduce the liberative potentials. Therefore, Pentecostals should always be vigilant and take extra efforts so that worship may not fall into human realm. Here we shall look into some of the pitfalls that plague the movement in its worship.

First of all, current models of worship in Pentecostal churches is usually organized around the singing of praises, which is termed as 'prayer and praise' or 'praise and worship'. As Simon Chan cautions, when worship is largely reduced to a string of praise ditties, the aim of worship subtly shifts from encountering God to mood creation and possibly psychological manipulation. A deep sense of reverence and the theological virtues of faith, hope and charity may be ignored. Worshippers are worked up or are told to work themselves up to have faith for one thing or another, especially healing. They are told that if only they really believe,

---

[62] Murray W. Dempster, "Evangelism, Social Concern, and the Kingdom of God", in *Called & Empowered: Global Mission in Pentecostal Perspective*, edited by Murray W. Dempster, Byron D. Klaus & Douglas Petersen (Michigan: Baker Academic, 1991), 36.

[63] Miller & Yamamori, *Global Pentecostalism*, 133.

the Lord will answer their prayer, that if they are not healed, it is a sign that they lack faith.[64]

Secondly, the tendency of many Pentecostals to assume that a highly emotional expression in worship automatically signals the presence and power of the Holy Spirit. Many congregations seem to be practicing what Kraft calls "emotional ritual". It is known that some Pentecostal leaders are teaching that until people have "worked themselves up" to a certain emotional level, the Holy Spirit will not begin his work. People need to know that the Holy Spirit is not so bound to one particular form of behaviour, be it emotion or non-emotion, as to require us to work ourselves up to get him to appear. According to Kraft, in fact often God's working is blocked in a person until he or she calms down emotionally.[65]

Thirdly, in the din and emotional expressions, at times, one can miss the real adoration and worship. Kraft notes that when Pentecostals gather, they are often very good at praising but not so good at worshiping. Pentecostals have the tradition of emphasising on praise of God, sometimes loudly and usually joyously. But the quieter, more devotional expressions of our adoration is often not so prominent in much of Pentecostal worship. This too is important, perhaps even more important than the louder expressions. Pentecostals should not miss the opportunity to add quiet devotion to the loud praise.[66]

Another pitfall that usually infects Pentecostal worship is the danger of triumphalism. Many a time, the contents of the songs sung generally refer to instantaneous change that leaves little room for a recognition that, for many people, change is a gradual process. Similarly, there is little understanding that for many Christians, there are periods of 'the dark night of the soul' when it is difficult to sense the presence of God at all.[67] As a result, people can end up living in a state of dualism. They can be experiencing the most difficult problems, and yet in church be singing of the potential of the Lord's deliverance and freedom from their problems. For some people, this dichotomy is described as 'speaking out in faith' the desires of one's heart, whilst believing that God will respond to such certainty; for others, it is viewed as living in denial. As Hudson affirms, "Our worship needs to be honest, expressing life as it is, not just as we wish it were. Biblically, alongside the psalms of glorious victory and procession, are the psalms of darkness and abandonment. Worship that is 'in spirit and in truth' must reflect both these experiences."[68] Another concern is related to

---

[64] Simon Chan, *Pentecostal Theology and the Christian Spiritual Tradition* (Sheffield: Sheffield Academic Press, 2000), 37.

[65] Charles H. Kraft, "A Third Wave Perspective on Pentecostal Missions", in *Called & Empowered*, 223.

[66] Kraft, "A Third Wave Perspective on Pentecostal Missions", 226.

[67] Hudson, "Worship: Singing a New Song", 196.

[68] Hudson, "Worship: Singing a New Song", 197.

the singing, is the fact that earlier hymns expressed a wide range of doctrinal truths and personal experiences of joy and sadness, hope and confusion, a close awareness of God and a sense of abandonment by God, triumph and fear, health and sickness. Many modern songs, however, are triumphant and even triumphalistic. Sometimes such an attitude results in a view of spiritual encounter with the devil in which songs is sung and can be assumed to be achieving spiritual victories. However, as Hudson puts it, "To presume that, because we are singing about spiritual warfare, we are actually engaged in it is fallacious."[69]

The danger of individualism is another mistake that crept into Pentecostal worship. The focus for many of the worship songs is the individual believer's personal walk with God, and so intercession can become limited to wholly personal matters, often relating to healing and wholeness. This tendency may insulate us from the pain that people bear and the situations that seem hopeless, even as we claim to be using the gifts of power and proclaim God's victory. It is significant to identify with those who suffer just as Christ suffered on the cross for others.[70] Finally, very often the Pentecostal worship becomes too expert or leader-centered. This is neither biblical nor healthy. God gives gifts to everyone, not simply to those who have been installed in certain offices. The doctrines of the "priesthood of all believers" (1 Pet. 2:5, 9) and the distribution of gifts to each of God's people (1 Cor. 12:6–7) should be carefully adhered to.[71]

Let us conclude here. We have glanced some of the unique characteristics of Pentecostal worship which brings liberation and transformation to the worshippers and also act as catalyst for the growth of the movement. The elements of worship such as Spirit experience and singing and music, vibrancy, prayer and so on provide the believers with spiritual strength, emotional release and stability and physical healing. The strength and vitality received through encounter experience empower believers to involve in God intended tasks in a broken world. Even though these factors root the movement in a unique position among other Christian denominations, at times over hype, emotionalism and human elements overtake the real reverence and act of worship. Occasionally worship slips into show off instead of divine presence and Spirit-move. Hence, Pentecostals need to take extra care to keep a healthy balance between deeply anchored spiritual fervour and a sane physical and emotional involvement, without discarding the vibrancy and exuberance of their worship. At any cost, the liberative and transformative nature of Pentecostal worship should not be missed or abandoned.

---

[69] Hudson, "Worship: Singing a New Song", 197.

[70] Hudson, "Worship: Singing a New Song", 200-201.

[71] Kraft, "A Third Wave Perspective on Pentecostal Missions", 224.

Chapter 8

Preaching and Testimony Communications for Liberation

Preaching is one of the most significant elements in Pentecostal spirituality and continuous to play a major role in the formation and rapid growth of the Pentecostal movement all over the world. Through preaching, Pentecostals disseminate the message of salvation, deliverance and eternal hope, bring many to their churches. In addition, Pentecostal preaching acts as a liberative communication in the majority world context where people suffer diseases, attack of evil spirits, poverty and oppression. The Pentecostal message of deliverance and blessing combined with signs and wonders such as miraculous healing, exorcisms and other gifts of the Spirit, attract afflicted populace into the Pentecostal fold. The dramatic style of preachers and storytelling method capture the attention of anyone who happens to just hear them. It is not only the style and method but the gospel message is presented with power and authority of the Holy Spirit that convicts people and change their lives.

Similarly, sharing of testimony is a vital way of communicating Pentecostal message to others. It is the testimonies shared by ordinary Pentecostals that enabled the Pentecostal movement to rapidly grow in the third world situation. Having experienced salvation and power of the Spirit, men and women, educated and uneducated, all alike share what they experienced in their lives. They share the miraculous healing they experienced, a deliverance through prayer and blessings received by faith to neighbours and friends. Such testimonies attract people who are going through sickness and other maladies and they join Pentecostal churches and receive recovery from their struggles. This method ushered Pentecostal growth in Indian context. Thus, Pentecostal preaching and sharing of testimonies can be termed as means of communication for liberation.

Anointed preaching, backed up by supernatural manifestations is the hallmark of Pentecostal movement and can be termed as its basic spirituality. F. J. May affirms that anointed preaching is the best possible method of quickening the pace of God's work in the world. Church history shows us again and again that in times of great revivals and spiritual renewals, powerful preaching has been a vital part of the movement.[1] Besides, the Pentecostal movement in its early decades was driven by a fervent eschatological expectation of the soon-coming kingdom of God. Therefore, proclamation gained the forefront of a vigorous effort to evangelize the world before the arrival of Christ in judgment and salvation.[2] Pentecostal preachers have been certain of their call. They have unwavering faith in the word of God and have relied totally on the power of the Holy Spirit to enable them to have effective delivery. As a result, Pentecostals have the fastest growing churches in the world. Ray H. Hughes, former president of the Church of God School of Theology in Cleveland, Tennessee, and a Pentecostal preacher of worldwide renown, says, "The man of God who is called and anointed of the Holy Spirit, and who will faithfully yield to the leading of the Spirit, has the same commission and enablement as was given the disciples of old."[3] A closer look at fast growing Pentecostal churches today would reveal that behind the aggressive evangelistic activity there is divinely inspired and anointed preaching, based on a sound theology, with a strong emphasis on the transforming power of the Word of God.[4]

Pentecostal and Charismatic preaching is a type of preaching that is different from all other forms of preaching. It is an approach to preaching that is not based on modern communication and homiletical theory, but instead draws out homiletical and hermeneutical principles found in Scripture. This approach is as old as the Bible itself and it does give missionaries and pastors homiletical and hermeneutical principles in preaching the gospel. Moreover, Pentecostals have a holistic approach to preaching and make their model the preaching ministry of Jesus and the apostles. It is a fresh yet old approach to preaching that has the potential to change one's preaching ministry. The Pentecostal approach to preaching has already proven its value to the Christian church by its growth.[5]

---

[1] F.J. May, "Supernatural Anointing and Church Growth", in *Church Growth the State of Art,* edited by C. Peter Wagner, Win Arn & Elmer L. Towns (Virginia: Liberty University, 1986), 140

[2] Frank D. Macchia, "The Struggle for Global Witness: Shifting Paradigms in Pentecostal Theology", in *The Globalization of Pentecostalism,* edited by M.W. Dempster, B.D. Klaus & D. Petersen (Carlisle: Regnum, 1999).

[3] Ray H. Hughes, *Pentecostal Preaching* (Cleveland, Tennessee: Pathway Press, 1981), 156.

[4] May, "Supernatural Anointing and Church Growth", 141.

[5] Aldwin Ragoonath, *Preach the Word: A Pentecostal Perspective* (Winnipeg, Canada: Agape Teaching Ministry of Canada, 2004), 5.

However, some have suggested that Pentecostals do not have a systematic homiletic.[6] Even some accuse Pentecostal preaching as emotionally charged and even manipulative. For instance, Ralph Turnbull terms it as "simplistic in style, abundantly illustrated from experience, manipulative in emotional appeal …"[7] His view exemplifies the Evangelical assessment of Pentecostal preaching. Many Pentecostal educators have also viewed Pentecostal preaching with a similar suspicion, and have attempted to reshape their students into a western Evangelical image.[8] Pentecostals, nevertheless are convinced that they have their own homiletic and their own way of communicating the gospel. As Rangoonath puts it, "If homiletics is an approach to preaching which makes the word of God plain to a group of people then certainly Pentecostals have an approach to preaching."[9] What is unique about Pentecostal preaching is, it is based on non-western, nonlinear, inductive, affective, and narrative strategies.[10] In addition, as Ray Hughes asserts, Pentecostal preaching is so unique in its nature and so encompassing in its power that no word other than "supernatural" seems adequate to describe it. Pentecostal sermons accompany signs, wonders, healings, and miracles such as happened during New Testament times. Not only will Pentecostal preaching produce the same miraculous results as those recorded in the New Testament, it will always produce them in keeping with the spirit and the tone of the New Testament.[11] Moreover, for Pentecostals the New Testament preaching is their model. They look to the preaching methods of Jesus recorded in the gospels and the means and ways apostles used in the book of Acts, for form and content. Therefore, in the following pages, we shall briefly look into the preaching methods of Jesus and the apostles to see the affinity of Pentecostal preaching to them. We shall also explore the nature of Pentecostal preaching and testimony and get a glimpse of how they bring liberation to masses.

Models for Pentecostal Preaching: Preaching of Jesus and Apostles

Pentecostals mostly follow the pattern of Jesus and the apostles for their preaching. As we turn to the New Testament, we see the power of anointed preaching as manifested in the lives of John the Baptist, Jesus and the apostles. The ministry of John the Baptist was accomplished through the proclamation. The themes of his preaching such as righteousness, justice, judgement and repentance were readily

---

[6] Ragoonath, *Preach the Word,* 5.

[7] Quoted in Lee Roy Martin, "Fire in the Bones: Pentecostal Prophetic Preaching", in *Toward a Pentecostal Theology of Preaching*, edited by Lee Roy Martin (Cleveland, Tennessee: CPT Press, 2015), 6.

[8] Martin, "Fire in the Bones", 6.

[9] Ragoonath, *Preach the Word,* 6.

[10] Martin, "Fire in the Bones", 6.

[11] Ray H. Hughes, "The Uniqueness of Pentecostal Preaching", in *Azuza Street & Beyond,* 2nd edition, edited by Grant McClung (Florida: Bridge-Logos, 2012), 117.

accepted by the ordinary people. He was scathing in his attack against authorities and religious leaders who would not repent their unrighteous deeds. Though the gospels did not record any miracles in the ministry of John the Baptist, it was reported by Matthew that he came with the power of Elijah (Matt. 11:13-15; Matt. 17:12-13) to prepare a new generation for the coming of the Messiah. It was his power of preaching that melted the hearts of the people to flock around him for the baptism of repentance. Jesus highly extolled the preaching of John the Baptist and considered him as the greatest of all prophets.

Jesus can be considered as a preacher *par excellence*. Luke records that Jesus began his ministry "in the power of the Spirit" (Luke 4:14). The first ministry activity of Jesus was preaching (Mark 1:14-15). The very purpose of his mission on earth was to preach the good news of the kingdom of God; "I must proclaim the good news of the kingdom of God to the other towns also, because that is why I was sent" (Luke 4:43). Matthew also says, "Jesus went about all Galilee, teaching in their synagogues, *preaching* the gospel of the kingdom, and healing all kinds of sickness and all kinds of disease among the people" (Matthew 4:23; Luke 4:43; Luke 8:1). His ministry of healing, exorcism and other miracles were the signs of the in-breaking of the kingdom of God.

His preaching was consisted of parables and stories that connected with ordinary folks and their life situation. The stories of the sower, lost sheep and coin, distribution of talents and so on, conveyed the message of the kingdom of God through people's everyday activities. This method of preaching easily conveyed the spiritual message to uneducated and ordinary villagers. The stories of the prodigal son and the good Samaritan definitely brought a new vista in his listeners, enabling them to transcend the patriarchal and closed cultural and religious mindset of the first century Jewish society. Moreover, Jesus often shocked the people using hyperbole - such as to cut off one's hand or pluck out one's eye (Matthew 5:29-30), to convey the seriousness of the message and to get attention of the people. Jesus also preached with authority and power unlike the Jewish teachers. Multitude gathered around him of thousands by walking for miles just to hear him. His followers listened him with utmost attention for hours and even days. The main purpose of his sermon was to save the lost and bring them to the kingdom of God, thus Jesus' sermons changed lives of the people. Besides, his preaching provoked the ire of political and religious leaders and they began looking for opportunity to kill him.

More than all of these, Jesus spoke directly to people's life situation - their needs, struggles, hurts and interests. In his sermon in the synagogue of Nazareth, he preached good news to the poor; Jesus pronounced: "The Spirit of the Lord is upon me, because he anointed me to preach the gospel to the poor". Then, he described what his anointed ministry would accomplish. He would heal the broken-hearted, proclaim release to the captives, and recovery of sight to the blind and he would set free those who are downtrodden. He conveyed the message of God's favour and compassion upon people, thus inaugurated a new eschaton of God's reign (the Nazareth Manifesto, Luke 4:18-19). The listeners were marvelled at "the gracious words coming from his mouth" (Luke 4:22). Through his preaching, Jesus touched "where it hurts", the nerve centre of the poor and downtrodden to liberate them. Consequently, Jesus' preaching was accompanied by dramatic miracles through which people were healed of diseases, delivered of evil spirits, and provided with their needs. Indeed, his preaching was libertive preaching.

The same could be said of the preaching of the disciples of Jesus. When we come to the book of Acts, Peter's sermon in the context of the outpouring of the Holy Spirit stands as a classical example of explaining and rationalising the supernatural phenomena of tongue speaking, prophecy and other signs to the people gathered there. We marvel at the astounding results of such a preaching and even later also, thousands believing, turning to the Lord and joined the church (Acts 2:41; 4:4). As he preached at the house of Cornelius, the "Holy Spirit fell upon all those who were listening to the message" (Acts 10:44). It was the powerful sign of confirmation of the acceptance of gentiles into the church community and work of the Holy Spirit into cultures and languages. We also see power of preaching of Stephen in which he presented the historical account of rebellious nature of Jews and judgment upon them for rejecting Jesus the messiah. This of course, infuriated the crowd and resulted in his killing but before breathed his last he was able to deliver the message. He stands a fiery model for Christian preaching. Similarly, by the preaching ministry of Philip, accompanied by signs and miracles in the city of Samaria, many were liberated from infirmities, spirit possessions and brought "great joy in the city" (Acts 8:4-8). Consequently, a Christian community was formed there; later apostle Peter and John visited there and prayed over them to receive the Holy Spirit (Acts 8:14-18).

The Apostle Paul's testimony and anointed preaching to prove Jesus as the messiah is the core of preaching of the Acts. His sermon in Antioch of Pisidia was outstanding in proving Jesus as the messiah and saviour and Luke records, "The next Sabbath almost whole city gathered to hear the word of the Lord" (Acts 13:44). When he went to the city of Corinth, he faced one of the greatest challenges in his entire career. Therefore, he determined to overcome his own weaknesses and fear by totally relying on the power of the Holy Spirit. He knew that he would never be successful against the power of darkness by using "superiority of speech or of wisdom". Instead, he depended entirely on the "demonstration of the Spirit and of power" (I Cor. 2:1, 4). He wanted the faith of his converts to stand, not in the wisdom of men, but in the power of God. Anointed preaching of the word of God, confirmed by signs, wonders and miracles, is absolutely necessary in order to have church growth, New Testament style.[12]

---

[12] May, "Supernatural Anointing and Church Growth", 141-142.

Paul used spiritual gifts in his evangelistic activities. He explained this fact in his testimony to the Corinthians concerning his initial efforts in their lives: "My message and my preaching were not in persuasive words of wisdom, but in demonstration of the Spirit and of power" (I Cor. 2:4). It appears that in Corinth, Paul combined proclamation with demonstration, as Christ had done throughout his ministry. Here we see both proclamation as well as God's mighty presence to perform miracles to bring people to church. The Word and works of God, coupled in an expression of God's divine will and mercy, culminate in the conversion of individuals as well as groups. John Wimber calls this type of ministry that Paul had in Corinth as power evangelism: a presentation of the gospel that is rational but also transcends the rational. The explanation of the gospel comes with a demonstration of God's power through signs and wonders. It is a spontaneous, Spirit inspired, empowered presentation of the gospel. It is usually preceded and undergirded by supernatural demonstrations of God's presence.[13] In Athens, though he was more contextual and philosophical, he had presented his case with beautiful exposition of natural theology and Christology, starting from an unknown God to the fact of resurrection and judgment through Jesus Christ. Though some commentators see his preaching there as less effective with meagre results, we received a mission methodology that contribute to evangelism among a highly religious and philosophical audiences. Hence, the brief discussion of the proclamations of Jesus and apostles obviously demonstrate that they were liberative in nature. Whoever heard Jesus' words, and accepted the message of new dispensation of God's rule, were delivered of their troubles and transformed into a new life. The apostolic proclamation of Christ with the power of the Spirit, accompanied with signs and wonders liberated the people all over the known world of those times, thus formed a new community, that is called the church. Many of these traits are seen in Pentecostal preaching.

Nature of Pentecostal Preaching and Testimony

Even though Pentecostals employ other means of communication, preaching and testimony still form the popular modes of communication. The one reason behind it is, anyone can convey the message of good news, irrespective of age, gender or education and anywhere, whether it is a crowded market place, street-corner, homes or churches. Similarly, personal testimony and the word of God is shared in all situations; whether it is at work place, while travelling or even in casual conversations. This is democratisation of ministry of preaching which was considered only as the privilege of clergy in denominational churches. Moreover, as Hollenweger suggests, Pentecostal theology is oral in nature and preaching is

---

[13] John Wimber, "Signs and Wonders in the Growth of the Church", in *Church Growth the State of Art*, 149.

the most suitable method for the dissemination of Pentecostal message.[14] Martin rightly asserts, "The orality of Pentecostalism has led, in part, to a celebration of preaching as a mode of divine revelation."[15]

Like the first Christian communities, early Pentecostalism was a "charismatic community which placed emphasis on *hearing*, not reading."[16] Early Pentecostals were mostly poor and this is true almost everywhere Pentecostal movement takes its new roots. They are oral, non-conceptual peoples who are often masters of story. They tell their own stories who are in their own condition. Therefore, Pentecostalism resembles more of the early disciples than religion taught in our schools and universities.[17] Early Christians conveyed the story of Jesus in oral form and their preaching was kerygmatic that exhibited the method of the storytelling and attracted the ordinary people to the new movement. They also shared their own testimonies which acted as powerful communication in the first century Jewish and gentile context. A cursory glance would reveal lot of similarities between the New Testament preaching and Pentecostal preaching in their form, content, use of supernatural elements and stories.

Pentecostals preach with lots of stories; stories of danger, disease, and death that often turn into stories of healing, hope, and happiness.[18] Pentecostal stories of conversion, success, and deliverance invite others to imagine their lives of conversion, success, and deliverance.[19] Stories communicate the truth of the gospel and the truth of our real lives. Stories open up new vistas for us to live in and open our eyes to new possibilities.[20] Pentecostals as storytellers create and envision worlds of transformation, hope, and wonder that people can live in. Stories give us our sense of self and help us move from our past to our future, toward the purpose of our lives. The Pentecostal story is that God is active in this world and that we can be a part of God's miraculous and prophetic work.[21]

Besides, one of the central elements of Pentecostal worship is the dynamic preaching, which is more than an intellectual exercise. In the fashion of a dialogue, the Pentecostal preacher challenges his congregation and, in turn, receives back their approval of the message with a barrage of "Amens", or "Alleluias". Religious

[14] Walter J. Hollenweger, "The Black Roots of Pentecostalism", in *Pentecostals After a Century,* edited by Allan Anderson & Walter Hollenweger (Sheffield: Sheffield Academic Press, 199), 36-43.

[15] Lee Roy Martin, "Introduction", in *Toward a Pentecostal Theology of Preaching*, 5.

[16] James K. A. Smith, "The Closing of the Book: Pentecostals, Evangelicals, and the Sacred Writings", *JPT* 11 (1997): 50.

[17] Walter Hollenweger, "After Twenty Years Research on Pentecostalism", *IRM* 75/297 (1986), 3–12.

[18] Paul Alexander, *Signs & Wonders: Why Pentecostalism is the World's Fastest Growing Faith* (San Francisco: Jossey Bass, 2009), 91.

[19] Alexander, *Signs & Wonders*, 93.

[20] Alexander, *Signs & Wonders*, 94.

[21] Alexander, *Signs & Wonders*, 83-84.

observers and non-Pentecostal commentators of Pentecostal worship have noted that the Pentecostal preaching has a distinct quality; "A good Pentecostal preacher is well worth hearing", says researcher Christian Lalive d'Epinay, "for he has a genius for communication..."[22] Similarly, Harvey Cox also mentions the dramatic nature of Pentecostal preaching he had witnessed as a young man in a "little church" in his home town; he says:

> I have to admit; his [the pastor's] sermons were masterpieces of suspense and melodrama, replete with vivid images from Revelation and Daniel of beasts and dragons and vials of fire - high octane material our more reserved Baptist minister usually steered away from. He also hopped and bounced around a lot, and he sometimes acted out two sides of a conversation between, for example, God and the devil, or David and Saul, mimicking their different voices. Frequently, he slid out from behind the pulpit and sauntered along the aisle as he spoke. It was dramaturgy at its best...[23]

Such presentations enable listeners often come to see themselves as re-invoking characters in a biblical drama whose episodes can be replayed again and again throughout history, as tokens echo an original type.[24] Dynamic nature of preaching results in not only attract people but also sent the message directly into the mind of the people to keep it for a long time.

Pentecostals grant a dignity to the preached Word and they wait in great expectancy as the Bible is preached. They want to hear and experience the Word from an anointed preacher rather than a trained professional. Pentecostals look for the inspiration that comes from actual persons who, by song and testimony, tell of what God is doing for them. Pentecostals feel that free and full lay participation in the church meetings offers a *practical* dimension to the church service which would otherwise be lacking. In church context the laity by their testimonies and life preach greater practical sermons than [the minister's] messages from the pulpit.[25] Moreover, Pentecostals expect all the supernatural manifestations of the Scriptures to be realized during the present era. This 're-experiencing' of the biblical text was further emphasized in the worship service by testimonies. These testimonies offered by laity provided evidence that God was continuing to work miracles in the present. The testimony not only served to provide evidence of God's miraculous power, but it also aided in the process of interpreting Scripture.

---

[22] Grant McClung, "Spontaneous Strategy of the Spirit", in *Azuza Street & Beyond,* 144.

[23] Harvey Cox, *Fire from Heaven* (Cambridge, MA: Da Capo Press, 1995), 10.

[24] Simon Coleman, *Globalisation of Charismatic Christianity: Spreading the Gospel of Prosperity* (Cambridge: Cambridge University Press, 2004), 125.

[25] Frederick Dale Bruner, *A Theology of the Holy Spirit: The Pentecostal Experience and the New Testament Witness* (Michigan: Eerdmans Publishing, 1970), 136.

The testimonies presented by the community helped shape the understanding of those who were attending the worship service.[26]

Furthermore, Pentecostal preaching is a Spirit empowered endeavour and involves signs and wonders; Hughes says, Pentecostal preaching is "a Spirit-endowed preaching which is pungent and penetrating."[27] Hughes claims that there is a "miracle element" present in Pentecostal preaching which makes it a powerful evangelistic force.[28] The empowerment from the baptism of the Holy Spirit and gifts of the Spirit make Pentecostal preaching so effective that listeners are attracted and delivered of their troubles. One of the reasons for massive growth of Yonggi Cho's church in Seol, South Korea, was the anointed preaching. According to Yonggi Cho, the message of hope and blessing need to be conveyed to the congregations. The message of a pastor has the same function as that cool water. Pastors are to mend the broken souls of those who have passed out because of sins, sorrow, afflictions, and meaningless lives, under the tree of God's love, and encourage them to build up a new life by giving them the message of living water through Jesus Christ.[29] The use spiritual gifts such as healing, prophecy, word of wisdom and knowledge in the Pentecostal preaching brings consolation, encouragement and also results in spiritual and social liberation.

Another significant element in Pentecostal Preaching along with the use of spiritual gifts is the confrontation of demonic powers. Pentecostals are very well aware of the fact that this world is in rebellion against God, infested with minions of Satan. They come to "steal, destroy and kill" people and keep them under their control. These forces perpetuate wickedness, hatred and violence. Hence, there can be no compromise between righteousness and wickedness. Pentecostal preaching confronts the agents of the devil, who perform black magic, witch-craft, and related activities, who make financial gains through demonic activities. We see the clear example of this power encounter in Paul's preaching ministry at Ephesus. Lot of people were delivered of evil spirits (Acts 19:11-12). Through a dramatic incident (vv. 13-16), many were joined with Paul and also burned their books that contain witch-craft. Later we see Paul's preaching impacted the city so dramatically that the silversmiths were hurt financially (Acts 19:23-41). Similar incidents are very common in Indian context. Although, often Pentecostal

---

[26] Kenneth J. Archer, *A Pentecostal Hermeneutic: Spirit, Scripture and Community* (Cleveland, Tennessee: CPT Press, 2009), 167-168.

[27] McClung, "Spontaneous Strategy of the Spirit", 144.

[28] In the chapter, "The Uniqueness of Pentecostal Preaching", Hughes describes some of the special characteristics of Pentecostal preaching: It (1) convicts of sin and produces revival, (2) moves men and women to be baptized with the Holy Ghost, (3) produces faith, (4) confronts demonic powers, (5) produces godly fear and respect for the church, and (6) is confirmed by the operation of the spiritual gifts. See Hughes, *Pentecostal Preaching,* 149-157.

[29] David Yonggi Cho, "The Secret Behind the World's Biggest Church", in *Azuza Street & Beyond,* 135.

preachers are attacked or even put into jail, for speaking against such evil deities, many are being liberated by such powerful preaching ministry.

Furthermore, Pentecostal preaching is prophetic. Even though the word "prophecy" normally understood in terms of predicting of the future events, the New Testament also attribute a sense of "forth-telling" which includes preaching. In the scriptural sense, the New Testament prophet is one empowered by authority of the Holy Spirit to declare the mind of God. This brings us to the more correct definition of prophecy, which makes the minister one who speaks for others. Moreover, a minister speaks with the authority of the Spirit and the source of message is also Spirit. Thus, the Holy Spirit moves upon the Pentecostal preacher and he speaks the revealed message in his own words. Sometimes the message comes by a revelation. At other times the Spirit reminds certain things he previously learned or known. Therefore, prophetic preaching does not preclude study and preparation (John 14:26). Sometimes the Spirit will lead the Pentecostal preachers in another direction with a word of knowledge or a special illumination to meet a specific need of someone in the congregation.[30] In pursuit of the prophetic ideal, Pentecostal preachers have preferred to call their preaching a 'message' rather than a 'sermon.'[31] Just as the prophetical message of the Old Testament, reproved, rebuked, comforted and exhorted, Pentecostal preaching conveys God's heart to the righteous as well as wicked. It comforts those who are troubled and experience sorrows; it corrects those who are in error and also liberates from clutches of spiritual and social oppression. Very often, Pentecostal preaching also evoke disfavour and ire of the listeners. Thus, Pentecostal preaching stands as "prophetic", and as a way of communicating God's mind to the people.

For Pentecostals, Bible is the source of their preaching. Bible is not only Scripture, but equivalent to the script for a play, with roles adopted by those who take its words to heart and to their Spirit.[32] Pentecostal take the word of God in literal sense and present the stories of biblical times and apply them here today. Early Pentecostals envisioned themselves as living in the continuation of "Bible days". Whatever is mentioned in the Bible, whether it is the deity of Jesus, divine healing or any other miracles are fully believed and anticipated. Therefore, in Pentecostal preaching the word of God literally presented in the power of the Spirit and all miracles, instructions and stories are taken into account and experienced. Moreover, in practical life, Pentecostals take Bible as a collection of stories that can be applied directly and indexically to the self, encouraging the believer to take a particular course of action, remain firm in the faith, discover the reason for a particular event and so on. In actuality the Bible is not just to be believed; it is to be lived.[33] This principle is actualised

[30] Hughes, *Pentecostal Preaching,*131-132.

[31] Martin, "Toward a Pentecostal Theology of Preaching", 47.

[32] Coleman, *Globalisation of Charismatic Christianity*, 126.

[33] Coleman, *Globalisation of Charismatic Christianity,* 126.

in Pentecostal context through sermons. Pentecostal preaching is not only built upon the word of God but also according to the leading of the Holy Spirit, rather than human assumptions. It depends upon the Spirit to convict and bring miraculous results. Even while the message was in progress, men or women have been known to cry out, to stand, and to run forward to an altar of prayer, conviction too heavy for them to wait.[34] Hughes reiterates three significant points in relation to Pentecostal preaching: (1) True Pentecostal preaching always centers in the Word; (2) Pentecostal preaching always exalts Jesus Christ; and (3) Pentecostal preaching is always directed and empowered by the Holy Spirit.[35]

The above mentioned characteristics of Pentecostal preaching are amply exemplified in the history of Pentecostal movement. We can see an array of Pentecostal preachers enact these characteristics in their ministry yester-years as well as contemporary setting. For instance, Maria Woodworth-Etter, who was a healing evangelist in America narrated the power of the Spirit tremendously worked in her ministry of preaching:

> Many times I have stood before congregations of thousands, preaching or singing, when the Holy Ghost fell upon them,..and swept over, wave after wave, till the multitudes would sway back and forth like the trees in a forest, or grain in a storm. Many of the tall oaks would be laid prostrate over the house or campground; Many shouted, others wept with a loud voice. Other times the power would sweep over the house in melting power. In a few minutes nearly everyone in the congregation would be weeping, saints and sinners. The solemnity of death would rest upon the people; you could not hear a sound nor see a move; the people were held by the power of God. These outpourings of the Holy Ghost were always followed by hundreds coming to Christ. The Lord has backed up His word, as I preached it on the apostolic line, with "signs and wonders" and demonstrations of the Spirit.[36]

The power of God manifested in her evangelistic meetings for healing and miracles and many were delivered of their troubles. Liardon narrates one such incident:

> One night, three people that had been deaf and dumb, all strangers to one another, stood at the altar, weeping, hugging and shouting because God had opened their ears and given them their speech. Many others looked on and wept, making their way to the altar to know God and be saved. One of the three formerly deaf and dumb went on to testify:

---

[34] Hughes, "The Uniqueness of Pentecostal Preaching", 118.

[35] Hughes, "The Uniqueness of Pentecostal Preaching", 118.

[36] Maria B. Woodworth Etter, *Signs and Wonders*, abridged edition, (Hants: The Revival Library, n. d), 24.

"When Sister Etter put her finger in mouth at the root of my tongue and then in my eyes, commanding a deaf and dumb spirit to come out, God instantly opened my ears and gave me my voice."[37]

In Pentecostal preaching, it was not the fine vocabulary or the right homiletic principles that energises the message, rather the anointing of the Spirit makes the sermon effective. John G. Lake, the famous healing evangelist who visited the Azuza street meeting commented about the preaching of William Seymour:

> He had the funniest vocabulary. But I want to tell you, there were doctors, lawyers, and professors, listening to the marvellous things coming from his lips. It was not what he said in words, it was what he said from his spirit to my heart that showed me he had more of God in his life than any man I had ever met up to that time. It was God in him that attracted the people.[38]

The preaching ministry of famous British evangelist Smith Wigglesworth, is an example of the power of spoken word that results in miracles; while he preached, powerful presence of the Holy Spirit would fill the audiences. In the beginning of his ministry, he was tarrying for the baptism of the Holy Spirit but did not receive it. Disappointed in his spirit, he decided to leave the church, but entered the parsonage to say goodbye to vicar's wife, Mrs Alexander Boddy. There he asked her to pray for him. As she prayed over him, the power of the Spirit instantly fell upon him. Instead of going home, Smith directly went to the congregation of Alexander Boddy (one of the founders of Pentecostal movement in England), interrupting the service, he begged to speak for a moment. When he finished his "sermon", fifty people were baptised in the Holy Spirit and spoke with other tongues. Later on Sunday the Lord gave him the passage in Isaiah 61:1-3 to preach from. He preached with great power and at the end of the service, a man stood and said he wanted the experience that Smith had. As the man sat down, he missed his chair and fell on the floor. In a short time, eleven people were on the floor laughing in the Spirit.[39]

Michael Bergunder relates some true stories that happened in an evangelistic conventions of Pentecostal and charismatic churches in south India where healings and other miracles changes the lives of the people and they join Pentecostal congregations. One visitor to a *Jesus Calls* convention testified that she had brought her sister "from far away and with much labour and difficulty". The girl had for three years been bound by black magic and she did not know who she was. There was no place we would not go, no gods we would not

---

[37] Roberts Liardon, *God's Generals: Why They Succeeded and Why Some Failed* (Tulsa, Oklahoma: Albury Publishing), 59-60.

[38] Liardon, *God's Generals*, 139.

[39] Liardon, *God's Generals*, 189.

implore to make her well. They all let her down. Out of the belief that she would be cured if she came here, we brought her with great difficulty. When it was time for prayer, . . . a power came down on her. Now she knows who she is and she has a complete cure.[40] In another incident, a 25-year-old student attended a Pentecostal convention by chance. He was suffering from slight pains that occurred during urination. While he was in the convention, the following words were spoken: "A., you will be cured of an abscess". The next morning, he perceived that the pain had ceased. He concluded that the healing had taken place the day before through prayer at the rally. On the basis of this insight, he left the Catholic Church and became a member of the Pentecostal church that had held the convention.[41]

Similarly, the testimonies of ordinary people have great effect in changing the lives of the people, delivering of their troubles and leading them into faith. A cursory glance into the history of growth of Pentecostal movement in India would show that more than pastors or full-time workers, it was the sharing of personal testimonies and word of God by ordinary faithful men and women that impacted a widespread growth.[42] Pentecostal believers very often share their salvation, divine healing and deliverance experiences to their friends and relatives. This way Pentecostal churches are growing rapidly among Tribals, Dalits and people in interior villages in north of India. Many are healed of their illness, delivered of attacks of evil spirits and blessed financially. Even the uneducated women testify their faith, the healing they received and the greatness of Jesus in their daily encounter with their neighbours and those who are in dire need. A woman whom I have spoken said this:

> In my village I testify to the women who are suffering from various diseases and other problems. I pray for them in the name of Jesus. I tell them Jesus would heal them. Even though I am illiterate I tell them He is greater than all gods. People believe it.[43]

Through preaching and testimony, Pentecostals proclaim Jesus Christ as the only true God and reject any claims of divinity of gods or spirits of their old religions. They proclaim the uniqueness of Jesus in a religious pluralistic society without fearing any consequence. This, of course, attract the ire of fanatic

---

[40] Michael Bergunder, "Miracle Healing and Exorcism in South Indian Pentecostalism", *Global Pentecostalism and Charismatic Healing,* edited by Candy Brown Gunther (New York: Oxford University Press, 2011), 296.

[41] Bergunder, "Miracle Healing and Exorcism ", 297.

[42] See my book on North Indian Pentecostal history; Shaibu Abraham, *The History of the Pentecostal Movement in North India: Unfolding its Social and Theological Contexts* (New Delhi: Christian World Imprints, 2017).

[43] Shaibu Abraham, *Pentecostal Christology: Empirical Approach in Indian Context* (New Delhi: Christian World Imprints, 2019), 124.

elements. It is usual that pastors and believers are being abused and persecuted for their testimony; opposition and attack continue in many places. Even though such incidents are common, the ordinary Pentecostal believers seldom cease to proclaim the greatness of Jesus. There are many stories, through the testimonies of believers suffering people came into Pentecostal churches and delivered of their trouble. For instance, a man was troubled by evil spirit attack and his wife and a child died of it. He later married again but she was also attacked by the same spirit. Then some people directed him to a Pentecostal church and the family was delivered from the attack of the demon.[44] Thus, Pentecostal preaching and testimonies shared by ordinary believers act as a communication of liberation and impact tremendous church growth in Indian context.

Preaching and Testimony in Pentecostal Theology

Now in this section, we will have a glimpse of how the above mentioned characteristics of Pentecostal preaching and testimony are explained by Pentecostal and larger theological enterprise in their recent presentations. We will limit the discussion with only some of the elements for the sake of brevity.

Oral-Narrative Preaching

The early Pentecostal way of doing theology was expressed by means of testimonies, songs, trances, inspired preaching and dance. Hollenweger notes that early Pentecostals primarily relied upon oral means of communication to express their theology and it involved orality of liturgy, narrative theology and witness. He describes oral quality of Third World Pentecostals:

> For them the medium of communication is, just as in biblical times, not the definition but the description, not the statement but the story, not the parables, not a systematic theology but a song, not the articulation of concepts but the celebration of banquets.[45]

He also compares first century Christianity and Pentecostal movement in relation to their oral nature. The founder of Christianity was a story-telling rabbi who belonged to the oral culture of the Middle East. Jesus was not a European and he never wrote a book, but taught with stories. The founder of Pentecostalism was a black ecumenist from the United States and black culture and spirituality are of oral in nature. Both movements owe their initial growth to the oral structure of their origins. The reason for Pentecostalism's breathtaking growth is their narrative *theology and witness.*[46]

---

[44] Abraham, *Pentecostal Christology*, 95.

[45] Hollenweger, "After Twenty Years", 10.

[46] Hollenweger, "The Black Roots of Pentecostalism", 36.

This oral-narrative dynamic allows for the Christian 'story' to be integrated with life experiences. It gives a 'voice' to every believer inasmuch as it is the responsibility of everyone to participate in the telling of his or her experience. An oral-narrative theology allows for theology to become part of the life of the community of faith. A story or narrative provides a means of enabling the person to make proper decisions as well as understanding the depth of human nature. Stories form who we become and affect our decisions and actions. Hence, belief is forged in the context of community with everyone having a voice in the ongoing dialectic of the kingdom of God.[47] In addition, truth is far less powerful when it is represented analytically, propositionally or systematically. As Hauerwas says, story of Jesus enables us to be part of divine story and find our true selves to be liberated from all the enslaving stories of this world.[48] Cheryl Bridges applies this in Pentecostal context:

> A true story is one that gives us the courage to go on and empowers us to know ourselves in a transformative way. Such a knowledge is like a skill that gives us the ability to know the world as it is and should be—it is a knowing that changes the self. False stories offer no transforming ability. For Pentecostals, it is their stories in relation to the stories of the Scriptures which give the ability to understand oneself and the world and God's critique on both. Stories provide for a fleshing-out, an understanding of how God is at work on the earth. Pentecostals utilize this form to give each other the 'courage to go on and the will to live in a transformative way.'[49]

Thus, stories have a remarkable ability to represent reality and a narrative style preaching enables the conscientization process and leads listeners into liberation.

Prophetic Preaching

Another significant aspect that to be discussed in Pentecostal preaching is its prophetic nature that forms the spirituality of Pentecostal movement. Pentecostal preachers claim to be called specially for prophetic ministry. Here the call narrative is fundamental and perceived similar to the Old Testament prophets. Pentecostal call narratives often include an element not found in other traditions – the experience of Spirit baptism. Spirit baptism is the quintessential prophetic encounter that transforms the believer, resulting in a reordering of all of life in

---

[47] Cheryl Bridges Johns, *Pentecostal Formation: A Pedagogy Among the Oppressed* (Eugene, OR: Wipf and Stock Publishers, 2010), 87-88, also see, S. Hauerwas and R. Bondi, *Truthfulness and Tragedy* (Notre Dame: University of Notre Dame Press, 1977), 71.

[48] Quoted in Alexander, *Signs & Wonders*, 83-84.

[49] Bridges Johns, *Pentecostal Formation*, 88;

terms of a derivative apocalyptic spirituality.[50] In one testimony after another, Pentecostal ministers have related their call narratives, telling how they were set apart as preachers of God's Word. Many of these preachers have testified to resisting the call and even running away from it, but they could not escape the forceful work of the Holy Spirit.[51] Bergunder presents a typical case; one respected pastor from Bangalore reported becoming ill after refusing a call from God to resign his job and enter full-time ministry:

> At the beginning of 1979 the Lord started to speak to me about my calling. Many times and strongly came the call: "Resign the job!" But, I did not because the family had a lot of financial problems . . . . But, anyhow, by September, God's dealing became heavier and heavier. And, [by] September end I was in hospital, October sixth, being on the threshold of death, I made a decision, a covenant with the Lord to fully serve him. When I made that decision the Lord healed me.[52]

The biblical prophets experienced dramatic encounters with God that 'radically transformed' them and initiated their entrance into prophetic ministry. These encounters are reported in the form of call narratives that bear similarities to the testimonies of many Pentecostal preachers. The prophetic calling fills the preacher with a compelling urge to proclaim the divine word. The apostle Paul declares, 'Although I preach the gospel, I have nothing to glory of; for necessity is laid upon me. Yes, woe is unto me, if I do not preach the gospel' (1 Cor. 9.16). When Peter and John were ordered by the Jewish authorities to cease preaching about Jesus, they replied, 'We cannot stop speaking what we have seen and heard' (Acts 4.20). The prophet Amos writes, 'I am not a prophet, neither a prophet's son ... but the Lord took me as I followed the flock, and the Lord said unto me, Go, prophesy unto my people Israel' (Amos 7.12-15). Jeremiah, facing opposition and persecution decided to quit but he says, 'I said I would not mention him, or speak any more in his name, but there is in my heart as it were a burning fire shut up in my bones, and I am weary with holding it in, and I cannot' (Jer. 20.9). Many of the Pentecostal preachers claim such conviction in their lives.

Martin, appropriating Abraham Heschel's portrayal of ministry of prophets, applies it in Pentecostal preaching ministry. He says that the prophet experiences pathos from two directions. As the messenger of God, the prophet is filled with God's passions; but, as a member of the community, the prophet suffers along with everyone else. In the presence of God [the prophet] takes the part of the people. In the presence of the people [the prophet] takes the part of God. The best prophetic preaching, therefore, is the communication of the pathos of God by a prophet who speaks from a position of solidarity with the people of God. When

[50] Martin, "Toward a Pentecostal Theology of Preaching", 45.

[51] Martin, "Toward a Pentecostal Theology of Preaching", 44-45.

[52] Bergunder, "Miracle Healing and Exorcism", 291.

engaged in prophetic criticizing, the prophet's words are outbursts of violent emotions in reaction to the evil and complacency of society. Even when engaged in prophetic energizing, powerful emotive expression is called for. Prophetic preaching challenges assumptions, interrupts apathetic slumber, exposes sin and hypocrisy, and requires repentance. Dispassionate modes of discourse cannot accomplish the goals of prophetic preaching. Therefore, a prophetic message will be delivered with passion and with an abundance of affective language.[53]

Dynamic Pentecostal Preaching

Charismatic Christianity is a religion of the Word. Powerfully charged language is read, spoken, written, memorised, prophesied, translated, pinned up on signs in houses and cars, and so it is believed. Having studied the spirituality of charismatic groups, Simon Coleman, an anthropologist says that Pentecostals and Charismatic believers sometimes refer to the Scriptures as their 'spiritual weapon'. The sacred text is treated as an intimate possession to be taken with the person as he or she goes about their daily lives, and its margins are usually heavily scored with notes taken from sermons, classes and personal reflections.[54] Besides, Coleman argues that, for Pentecostals and many other conservatives, devotion to the Bible implies dramatization – bringing the word to life, certainly in preaching but also in one's life. The power of Scripture and other forms of inspired language is validated through inductive strategies that seek to assess the effects of language on the self and the material environment. The application of literalism and doctrines of inerrancy in relation to the Bible is as much about embodying and 'living out' the text in a self-reinforcing process of spiritual authentication as it is about the verbalised assertion that everything the Bible says is un-problematically 'true.'[55]

Coleman uses various categories such as 'dramatisation, internalisation and externalisation' to explain the way the word of God is appropriated and applied among Pentecostals. 'Dramatisation' in Pentecostal setting implies the *acting out* of religious – and ultimately biblically derived – ideals in terms of personal conduct and behaviour. 'Internalisation' refers to the process of *incorporating* language within the self in a way that is even more embodied. It is a form of self-inscription (as opposed to description) that leads believers to understand themselves as 'words made flesh'. 'Externalisation', refers to the deployment of language as a *performative* force in order to change physical, social and material circumstances.[56] This dynamic use of the word of God, obviously leads into a liberative spirituality.

---

[53] Martin, "Toward a Pentecostal Theology of Preaching", 52-53. Abraham Heschel, *The Prophets* (New York: Harper & Row, 1962).

[54] Coleman, *Globalisation of Charismatic Christianity*, 117.

[55] Coleman, *Globalisation of Charismatic Christianity*, 118.

[56] Coleman, *Globalisation of Charismatic Christianity*, 118.

Testimony

As we have already explored, Pentecostalism is rooted in oral culture, rather than literary culture.[57] One of the forms *par excellence* of communication of the Pentecostal religious experience is the personal testimony. It is directed both inward toward the community of believers and outward toward the world.[58] Pentecostals make their theological-world with their personal testimonies, what God has wrought in their lives. Telling of one's personal story of God's activity is central to the ordinary expression of faith.[59] It attempts to represent in verbal form the shape of a life.[60] Moreover, testimony not only has the capacity to generate the knowledge, but also gives proper weight to our dual nature as both socially indebted and individually rational creatures.[61] In Pentecostal churches, and in their neighbourhood, ordinary members articulate their theological world with their testimonies. There is a popular saying among Indian Pentecostals that 'a testimony begets another testimony'. In the testimonial narrative, one communicates his experience to another or to others.[62]

Pentecostal testimony could be said to function by means of three interrelated modes: personal story, congregational story and denominational story.[63] Along with the testimonies of believers, the sermons, missionary stories, and worship as well as related activities in the local church contribute to the larger testimony of the community. They include stories of healing, exorcism, and miraculous elements. These testimonies form the bedrock of Pentecostal spirituality and theology in third world context, since the gospel stories are similarly formed by testimony.[64] These testimonies reflect a combination of personal values, corporate beliefs and particular circumstances of ordinary people. Cartledge argues that testimony is a means of social knowledge construction which integrates other forms of knowledge such as perception, memory, consciousness and reason. In Pentecostal spirituality it acts as a

---

[57] Walter J. Hollenweger, *Pentecostalism: Origins and Developments Worldwide* (Peabody: Hendrickson Publishers, 1997), 18.

[58] No Author, "Pentecostal Conversion in the Popular Perception of the Sacred: Some Methodological Elements for its Analysis", *Voices from the Third World* XIV/2 (December 1991): 55.

[59] Mark J. Cartledge, *Testimony in the Spirit* (Farnham: Ashgate, 2010), 17; Alan Jacobs, *Looking Before and After: Testimony and the Christian Life* (Michigan: Eerdmans, 2008).

[60] Jacobs, *Looking Before and After*, 24.

[61] Jennifer Lackey, *Learning from Words: Testimony as a Source of Knowledge* (Oxford: Oxford University Press, 2010), 3; Jan Vansina, *Oral Tradition: A Study in Historical Methodology*, translated by H.M. Wright (New Jersey: Transaction Publishers, 2006), 47-113.

[62] No Author, "Pentecostal Conversion in the Popular Perception", 55.

[63] Cartledge, *Testimony in the Spirit,* 17.

[64] The Gospels themselves are the testimony of the eye witness; see Richard J. Bauckham, *Jesus and the Eyewitnesses: The Gospels as Eyewitness Testimony* (Michigan: Eerdmans, 2006), 5; also see Richard J. Bauckham, *The Gospels as Eyewitness Testimony* (Cambridge: Grove Books, 2008).

mechanism of reinforcement and commitment and also as a means of integrating social knowledge enabling us to enter into the world of Pentecostal theology.[65]

According to Coleman, many narrative forms are deployed in faith contexts. Part of the process of gaining identity in a congregation is the development and constant honing of a personal account of conversion, depicting how one became born-again into a new life. One effect of such practices is the integration of a shared religious language into the idiosyncratic details of the person's life history. The convert learns that their previous life was one of 'darkness' as opposed to present enlightenment and revelation. 'Something lacking' has been replaced by plenitude, as identity is discovered through the 'full Gospel' and 'in Christ'. God, 'has a plan' for every believer's life. Conversion narratives are used to describe the self to witnessing to the unsaved, and are frequently topped up by testimonies of more recent miracles that may have occurred. Thus the use of autobiography – and self objectification as a character in such narratives – illustrates the ideal of a personal relationship with God but is also deployed as a mode of persuasive discourse.[66]

As we end our discussion, let me give some suggestions to improve the Pentecostal preaching, the very core of Pentecostal spirituality. These suggestions are neither exhaustive nor foolproof but rather drawn out from my observations. *First of all*, Pentecostal preaching needs to be more compassionate, avoiding to be unnecessarily judgemental but "touch where it hurts" to empower listeners. This is essential in a religiously pluralistic society like India, where Pentecostal preaching and sharing of testimony time and again become a cause of animosity and strife, escalating into violence against Pentecostals by fanatic elements. Therefore, wherever it is possible, peace and tranquillity be preserved without compromising the very core of Pentecostal message and uniqueness of Jesus Christ. *Secondly*, though Pentecostal sermons are anointed, the "prophetic" nature is in decline. Pentecostals seldom preach against poverty, oppressions as well as other maladies in society and inequalities in churches. It seems that *status quo* silence is crept in. It is imperative that preachers be empowered to speak against ills of society and church, in the power of the Spirit. *Thirdly*, it is observed that the gusto, theatrical and high decibel presentations are misconceived as anointed and prophetic preaching. Content and clarity of the divine message is lost in the din. Pentecostal believers are so tuned that even they shout "halleluiahs" to irrelevant things presented. Often Pentecostal preaching dwells upon peripheries, not presenting the deeper meaning of the text. Preachers are to be trained to preach the Word with deeper knowledge of the text with the power of the Spirit, exercising spiritual gifts without manipulating the listeners. *Fourthly*, the lay participation in preaching should encouraged which is in decline. There is a lure among Pentecostals to

---

[65] Mark J. Cartledge, *Practical Theology: Charismatic and Empirical Perspectives* (Waynesboro, GA: Paternoster Press, 2003), 52-57.

[66] Coleman, *Globalisation of Charismatic Christianity*, 119.

attribute all ecclesial roles to clergy, similar to other denominational practices. Ordinary believers are better suited to preach the Word and share their personal testimony to outsiders. Moreover, laity be encouraged and given enough training to harness the spiritual resources in the Pentecostal community. *Finally*, in Bible colleges and seminaries, there is a tendency to pin down sermons to a three point affair in consonance with the western protestant mode of preaching, diluting the vibrancy and dramatic nature which can be counterproductive in third world context. Pentecostal preaching should be accompanied divine healing, exorcism, word of knowledge and so on, to bring listeners into liberation.

Let us conclude our discussion; it obvious from the discussion that Pentecostal preaching has close affinity to methods and content of proclamations of Jesus and apostles and employs unique homiletical principles unlike the Evangelical tradition. It employs dramatic presentation, narrative style and stories, coupled with signs and wonders. It attracts the attention of all, whether highly educated or ordinary, affects a renewed perception to change their life and surrounding. It enacts radical changes in the life situations of the poor and downtrodden to lift them into a higher pedestal. It stands as a point of contact with non-Pentecostals and leads them into Pentecostal congregation. Pentecostal preaching, hence, forms the basic spirituality of Pentecostal movement and acts as communication for liberation.

Chapter 9

Eschatology
Urgency for Liberation

Pentecostalism can be rightly termed as an apocalyptic movement and the physical, literal return of Jesus to the earth is an important feature of Pentecostal spirituality. Pentecostals strongly believe that when Jesus Christ returns, the Christians who live a holy life will be taken up to be with the Lord and the non-believers will be left behind. Moreover, Pentecostals realise that Jesus may return at any time like a thief and therefore, they ought to be ready always. This understanding was deeply ingrained in Pentecostal spirituality from the origin of the movement and even after a century, most of the Pentecostals hold it firmly. This great hope impelled early Pentecostals to live a separated and holy life from the world and its system and they were eager to bring as many people as they can, to Pentecostal fold before the return of Christ. Such lifestyle and missionary fervour resulted in Pentecostals to go out as cross-cultural missionaries to the end of the earth and attracted millions of ordinary people to the movement everywhere. One of the reasons for the magnificent growth of the movement is its eschatological fervour and resultant evangelism and mission. McClung underline this fact, "Eschatological urgency is at the heart of understanding the missionary fervour of early Pentecostalism."[1] Eschatology for Pentecostals is not simply about the end times as the last chapter of a theological system. It is a living hope that affects the entire Christian life.

[1] Murray W. Dempster, "Eschatology, Spirit Baptism, and Inclusiveness: An Exploration into the Hallmarks of a Pentecostal Social Ethic", in *Perspectives in Pentecostal Eschatologies: World without End*, edited by Peter Althouse & Robby Waddell (Eugene, Oregon: Witf & Stock Publishers, 2012), 157.

Christ as the coming king integrates and defines Christ's saving work, Spirit baptism, and healing.[2] The essence and relevance of Pentecostal eschatology can be termed as this; a liberating hope, a liberating lifestyle and a liberating mission. Hence, eschatological hope is a liberating spirituality in Pentecostalism.

Macchia affirms that eschatology may be of more importance to the essence of Pentecostalism than the baptism in the Spirit.[3] The Pentecostal movement arose in an atmosphere of fervent expectation of the second coming of Jesus. The powerful outpouring of the Holy Spirit all over the world in the beginning of the twentieth century understood as the fulfilment of 'latter rain' promise and signalled the beginning of the 'last days'. The experience of the baptism of the Holy Spirit and the tongues were considered as the visible signs of the impending coming of Christ and the beginning of the glorious eternity. It was frequently reported that messages in tongues from around the world were being interpreted as 'Jesus is coming soon'. The very fact that people all across the world were seeking God for the baptism of the Holy Spirit indicated that 'the Lord is preparing His people for His soon coming'. A testimony in the *Apostolic Faith* concludes with these remarks:

> Surely the glorious coming of our blessed Lord is very near, and all this supernatural work of God is needed for the work to be completed. This is only the beginning of the gracious latter rain, which our risen Lord will pour out upon all flesh, and as the Holy Spirit shall temper each vessel meet for service, He will fully restore all the gifts, or rather manifest each as needed. For all is inherent in Himself, and all thus baptized will indeed be one. The Holy Spirit is now leading us into much prayerful study of His Word. He makes Christ increasingly all in all,..and the coming of the Lord increasingly real.[4]

As Ernst Käsemann affirmed, that apocalypticism is the mother of all Christian theology, Land applies the concept to Pentecostal eschatology and says, "Pentecostals were adopted by and adopted this 'mother' and became sons and daughters, prophets and prophetesses of the new order of the Latter Rain of the Spirit."[5] The participants at Azusa Street located themselves "in the evening of the dispensation of the Holy Ghost" (the day of Pentecost being "the morning"). For early Pentecostals, as John the Baptist warned people to prepare the way of the

---

[2] Frank D. Macchia, "Pentecostal and Charismatic Theology", in *The Oxford Handbook of Eschatology*, edited by Jerry L. Walls (Oxford: Oxford University Press, 2008), 354-355.

[3] Frank D. Macchia, *Baptised in the Spirit: A Global Pentecostal Theology* (Grand Rapids, Michigan: Zondervan, 2006), 38-40.

[4] Larry R. McQueen, *Toward a Pentecostal Eschatology: Discerning the Way Forward* (Dorset, UK: Deo Publishing, 2012), 64-65; *Apostolic Faith* 1/5 (Jan, 1907), 2.

[5] Steven J. Land, *Pentecostal Spirituality: A Passion for the Kingdom* (Sheffield, England: Sheffield Academic Press, 1993), 63.

Lord, so "the voice of warning is going out to the world today to prepare for the Second Coming of the Lord Jesus Christ."[6]

This imminent expectation is revealed in the titles of early Pentecostal journals: 'The Bridal Call', 'The Last Trump', 'I come quickly', 'The Evening Light and Church of God Evangel', 'Maranatha', 'The Midnight Cry', 'The End-Time Messenger', 'The Bridegroom's Messenger', 'Trumpet of Zion' (*Seeyon Kahalam*, one of the earliest Malayalam Pentecostal magazines) and so on.[7] The *Apostolic Faith* wrote,

> How we rejoice at the hope, each day bringing to us a deeper experience and a brighter assurance that we, ourselves, will never see the grave! His approach is so nigh at hand, one almost thinks they can hear the songs of the angels who are to accompany Him in His coming. Without a shadow of a doubt, we are living in the latter days and that "Latter Rain" is being poured upon us...[8]

The sense of Jesus' imminent return was woven tightly into the spiritual experience of the participants and it permeated the personal testimonies, poems, letters, reports of tongues-speech, and articles as a constant reminder that 'Jesus is coming soon.'[9]

As the movement spread throughout the world, the message was the same. Pentecostals all over the world have viewed the return of Jesus as a major stimulus to Christian service, holiness (1 Jn. 3.3) and, in particular, evangelism (Mt. 24.14). They also emphasize the association of the return of Jesus with the judgement of believers (Mt. 25.14-30; 1 Cor.14.9-15).[10] William Faupel aptly asserts that eschatology forms the integrating theme of Pentecostal theology.[11] In the following pages, we shall have a glimpse of the content and shape of Pentecostal eschatology. First of all, an overview of early Pentecostal eschatology will be presented, followed by the origin and development of eschatology in the movement. In addition we shall explore the unique nature of Pentecostal eschatology that makes it a liberative spirituality.

---

[6] Larry R. McQueen, "Early Pentecostal Eschatology in the Light of *The Apostolic Faith*, 1906–1908", in *Perspectives in Pentecostal Eschatologies: World without End*, 142; *Apostolic Faith* 1.2 (Oct, 1906), 3.

[7] Walter J. Hollenweger, *The Pentecostals: The Charismatic Movement in the Churches* (Minnesota: Agsburg Publishing House, 1972), 415.

[8] McQueen, "Early Pentecostal Eschatology", 142; *Apostolic Faith* 1.9 (Jun–Sept, 1907), 4.

[9] McQueen, *Toward a Pentecostal Eschatology*, 63.

[10] Keith Warrington, *Pentecostal Theology: A Theology of Encounter* (London: T&T Clark, 2008), 313.

[11] D. William Faupel, *Everlasting Gospel: The Significance of Eschatology in the Development of Pentecostal Thought*, (Sheffield: Sheffield Academic Press, 1996), 32.

Overview of Eschatology

According to the Pentecostal understanding of future events, the second coming of Christ and consummation of God's plan of salvation will take place in the following stages: the rapture of the church; great tribulation under the Antichrist; the return of Christ to redeem Israel and to set up the millennial kingdom of peace; the resurrection of the dead for the last judgment; the destruction and re-creation of heaven and earth, the new Jerusalem, God as all in all. Sometimes the details of the timetable for the final age are disputed.[12] However, many of these beliefs are shared with other, especially fundamentalist, believers. During the earliest years of Pentecostalism, its adherents adopted the eschatological vision of Fundamentalism or Dispensationalism.[13] We may summarise the Pentecostal eschatological scheme as follows: first of all, the fulfilment of prophecies of the restoration of Israel prepares the world for the coming of Jesus Christ.[14] The basis for this is Old Testament scriptures such as Isaiah 66 and Zechariah 14 which indicated that one day God's people would be re-gathered to the land that God had promised them. In Matthew 24:32-34, Jesus used the example of the fig tree, reminding his hearers that one can tell the approach of summer by the emergence of its leaves. Israel's presence in Jerusalem once again as a result of gains in the Yom Kippur war was seen as a fulfilment of this prophecy.[15] The formation of the nation of Israel in 1948 had brought great expectation of the second coming. Many had predicted the coming of Jesus in that generation itself.

The biblical basis of the second coming is found in the words of the Lord himself and in the teaching of his apostles. Often quoted Bible verses are: "Keep awake therefore, for you do not know on what day your Lord is coming... Therefore you also must be ready, for the Son of Man is coming at an unexpected hour" (Matt. 24:42-44); "For the Lord Himself, with a cry of command, with the archangel's call and with the sound of God's trumpet, will descend from heaven, and the dead in Christ will rise first. Then we who are alive, who are left, will be caught up in the clouds together with them to meet the Lord in the air; and so we will be with the Lord forever" (1 Thess. 4:16-17); "But our citizenship is in

---

[12] Hollenweger, *The Pentecostals*, 415.

[13] Warrington, *Pentecostal Theology*, 309.

[14] I have heard some of the popular Pentecostal preachers even justifying the contemporary violence and bloodshed perpetuated by the state of Israel upon the population of surrounding regions, in the name of prophetic fulfilment. This is certainly contrary to what Jesus was taught and the original Pentecostal spirituality.

[15] James J. Glass, "Eschatology: A Clear and Present Danger — A Sure and Certain Hope", in *Pentecostal Perspectives*, edited by Keith Warrington (Cumbria, UK: Paternoster Press, 1998), 127-129, 131-132. Glass says: "Some teachers interpreted the fig tree as a reference to Israel: flourishing fig tree = flourishing Israel. This was then seen as a reference to the restoration, while 'this generation' was understood as the generation that would witness the restoration and see the Lord's return. One can imagine the excitement caused when Israel became a nation once again in 1948. It goes a long way to accounting for books with titles such as 'Christ Returns By 1988.'"

heaven. And we eagerly await a Saviour from there, the Lord Jesus Christ, who, by the power that enables him to bring everything under his control, will transform our lowly bodies so that they will be like his glorious body" (Phil. 3:20). These verses are referred to Jesus' coming for His Church, an event commonly known as the "Rapture". This coming of Christ is not directly to the earth but in the air, and not of coming to judge the world but to deliver the church. At that moment the dead in Christ will be raised and living Christians will be caught up to meet the Lord in the air and be with him forever. In this resurrection, those who have died in Christ will have their redeemed souls and spirits united with a body similar to Christ's glorified body. Christians living at the time of this event will not die, but will be changed to be like Christ. Nobody knows the day or the hour when this will take place. Adherents of this view are classed as 'pre-tribulationists' in that they believe Christians are taken up from the earth to meet the Lord before the onset of the great tribulation. This is the majority view in Classical Pentecostalism.[16]

After the Rapture of the Church, Christians will be brought before the judgment seat of Christ. He will reward them on the basis of the works they have accomplished. The Rapture will also inaugurate a period that the Bible characterizes as the "great day of His wrath", "the great tribulation" and the "time of Jacob's trouble". The great tribulation is held to be seven years in duration (Rev. 7:14; 13:5; Dan. 7:25; 9:27). At the outset of the tribulation, Antichrist is revealed. His accession to world power initially heralds peace and prosperity for the world but unparalleled woe for the 144,000 Jews whom God supernaturally turns to Christ (Rev. 7:8 ff). This time of unprecedented difficulty will affect Israel and all nations. Its purpose will be to prepare Israel for her Messiah. Conditions gradually degenerate as God pours out his judgement (Rev. 6; 8; 9) and the peace initiated by Antichrist is eventually shattered and the nations of the earth converge on the plain of Megiddo for the battle of Armageddon (Rev. 16:16). Then Jesus Christ will return with the hosts of heaven as well as the Church and will defeat antichrist and his army and inaugurate his millennial reign (Isa. 11; Rev. 20). At this Second Coming, the Antichrist will be cast into the Lake of Fire and Satan will be bound for a thousand years (Rev. 20:2). The nations and their representatives will be judged. Israel will be restored to her land, never more to be removed. Christ will reign with firmness and equity. His kingdom will be marked

[16] Others have believed that the Scriptures teach a mid-tribulation rapture, while others prefer a post-tribulation rapture. The main attack on pre-tribulationalism is that firstly, the second advent is not pictured elsewhere in scripture as a two-stage event, while secondly, it is nowhere recorded that the church will be taken from the world before the Lord comes again. One main assumption of pre-tribulationism is that the church, since there is no mention of it being on the earth from chapter four of Revelation onwards, must therefore have been raptured. This interpretation of Revelation is facilitated by understanding the address to the seven churches in Asia Minor not simply as an address to seven local churches but also as an address to the universal body of Christ in seven different ages. See, Glass, "Eschatology: A Clear and Present Danger", 130.

by material and spiritual blessing, since the curse upon the earth will be removed. At the end of the thousand years, Satan is loosed and the nations rebel against the Messiah (Rev. 20:7-8). God will crush this uprising in the last battle of the ages and Satan will be thrown into the lake of fire. The second resurrection then takes place and the unrighteous dead are raised to stand before God (v. 5, 11-13a), judged and cast into the lake of fire along with Satan. The place where they suffer will be final and everlasting punishment (v. 13b-15). The earth is finally destroyed and a new heaven and earth are brought into existence. Then the New Jerusalem, the Holy City of God will come down out of heaven and saints will enjoy the presence of God forever (21:1-27).[17]

The Origin and Development of Eschatology

Pentecostal movement came out of the nineteenth century Holiness movement, which in turn is rooted in the Methodism of John Wesley. The Holiness movement was a radical movement, more than any other streams of nineteenth century evangelicalism. As James Glass puts it, it was a movement of crisis; the crisis of conversion; the crisis of baptism in the Spirit. It was a movement of revival that expected God to break into people's lives, and even the whole of society. Its eschatology was similarly radical. God would 'rend the heavens' and rule the earth either by means of the church or by the personal advent of Jesus to establish his kingdom. Inheriting the ethos and nature of the Holiness Movement, Pentecostalism too became a radical spiritual movement and embraced a radical eschatology.[18] Many leaders in the Holiness movement came to Azusa Street to 'receive their Pentecost', then took the message home to share with their churches and fellow ministers. In this way, several Holiness groups were swept into the emerging Pentecostal movement.[19]

Additionally, Pentecostals inherited the 'full gospel' from A. B. Simpson and other spiritual leaders in which Jesus was understood as the coming king. Pentecostals also read the scripture as the final authority for the future events and applied the eschatological references in the Bible literally. Pentecostals were also influenced by the dispensationalist teaching because some of the early Pentecostals had come from the Brethren churches. However, according to Glass, there was not a uniform eschatological outlook in the Holiness movement. Postmillenialism and premillenialism were both espoused by proponents of Holiness teaching. Towards the end of the century, premillenialism was becoming increasingly accepted. The shift in outlook was due to the changing social conditions and the theological relativism in religious circle.[20]

---

[17] Warrington, *Pentecostal Theology*, 314-315; Glass, "Eschatology: A Clear and Present Danger", 131-132.

[18] Glass, "Eschatology: A Clear and Present Danger", 133.

[19] McQueen, *Toward a Pentecostal Eschatology*, 61.

[20] Glass, "Eschatology: A Clear and Present Danger", 132-133.

This eschatological doctrine and fervour were taken over by the emerging Pentecostal movement. For Pentecostals, the "latter rain" of the Spirit had come to restore apostolic power (the power of Pentecost as the former rain) along with extraordinary gifts of the Spirit. They believed that the outpouring of the Spirit in the early twentieth century was the answer to the eschatological expectations of the late nineteenth-century Holiness movement. The early adherents understood their movement as the final empowerment for end-time missions. At first, many believed that the gift of tongues would be the supernatural means whereby all the nations would be quickly evangelized in order that Christ may return. The revival was a sure sign that the end was near.[21] Quoting *The Pentecostal Evangel,* Faupel puts it succinctly, "Salvation, the Baptism in the Holy Spirit, Divine Healing, the ministrations of the Holy Spirit among us are features of a program. ...The Second Coming of Lord Jesus Christ is not a feature of the program...it is THE program."[22] Thus, eschatology stood as the cornerstone of Pentecostal spirituality.

However, the emergence of the futurist premillennialism (pretribulation premillennialism) as we see today in Pentecostal movement arose in the early 1830s among the Plymouth Brethren, propagated most prominently by John Nelson Darby. The view was popularised by the publication of a monthly periodical (beginning in 1863), and the propagation of the teaching at various Bible and prophecy conferences (1875-1900).[23] Explaining 1 Thess. 4.16-17, Darby contended that there would be a rapture of the church prior to a seven-year tribulation period during which the Antichrist would be revealed. At the end of the seven years, Christ would return with his saints and, in the great battle of Armageddon, defeat the Satanic force. A thousand-year period would follow in which Christ would reign on earth with his saints. Satan would then be released for a season to test those who had not been raptured. The great white throne judgment would then take place when those judged righteous would be sent to Heaven and those found unrighteous would be doomed to Hell.[24]

The popularity of pretribulationist premillennialism among Pentecostals was largely due to the fact that it was the majority view of those who joined the movements from other evangelical denominations. Moreover, new scientific inventions and discoveries were considered augmenting the rule of the antichrist and coming tribulation. At the same time, an increase in immorality worldwide, diabolic and antichristian activities were also counted as the sure signs of the 'end of days'. The majority of premillennialists believed that most of the contents of

---

[21] McQueen, *Toward a Pentecostal Eschatology*, 9-10. Faupel, *Everlasting Gospel,* 113; J.R. Goff, Jr, "Closing Out the Church Age: Pentecostals Face the Twenty- First Century", *Pneuma* 14.1 (Spring, 1992): 7-21.

[22] Faupel, *Everlasting Gospel,* 43; D. H. Mcdowell, "The Purpose for the Second Coming of the Lord", *Pentecostal Evangel* (2 May 1925), 2.

[23] McQueen, *Toward a Pentecostal Eschatology*, 8.

[24] Faupel, *The Everlasting Gospel,* 29-30.

the book of Revelation are yet to be fulfilled, and going to happen imminently.[25] Some have suggested the dates of coming of Christ by carefully investigating the dispensational scheme. I have heard some experts in eschatology predicting the coming of Christ within few years, presenting all the biblical evidences and contemporary happenings. Even some countries had named as the place of rising of antichrist. Moreover, in order to prove and establish pre-tribulation premillennialism, Pentecostals have been identified many individuals as well as organisations as the antichrist: the Pope, Saddam Husain, the former ruler of Iraq, WCC, European Union, UN, NATO, and so on. These entities were considered as the forerunners of a one world government and a pseudo-church or a reconstituted form of the Roman Empire (Rev. 12.3; 13.1,17).[26] Glass correctly diagnoses the negative effects of such activities, despite these teachings created eager expectation for the second coming of the Lord:

> So-called experts on biblical prophecy often made startling predictions and the study of the prophetic scriptures gave way to unbiblical speculation. Prophetic teachers sometimes claimed that the Bible was as up to date as today's newspaper, yet some of their expositions were soon as out of date as yesterday's newspaper. This kind of sensationalism did and does great harm to the study of Bible prophecy and eventually produces frustration and disillusionment in those who follow such teaching. This might well explain a dearth of preaching on the Lord's return; the reaction against sensationalism may have been one against Bible prophecy as well.[27]

Besides, Dispensationalism is undergirded by a cessation doctrine, which argues that all the spectacular charismatic gifts ceased in the apostolic age. The experience of the Baptism of the Holy Spirit, tongue speaking, use of spiritual gifts were considered as gibberish or out rightly demonic. The wedding of dispensationalism to Pentecostal Pneumatology resulted in undermining of Pentecostal ecclesiology and the doctrine of Spirit baptism. The meaning of the blessed hope thus changed from the advent of the Second Coming to this new view of the rapture. Passive withdrawal from society thus replaced the original vision of hope in Pentecostal eschatology.[28] McQueen bluntly puts its effect, "The classical dispensationalism is one of the reasons for the denial of spiritual gifts in the Church today, which is, in essence, a denial of one of the core components

---

[25] Warrington, *Pentecostal Theology*, 310.

[26] Warrington, *Pentecostal Theology*, 311.

[27] Glass, "Eschatology: A Clear and Present Danger", 144.

[28] Peter Althouse, "The Landscape of Pentecostal and Charismatic Eschatology", in *Perspectives in Pentecostal Eschatologies*, 15.

of Pentecostal spirituality."[29] Thus, the liberative edge of the movement was undermined by the wholesale adoption of dispensationalism.

In the early period of Pentecostal movement, most of the classical Pentecostal denominations of the world subscribed to the dispensational eschatological scheme.[30] However, there were certain voices and movements that had kept the original liberative Pentecostal eschatology. Instead of passive withdrawal from society in anticipation of a secret rapture and the expression of divine judgment on the wicked, early classical Pentecostals anticipated an intensification of the charismatic outpouring of the Spirit in expectation of a final, glorious harvest of souls prior to the coming of the Lord.[31] Similarly, Macchia endorses that the Pentecostal priority with regard to eschatology was the empowerment of the Spirit for faithful life and mission rather than useless speculation about end-time doomsday scenarios. Their belief in a proliferation of apostolic signs and wonders amid an empowered church would also run contrary to dispensationalist teaching.[32] Compartmentalizing the relevance of the biblical text into historical periods moves contrary to the thrust of Pentecostal hermeneutics. In addition, Pentecostals see the age of the church as the era of the Spirit promised to Israel in the Old Testament (e.g., Joel 2:28). They would not see the church as a hiatus in between such a promise and its fulfilment later in the millennium.[33] Sheppard argues persuasively that Pentecostalism accepted certain features of the end-time schema from the dispensationalists early on but did not swallow its larger hermeneutical implications until they attempted later to gain the acceptance of conservative evangelical churches. Certainly there is an "uneasy relationship" between dispensationalism and Pentecostal eschatology.[34]

As a result of this theological difference, Pentecostals modified the dispensational script so that to maintain their understanding of the work of the Holy Spirit.[35] Wacker, for instance, proposes that Pentecostalism adopted the framework of classical dispensationalism but modified it in three major ways. First, Pentecostals claimed that only those believers who were baptized in the Holy Spirit would be taken up in the rapture. Second, they believed that all of the world

---

[29] McQueen, *Toward a Pentecostal Eschatology*, 57.

[30] The denominations such as Church of God (Cleveland), Church of God in Christ, Assemblies of God, International Church of the Foursquare Gospel, Pentecostal Assemblies of Canada, and a variety of Apostolic denominations follow this pattern. In India, all the classical Pentecostals subscribe to dispensationalism.

[31] Althouse, "The Landscape of Pentecostal and Charismatic Eschatology", 15.

[32] Macchia, "Pentecostal and Charismatic Theology", 357-358.

[33] Macchia, "Pentecostal and Charismatic Theology", 357.

[34] Gerald T. Sheppard, "Pentecostalism and the Hermeneutics of Dispensationalism", *Pneuma* 6:2 (Fall 1984), 9–10, 32–33 and 76; Macchia, "Pentecostal and Charismatic Theology", 357-358.

[35] McQueen, *Toward a Pentecostal Eschatology*, 57.

must hear the Pentecostal message (the full gospel) before Christ would come to take away his bride. Third, the present age of the Church was the fulfilment of God's plan for history, being marked in its beginning and ending periods with the outpouring of the Spirit. Thus, the restoration of miracles and other gifts of the Spirit, which had ceased according to the dispensationalists, became the primary sign that the present age was drawing to a close.[36]

In the history of Pentecostal movement various modifications and approaches have emerged in Pentecostal eschatology. Althouse presents three different eschatological positions in the history of the movement: the first was a latter rain eschatology, which anticipated a wondrous outpouring of the Spirit unseen since apostolic days. The belief was that as the new age dawned that the Spirit would pour out spiritual gifts to empower Christians to prepare for the kingdom. The second was the rise of dispensational millennialism (what Althouse calls fundamentalist dispensationalism) in the mid-twentieth century. The third phase is ongoing, in which Pentecostals are dissatisfied with dispensationalism and are articulating a proleptic eschatology, which focuses on the already-not yet, or the inauguration and fulfilment of the eschaton.[37] In addition, according to Warrington, a significant minority of Pentecostals prefer an amillennial perspective. It understands the 1000 years of Rev. 20:1-7 as symbolic of the era from the death of Jesus to his return and does not accord to Israel as much prophetic significance, believing that Israel is no longer God's chosen nation because the Church has taken that position.[38]

Despite eschatology served as the catalyst to bring Pentecostalism to birth and the *development* of Pentecostal thought, the original vision was considerably waned away in the movement.[39] Warrington rightly identifies that Pentecostals are now much more prepared to analyse and question their beliefs; that is not to suggest that they have rejected or will reject them. He argues that now Pentecostals are questioning some of the extreme ideas in eschatological scheme:

> [Pentecostals] are prepared to ask questions of some of "the eschatological shibboleths of their forefathers" and in so doing, some of them have arrived at different conclusions. Although, premillenrialism introduced a fervent drive to evangelize the world, recent decades

[36] Grant Wacker, *Heaven Below: Early Pentecostalism and American Culture* (Cambridge, MA: Harvard University Press, 2001), 251-65.

[37] Peter Althouse, "Pentecostal Eschatology in Context: The Eschatological Orientation of the Full Gospel", in *Perspectives in Pentecostal Eschatologies*, 210-211. The coming up of the fundamentalist dispensationalism was in part a reaction to the 1940's Latter Rain movement. It was a divisive movement that used latter rain theology to castigate established Pentecostal denominations, and also in part due to the evangelicalization of Pentecostalism, in which dispensational millennialism played a major role in reshaping Pentecostal theology.

[38] Warrington, *Pentecostal Theology*, 311.

[39] McQueen, *Toward a Pentecostal Eschatology*, 10.

> have seen a demise in this fervour and, perhaps coincidentally, in the adherence to premillennialism. The fact that Jesus has not come back after decades of certainty and the upward mobility of many Pentecostals have resulted in a cooling of the ardour to expect the rapture at any moment.[40]

Having seen an overview, origin and development of the eschatology of the movement and the declining trend as well, now we shall explore some of the unique aspects of Pentecostal eschatology that make Pentecostalism a liberative movement.

Christ-Centric Eschatology

Pentecostal eschatology is firmly connected to Pentecostal Christology. The way in which Pentecostals understand Christ, points to a high Christology. Besides, for Pentecostals Christology is not merely a doctrine but an intimate experience, hence it is an experiential Christology. Just as Pentecostals understand and experience Jesus Christ as the saviour, healer and the baptiser of the Holy Spirit, they also experience Jesus as the coming king. Therefore, when they read Bible, the references that point to the second coming of Jesus is understood literally and applied in their life and also proclaimed. In the early period of Pentecostal movement, the preaching of Christ's birth, death, resurrection and Second Coming was naturally extended to include, "His reigning in His millennial kingdom, and His white throne judgment, and then the new heavens and earth and the New Jerusalem coming down from God out of heaven, when He shall have put all enemies under His feet and He shall reign eternally, and we shall abide with Him forever and ever."[41] Moreover, all the other elements of the 'full gospel'- salvation, healing, Spirit baptism-are closely connected to the second coming of Christ. For instance, the development of the doctrine of the baptism in the Spirit, and speaking in tongues as the "Bible evidence" of Spirit baptism, was oriented to a great end-time revival preceding the coming of the Lord. For Charles Parham, speaking in tongues was a supernatural endowment to speak the languages of the world, in order for the gospel to be preached to all nations as the last sign ushering in the return of Christ. In other words, both the urgency in preaching the gospel to the whole world and the supernatural endowment of speaking in tongues were eschatological.[42] Similarly, the preaching of regeneration, the restoration of humanity back to God, the outpouring and the Baptism of the Holy Spirit upon believers, the working of signs and wonders and miracles are all leading up to the coming of Jesus.[43]

---

[40] Warrington, *Pentecostal Theology*, 313.

[41] McQueen, "Early Pentecostal Eschatology", 143; *Apostolic Faith* 1.6 (Oct 1907), 7.

[42] Althouse, "Pentecostal Eschatology in Context", 206

[43] Althouse, "Pentecostal Eschatology in Context", 207.

Obviously, this emphasis on the person and work of Christ in the Pentecostal movement has been a shaping factor in Pentecostal eschatology. Therefore, Glass terms Pentecostal eschatology as a Christological concern and surmises that the high Christology of Pentecostalism may well have pushed Pentecostal eschatology in a literalist direction.[44] Very often Pentecostals interpret eschatological references literally and end up in presenting unbiblical pictures. Nonetheless, they have a great zeal for the return of Christ and wish to bring as many as people to Pentecostal churches to prepare them as the bride of Christ. Likewise, they believe all the eschatological passages in literal sense and wait them to happen as it is portrayed in the scripture. As Glass puts it, "A non-literalist eschatology may thus be viewed as being detrimental to the status of Christ; the more literal the eschatology, the more dignity and glory accorded to Christ."[45] Thus, Pentecostal eschatology is thoroughly Christological.

Spirit-Centric Eschatology

Another significant character of Pentecostal eschatology is its strong connection to the work of the Holy Spirit. Here the baptism of the Holy Spirit and spiritual gifts are understood as the preparation for the coming of Christ. Early Pentecostal journals are replete with portrayals of references of connection between the baptism of the Spirit and the coming of Christ. For instance, McQueen quotes *The Apostolic Faith*, "In my mind this is the key to the present revival, with its speaking in tongues and other signs and wonders, that the coming of our blessed Lord is very near, and the Holy Spirit is here working in apostolic fashion to get the bride ready for meeting the Bridegroom."[46] Most frequently used metaphor in relation to the coming of Christ in *The Apostolic Faith* is that of the bride of Christ viewed in the contexts of the parable of the ten virgins (Mt. 25.1-13) and the marriage supper of the Lamb (Rev. 19.9). This complex images provided a comprehensive framework of connection between the baptism in the Holy Spirit and anticipated future fulfilment. McQueen underlines that in the eschatology of Azusa Street, the baptism in the Holy Spirit was 'the real type' of the 'double portion' of oil obtained by the wise virgins in the parable of the ten virgins. Thus, only those who were baptized in the Spirit were thought to be prepared to meet the coming Bridegroom and attend the marriage supper.[47] Another prominent image used among early Pentecostals to refer to the baptism in the Holy Spirit is that of the seal of God in the forehead (Rev. 7.1-3). Seymour wrote, "I am so glad that the Lord is holding back the winds until the angel has sealed all of the saints of the living God in their foreheads, the baptism of the Holy Ghost."[48] We also

[44] Glass, "Eschatology: A Clear and Present Danger", 136.

[45] Glass, "Eschatology: A Clear and Present Danger", 136.

[46] McQueen, *Toward a Pentecostal Eschatology*, 79.

[47] McQueen, *Toward a Pentecostal Eschatology*, 66; *Apostolic Faith* 1.5 (Jan, 1907), 2.

[48] McQueen, *Toward a Pentecostal Eschatology*, 68; *Apostolic Faith* 1.9 (Jun-Sep, 1907), 4.

see images that are taken out of the book of Revelation. For example, 'Full Over-comers' (Rev. 14:38); the 144,000 that appear with the Lamb on Mount Zion (Rev. 14.1) are identified as 'full over-comers' who were ready to go in the rapture with Christ to the marriage supper.[49]

Besides, Pentecostals typically make a connection between the empowerment of Spirit baptism and eschatological urgency for the church's global mission to spread the gospel. Early Pentecostals connected Joel's prophecy in Acts (Peter's sermon in the day of Pentecost) with various other Old Testament prophetic verses, which distinguished between the time of "the latter rain" and "the former rain" in the cycle of the annual agrarian harvest. By such a hermeneutical arrangement of biblical texts, Pentecostals portrayed the coming of the Spirit in the upper room in Jerusalem as "the former rain" and the coming of the Spirit at the Azusa Street Mission in Los Angeles as "the latter rain". As a consequence of this logic, Pentecostals believed that "the latter rain" outpouring of the Spirit at Azusa Street and beyond was a telltale "sign" of the impending return of Jesus Christ.[50] The natural corollary of this understanding was obvious; early Pentecostals, even ordinary believers became global missionaries.

Similarly, the gift of tongues is also understood in relation to eschatology in Pentecostal theology. Macchia interprets tongues within the context of eschatology as theophanic, sacramental and ecumenical. He further explains:

> The Pentecost narrative of Acts 2 is an eschatological event, in which the coming of the resurrection Spirit renews the covenantal community in anticipation of the parousia, and tongues is a theophanic sign of divine self-disclosure like that of the burning bush in the calling of Moses and the giving of the Law. As an eschatological foretaste, speaking in tongues is a cry for liberation, a "cry of abandonment", which symbolizes the liberating force of the Spirit in breaking down racial, gender and class barriers. Glossolalia embodies an equalizing impulse in levelling all languages and human strivings, pointing to the inauguration of divine justice and mercy in its "groaning" for the suffering of creation yearning for liberation.[51]

Thus, having experienced the gift of tongues, Pentecostals became the carriers of the message of liberation.

Another important elements to explore in relation to the work of the Spirit and eschatology is divine healing. Pentecostal theologians consider divine healing of the body as the visible sign of imminent 'eschatological redemption'. Macchia explains the healing of the body as the foretaste of the final resurrection

---

[49] McQueen, *Toward a Pentecostal Eschatology*, 69.

[50] Dempster, "Eschatology, Spirit Baptism, and Inclusiveness", 156.

[51] Althouse, "Pentecostal Eschatology in Context", 220.

of the body and advocates to see sickness and healing in the context of Christian hope for the redemption and liberation of all of creation.[52] In the same way, Land explains divine healings as "sign of the eschatological breaking in of the kingdom of God and last days restoration for the proclamation of the gospel of the kingdom in all the earth."[53] Divine healing is a partial realization of the resurrection because the resurrection of Christ and the outpouring of the Spirit have already been inaugurated and God's reign is already here and calls Christians to both expectation and participation in the kingdom. Moreover, healing cast in the light of the eschaton as its partial realization, also has social-political implications as Christians work in service to God's righteousness to change the material conditions of the world.[54] The implication of divine healing is not only about the resurrection of believers, it has wider ramification for rest of the creation (ecology). Althouse envisions healing as a sign of creation's eschatological transformation in the context of the proleptic eschatology and has implications for ecological responsibility. Creation is the context from which God's eschatological transformation will emerge, thereby calling us to participate in the care of God's good creation, as we await its apocalyptic transformation.[55] Thus, Pentecostals understand divine healing "a means of achieving deeper solidarity with the oppressed and the suffering creation as well as with the Spirit of redemption at work in healing."[56]

Mission-Centric Eschatology

Another significant aspect of Pentecostal eschatology is its missionary thrust. Apocalyptic vision of Pentecostals impelled them on a world-wide mission to spread the "full gospel" message because they considered that the time is short. Pentecostal missiologist Grant McClung rightly identifies the reason behind the missionary passion of early Pentecostals. The premillennial dispensational belief in the imminent return of Jesus Christ coupled with the experience of Spirit baptism for empowerment of believers to "Go into all the world and preach the gospel to all creation" (Mark 16:15) combined to forge a potent motivational force for world evangelism.[57] The global aspect of the mission was captured in the following announcement: "One token of the Lord's coming is that He is melting all races and nations together, and they are filled with the power and glory of God. He is baptizing by one spirit into one body and making up a people that

---

[52] Frank D. Macchia, "The Struggle for Global Witness: Shifting Paradigms in Pentecostal Theology", *The Globalization of Pentecostalism*, edited by M.W. Dempster, B. D. Klaus & D. Petersen (Carlisle: Regnum, 1999), 21.

[53] Land, *Pentecostal Spirituality*, 95.

[54] Althouse, "Pentecostal Eschatology in Context", 213.

[55] Althouse, "Pentecostal Eschatology in Context", 214.

[56] Macchia, "The Struggle for Global Witness", 22.

[57] Dempster, "Eschatology, Spirit Baptism, and Inclusiveness", 157.

will be ready to meet Him when He comes."[58] Similarly, another early writer expressed the urgency of the hour: "With almost a billion souls yet unreached by the gospel, O how we ought to haste to the ends of the earth with the glad news of salvation before it is too late."[59] To carry out such critical mission, first generation Pentecostals were equipped with spiritual gifts. For them the nine-fold gifts (I Cor.14), with which they were equipped assured that their message came directly from God. Not only did these gifts function as authenticating signs, they were also understood as God's means of enabling his chosen people to accomplish their task. To hasten that day, they eagerly sought to proclaim with authority and power 'this Gospel of the Kingdom.'[60]

As we have already seen, for Pentecostals, the signs and miracles were indications that they were living and participating in the "latter rain", in a "time before the time", in which Jesus would return. The Spirit was readying the world for the Second Coming of Christ, and those who knew and experienced this spiritual reality were called to share their faith in preparation of the "marriage supper of the Lamb". Belief in Christ's immediate return was a catalyst for sacrificial mission endeavours, which included coming out for cross-cultural missions, ready to experience hardship for the gospel.[61] McQueen summarises Wacker's explanation for the reasons for imminent missionary conscious among the early Pentecostals. Pentecostals foresaw an impending crisis and imminent doom for the world because of military rhetoric of powerful nations. However, they believed that for the true believer the end was filled with hope because the coming of Jesus meant that their suffering would end. Since, the coming catastrophe meant that time was short to do God's work and therefore the missionary zeal of early Pentecostals developed a world missionary consciousness and crossed many cultural barriers.[62]

Furthermore, as Faupel notes, many early Pentecostals believed their evangelistic practices could in fact hasten Christ's return. Though perhaps naive, Pentecostals believed that Christ's return would be preceded by the preaching of the gospel unto the ends of the earth. Castelo sounds similar, "Past expectation of the immediacy of Jesus' Second Coming and the fervour this created are logically precarious when they assume human creatures can force God's hand. Many early Pentecostals mistakenly believed that their work could hasten Jesus' return if all the signs of the last days, especially the preaching of the gospel to all nations,

---

[58] McQueen, "Early Pentecostal Eschatology", 151; *Apostolic Faith* 1.6 (Feb–Mar, 1907), 7.

[59] Faupel, *The Everlasting Gospel*, 21; "The Latter Days", *Word and Work* 29 (September, 1907), 231.

[60] Faupel, *The Everlasting Gospel*, 22-24.

[61] Daniel Castelo, "Patience as a Theological Virtue: A Challenge to Pentecostal Eschatology", in *Perspectives in Pentecostal Eschatologies*, 233-234; Faupel, *Everlasting Gospel*, 20.

[62] McQueen, *Toward a Pentecostal Eschatology*, 12.

are fulfilled."[63] For all the "escapist" tendencies within Pentecostalism, on this point they tended to be quite optimistic about how human efforts could influence salvation history to reach its completion.[64] *The Apostolic Faith* summarized it best: "This Gospel, the full Gospel of Jesus must be preached in all the earth for a witness then shall the end come."[65]

Community-Centric Mission Eschatology

It is argued by Pentecostals as well as outsiders that Biblical eschatology organized around a dispensational framework, as it has existed in Pentecostal understanding, is a major, perhaps the major, theological factor that has sparked and perpetuated the controversy over the social involvement of the church. Some observe that the eschatological fervour among Pentecostals unwittingly promoted a withdrawal of church from social involvement because such social concern might sidetrack the church from its priority of evangelistic mission.[66] Dwight J. Wilson characterized the impact of premillennial dispensational eschatology in forming the predominant Pentecostal mindset on social ministry: "Since the end is near, they are indifferent to social change and have rejected the reformist methods of the optimistic postmillennialists and have concentrated on 'snatching brands from the fire' and letting social reforms result from humankind being born again."[67] Moreover, belief in the imminent return of Jesus Christ had the latent function of producing within the Pentecostal movement a spirit of social quietism.[68]

However, in contrast to above observations, many of Pentecostal theologians strongly assert that contrary to the popular perception, the eschatological fervour among Pentecostals in reality propelled them to closely involve in alleviating the social evils in their surroundings. Along the same line of argument, Dempster demonstrates that belief in the triumphant return of Jesus Christ, when it is grounded in Jesus' own mission, ministry, and message about the kingdom of God, actually entails an eschatological warrant and a moral mandate for the church's engagement with society. According to him, the eschatologically driven focus on evangelism did not keep ministers and missionaries from developing social programs. Despite the eschatological beliefs at the theological level, church leaders at the practical level who ministered at home in decaying urban centers or abroad in various geographical regions marked by hunger, disease, and poverty developed social programs to meet

---

[63] Castelo, "Patience as a Theological Virtue", 242.

[64] Castelo, "Patience as a Theological Virtue", 242.

[65] McQueen, *Toward a Pentecostal Eschatology*, 73; *Apostolic Faith* 1.10 (Sep, 1907), 1.

[66] Dempster, "Eschatology, Spirit Baptism, and Inclusiveness", 157.

[67] Dwight J. Wilson, "Eschatology, Pentecostal Perspectives on", in *DPCM*, edited by S.M. Burgess & G.B. McGee (Michigan: Zondervan, 1988), 267.

[68] Dempster, "Eschatology, Spirit Baptism, and Inclusiveness", 157.

human need.[69] Similarly, Althouse affirms that the proleptic tension situates Pentecostalism within the socio-historical framework, which inspires believers to acts of social benevolence and justice. Issues in the world such as racism, poverty, chauvinism, or spiritual lostness were addressed within the context of its eschatological impulse, so that a reconciled church would realize racial equality, social justice, women in ministry and mission.[70]

This was true all over the world. A cursory glance into the history of Pentecostal movement worldwide would prove that early Pentecostals were socially active and contributed to the alleviation of pain and suffering of the poor and the downtrodden. For instance, in India early Pentecostal missionaries from the West established schools and orphanages along with mission stations. They had extensive social activities to help the natives. Burgess testifies the efforts of early Pentecostal missionaries:

> [Because] of difficulties faced in evangelizing North India, there turned to establishing institutions such as orphanages, industrial schools, elementary schools, correspondence schools, radio programs, leper asylums and dispensaries. The Assemblies of God developed the most extensive system of institutions, primarily centered in the Gangetic plain (North India).[71]

Dempster also corroborates the trend, "From the early days of the movement, church leaders established orphanages, hospices, rescue homes, and asylum for leprosy affected people as expressions of Christian compassion for the homeless, the poor, the hungry, and the outcasts of society. In more recent times, social programs have expanded beyond social welfare programs to include involvement designed to change the unjust social conditions that perpetuate human ills such as poverty and hunger."[72]

It is obvious that even though early Pentecostal eschatological expressions had certain negative elements in them due to over dependence on dispensationalism, it had wide range of effects in the formation and explication of Pentecostal theology, mission and worldwide growth of the movement. As we have seen, over reliance on Premillennialism and its schemes somehow steered away early Pentecostals from the biblical paradigm of 'already not-yet'

---

[69] Dempster, "Eschatology, Spirit Baptism, and Inclusiveness", 158.

[70] Althouse, "Pentecostal Eschatology in Context", 209.

[71] These include an orphanage and girls school at FBettiah, a girls' orphanage at Purulia, the James Harvey boys school at Nawabganj, a leper work at Uska Bazar begun in 1911 by Minnie Abrams, the "Baby Fold" at Rupaidiha, a girls' industrial school at Siswa Bazar. Stanley M. Burgess, "Pentecostalism in India: An Overview", *AJPS* 4/1 (2001): 92-93. Also see G. B. McGee, "Pentecostal Phenomena and Revivals in India: Implication for Indigenous Church Leadership" *IBMR* 20/3 (July, 1996), 124.

[72] Dempster, "Eschatology, Spirit Baptism, and Inclusiveness", 158.

for an over emphasised eschatology. However, in practical applications, their eschatological understanding was certainly in accordance with the biblical principles - the Christological notions they proclaimed and also the mission of the church that ensued following the eschatological ideals. Moreover, their eschatological urgency and fervour that resulted in rapid missionary activities and social programmes, lifted up many from the wretched conditions. Thus, eschatology played a liberative and transformative role in Pentecostal spirituality and it is true even today.

Nevertheless, it has been observed that Pentecostals of the twenty first century have lost the eschatological fervour of their forefathers in larger degree and hence has a weakened liberative thrust. Castelo bemoans, "Contemporary Pentecostals now live in a time when eschatological fervour has diminished. Reference is rarely made to Jesus' Second Coming in today's Pentecostal contexts."[73] If early Pentecostals had an 'over-sized eschatology' and over emphasis on it, today's Pentecostals have an extreme opposite position. In reality, Pentecostal eschatological expectancy is in tatters, especially in those contexts in which Pentecostalism has settled for an extended period of time. The less emphatic belief in the imminent return of Jesus has resulted in the topic of the second coming being less preached than it once was. It has been put on the shelf to become dusty, now and again being retrieved for a Bible study or a reminder that Jesus is coming again sometime in the future.[74] According to Castelo, a shift in Pentecostal theology has taken place so that Pentecostal self-understanding now revolves around the role of glossolalia in the baptism of the Spirit, or the Spirit's activity in charismatic expression, rather than the end-time expectation of the kingdom in which the manifestation of tongues plays a role.[75] He raises questions related to Pentecostal identity and self understanding in the context of waning away of eschatological expectancy: How do Pentecostals understand their history and their future in light of Christ's own eschatological tarrying? Christ has not yet returned despite expectations, so how can current Pentecostals deal with their heritage of eschatological fervour in light of the Lord's own patience in delaying the parousia?[76] These questions are pertinent and ought to be answered. Therefore, here we shall look into some of the way in which Pentecostals can regain their eschatological passion and improve their eschatological notions so that it may contribute to the extension of the kingdom of God and enhance the liberative potentials of the movement.

The faith in the second coming of Christ is the cornerstone of Christianity and so is indispensible for the existence and growth of Pentecostal movement. Therefore, it is paramount to reignite the lost fervour eschatological passion for

---

[73] Castelo, "Patience as a Theological Virtue", 234.

[74] Warrington, *Pentecostal Theology*, 321.

[75] Castelo, "Patience as a Theological Virtue", 234.

[76] Castelo, "Patience as a Theological Virtue", 234.

a healthy Christian life as well as the healthy growth of the movement. However, today's Pentecostals generally show apathetic attitude towards the great hope that existed among their Pentecostal forefathers. Many of them in wealthy nations are well settled and look for a better and prosperous future, except new converts in the Majority world. It is also a fact that early Pentecostals were overemphasised their expectation of the second coming of Christ as the first century Christians. What they had predicted and churned out of the biblical passages in their eschatological excitement due to the assimilation of dispensational schema sound less useful today. Therefore, there is an urgent need of a balanced eschatology which would help believers to keep their hope burning, at same time equipping them to involve in their surroundings.

The first question comes before us is, how can Pentecostals integrate an otherworldly eschatology into a prophetic one so as to avoid succumbing to fundamentalist escapism and a one-sided otherworldliness? As we look back to the history of Pentecostal movement, it is obvious that early Pentecostals were wrong about some of the details of their eschatology, but they were right to expect and live in light of the eschatological kingdom. The task for contemporary Pentecostals, and especially Pentecostal scholars, is to preserve those positive features of early Pentecostal expectancy without succumbing to end-time scenarios based in hypothetical assumptions.[77] Dempster advocates Pentecostals to view the Pentecost as the link between Jesus' proclamation of the justice and mercy of the kingdom of God and the redemption proclaimed by the church. He explains,

> When couched within the prophetic tradition, the eschatological continuity between the 'already' and the 'not yet' kingdom[s] implies that the apocalyptic act at the end of this age will not be one of total *annihilation* of the world but one of total *transformation* of the world.[78]

Moreover, Dempster shows the model of eschatology that was presented by Jesus in his earthly ministry that emphasised both present and future kingdom of God. This can be a viable model for contemporary Pentecostals.

> ...when Jesus announced that he would inaugurate God's reign again in human history through his ministry, he declared the eschatological kingdom was related to both present time and future time...It seems clear that the kingdom of God was present for Jesus, and it seems equally clear that the kingdom of God was future for Jesus. The kingdom of God, according to Jesus, was both a present reality and a future reality. The kingdom of God was "already" present in the

[77] Castelo, "Patience as a Theological Virtue", 242.

[78] Murray W. Dempster, "Christian Social Concern in Pentecostal Perspective: Reformulating Pentecostal Eschatology", *JPT* 2 (Apr. 1993), 62.

> messianic signs associated with his ministry but "not yet" consummated in the transformation of a new heaven and a new earth. For Jesus the kingdom of God was "now" and "not yet.[79]

Similarly, Land advocates that "Pentecostals should focus their attention and theological efforts on understanding God as the eschatological trinitarian presence and not on speculation concerning end-time sequences."[80] The central message of the eschatological hope is that it will usher in the complete rule of God that is being established already in this world through the Church. Pentecostals should concentrate not just on being removed from the sin and depravity of this world but also how best to introduce the Kingdom of God and righteousness into society prior to any return of Jesus.[81]

Glass advocates that when eschatology is given its proper place within the theology and practice of the Pentecostal community as an encouragement to holiness and a ground of hope for the future, then whatever millenialist shape it takes will matter less. This might mean that the incarnation, crucifixion and resurrection of Christ and the coming of the Holy Spirit would have as formative a role in shaping the Pentecostal worldview as the parousia. This would allow Pentecostals to interpret and understand their role in society from a wider theological perspective without sacrificing their distinctive contributions to eschatology.[82] Besides, in the context of contemporary issues of environmental destructions and annihilation, Pentecostal theology must be rearticulated within the context of eschatological hope, in a way that the future hope of the entire cosmos is accessible in the present. In other words, the world and creation together is the context for eschatology and therefore any holistic eschatological construction must be founded in a creational eschatology.[83]

Finally, as the coming of Jesus is tarried, it is essential for Pentecostal to practice patience through their activities.[84] According to Castelo, one such activity is pursuing lament within Pentecostal communal life. The practice of lament can help Pentecostals be a more truthful community, one that lives in transparency to and vulnerability before God and one another in the context of tarrying for the coming of Christ.

> In acknowledging that..Christ has not returned as expected, or that one is not healed or apparently shown blessing, Pentecostals can recognize in concrete circumstances the promise of hope...I believe Pentecostals have avoided talk of lament in their public

[79] Dempster, "Eschatology, Spirit Baptism, and Inclusiveness", 164.

[80] Land, *Pentecostal Spirituality*, 28.

[81] Warrington, *Pentecostal Theology*, 322-323.

[82] Glass, "Eschatology: A Clear and Present Danger", 145.

[83] Althouse, "Pentecostal Eschatology in Context", 206.

[84] Castelo, "Patience as a Theological Virtue", 243.

> pronouncements for fear that doing so would be perceived as a sign of inadequate faith. Pentecostals ought to realize that being a community of hope implies being a patient people who participate in the *koinonia* of one another's sufferings, hoping for their soon-returning Lord in the midst of their plight.[85]

As we conclude our discussion of Pentecostal eschatology, it is obvious that early Pentecostals expected and proclaimed a scheme of eschatological events that was borrowed from Dispensationalism. It is also a fact that following the scheme had created a heightened excitement that had resulted in unbiblical predictions regarding the second coming of Jesus. Nonetheless, early Pentecostal carried out a mission that was unparallel in the history of the church due to their expectancy and that mission was a liberative mission. However, after a century, the fervour has considerably declined and today we seldom hear the proclamation of the coming of Jesus. It is vital to reignite the lost expectancy of the coming the Lord as it is the cornerstone of Christian faith. However, instead of chasing a timetable of apocalyptic future events, Pentecostals should closely study the biblical passages that Jesus taught about his second coming and also construct their hope in the light of the teaching of the entire scripture. It is also significant to pursue holiness, integrity, watchfulness in personal and community life which are paramount for preparation of the coming of the Lord. In addition, the missionary thrust that was created among the early Pentecostals by their eschatological fervour be brought back to contemporary Pentecostals to liberate their compatriots who are living in wretched conditions. Certainly, a balanced understanding of eschatology will help the movement to articulate its spirituality, theology and mission in the right direction.

---

[85] Castelo, "Patience as a Theological Virtue", 243.

Chapter 10

Conclusion

Pentecostalism is a spiritual movement and sure, its spirituality is a liberative spirituality. In the preceding pages, we have investigated various elements of Pentecostal spirituality and it is obvious that the inherent power they possess lead suffering masses into liberation, especially in the third world situation. Pentecostals are privileged to inherit such a spirituality that liberated them as well as propel them to liberate others. The Full Gospel, the popular Christology of Pentecostal movement, when it was preached in the power of the Spirit, millions all over the world not only have joined Pentecostal movement but also their lives were transformed for a better future. Even though the message of the Full Gospel was proclaimed by the weak and lowly Pentecostals, its power to liberate the suffering masses was substantial. The elements of this message, Jesus as saviour, healer, Spirit baptiser and so on, enacted transformative and revolutionary changes in listeners. In the same way, Pentecostal holiness that originates in conversion and covers the whole span of the Christian experience in constant growth and cleansing, transformed lives and surrounding of believers. It is a state of separation and purity wherein souls move toward the perfect likeness of Christ. Therefore, Pentecostals were ready sacrifice their worldly possessions and comfort for the sake of newfound sanctified experience. This holiness, Pentecostals cherished as individual and community, shaped their lifestyle and activities in a hostile and hurting world, enabled them to keep pure and also disseminate a contagious purity and liberative holiness in the society. Besides the experience of salvation created an egalitarian vision among them to act against racism, caste system, other social anomalies and involve in social ministries.

Similarly, the experience of the baptism of the Holy Spirit, a New Testament spiritual phenomenon, equipped them with power and energy to carry out cross-cultural and foreign missions. While most other Christians have considered this outpouring of the Holy Spirit to be highly unusual, the Pentecostals cherished it as a divine grace with a powerful and energizing ministry of the Holy Spirit, to carry out the miraculous. This is interpreted as a rediscovery of the spiritual gifts of New Testament times and their restoration to ordinary Christian life and ministry. Pentecostals were empowered to involve in daring missionary endeavours, and rescue many from the wretched conditions. Thus, for the Pentecostal believers evangelism and mission are by default a life-style. It is not anything carried out by special agencies or highly trained experts. Rather, evangelism and mission are deeply ingrained in the psyche and daily life of the believers and they proclaim salvation through Christ without any hesitation. This way of communicating and sharing of life-experiences explains the rapid proliferation of Pentecostal churches all over the world and made Pentecostalism the fastest growing religious movement on the globe. The use of the spiritual gifts like healing, exorcism, prophecy and others, not only propelled the growth of the movement but also liberated masses, in particular in the majority world setting. The message of the Kingdom of God is proclaimed and proved through signs and wonders and *charismata* act as tools of liberation. It is obvious that exercising of Pentecostal spirituality enacts liberative changes in the lives of ordinary people and they join Pentecostal churches.

Equally, spontaneous and lively worship of Pentecostal movement generate reverence and piety. The participants of Pentecostal worship encounter God through the agency of the Holy Spirit. Energetic worship with involvement of whole of a person, captivating music, prayer and praise lead to physical and emotional healing. Here a new vista is created in the life of the participants and in most cases, an indelible mark is ingrained in one's life. Similarly, Pentecostal preaching, with a story telling style and dramatic presentation with the power of the Holy Spirit, obviously breaks into the life of the listeners and shatter the old worldview and enforce a new vision of reality. It brings radical changes in the life of the ordinary people to liberate them. Besides, Pentecostal eschatology instils a new hope of the advent of Christ, resultant holy life and drives them for an urgent end-time mission that liberates many. Thus, Pentecostal spirituality fetches new lease of life to thousands of people and steers the movement in the forefront of other Christian denominations and religious setting of the world.

However, after a century of the origin of the movement, in many places, especially where Pentecostalism is old, the vibrancy and radical nature of the movement is significantly in decline. The primary reason for this state of affair is, as we have seen, less emphasis on its spirituality in the recent history of the movement. Many of the revolutionary ideals we have explored either waned away or watered down. For instance, Pentecostal spirituality of emphasising the personal integrity and holiness in individual believer's life as well as the community life, is not visible as of the beginning period. Many of the practices which were considered to be unholy earlier slowly creeping back into the movement. The fraternal feeling and egalitarian attitudes are waning away, but instead superiority and caste feeling abound. Many in the leadership of the Pentecostal denominations are marred by court cases, allegations of financial misappropriations and moral failings. Instead of emphasizing on the internal integrity and ethical standard of biblical teaching, Pentecostals are now more concerned about the outward appearances. It seems that the power of holiness that attracted others is missing from Pentecostal movement as a whole.

Similarly, in the case of baptism in the Holy Spirit, Pentecostals themselves do not fully understand the meaning of the pouring forth of the Spirit as divine favour and power upon his chosen people for restoration of humanity to God. Instead of using the power of the Spirit for mission of the church and larger purpose of God in the world, Pentecostals tend to more individualistic in their outlook. The urgency and importance given to evangelism and mission in the earlier period is not visible today, rather Pentecostal denominations are more focused on erecting structures. The eschatological urgency and great expectation of the second coming of Christ is waned away significantly, if not totally.

Antidote to this state of affair is to recapture the original fervour of Pentecostal spirituality. There is an urgent need to rediscover and reemphasise the elements of Pentecostal spirituality which we have explored, for well being of the church and the world, which will propel the community to be a spiritual and social force in the 21st century.

Bibliography

Abraham, K. E. *K.E. Abraham, A Servant of Jesus Christ: Autobiography.* Translated by Finny Jacob. Kumbanad, Kerala: India Gospel Outreach, 2016.

_______ *Yeshu Kristhuvinte Eliya Dasan* (*Autobiography of Pastor K. E. Abraham*), 3rd edition. Kumbanad, India: K. E. Abraham Foundation Publications, 2001.

Abraham, P. G. *Caste and Christianity: A Pentecostal Perspective.* Kumbhaza, India: Crown Books, 2003.

Abraham, Shaibu. "Holy Spirit in the Pentecostal Mission Praxis in India: A Paradigm for Mission in Pluralistic Context". In *The Holy Spirit and Christian Mission in a Pluralistic Context.* Edited by Roji T. George. Bangalore: SAIACS, 2017.

_______ "Jesus the Exorcist: The Emerging Pentecostal Christology in India". In *Pentecostalism: Polyphonic Discourses.* Edited by Rajeevan Mathew Thomas & Josfin Raj S.R. Delhi/Kerala: ISPCK/New Life Bible Seminary, 2019.

_______ "Jesus the Healer: Ordinary Indian Pentecostal Christology". *SATHRI Journal* IX/2 (October 2015): 58-74.

_______ *Pentecostal Christology: Empirical Approach in Indian Context.* New Delhi: Christian World Imprints, 2019.

_______ *Pentecostal Theology of Liberation: Holy Spirit and Holiness in the Society.* New Delhi: Christian World Imprints, 2014.

_______ *The History of the Pentecostal Movement in North India: Unfolding its Social and Theological Contexts.* New Delhi: Christian World Imprints, 2017.

Abrams, Minnie F. *The Baptism of the Holy Ghost and Fire.* Maharashtra, Kedgaon: Mukti Mission, 1906.

Adewuya, J. Ayodeji. "Holiness: Reclaiming the Doctrine". In *Issues in Contemporary Pentecostalism.* Edited by R. Keith Whitt & French L. Arrington. Cleveland, Tennessee: Pathway Press, 2012.

Aigbe, Sunday. "Pentecostal Mission and Tribal People Groups". In *Called & Empowered: Global Mission in Pentecostal Perspective*. Edited by Murray W. Dempster, Byron D. Klaus & Douglas Petersen. Michigan: Baker Academic, 1991.

Albin, T. R. "Wesley, John". In *New Dictionary of Theology*. Edited by Sinclair B. Ferguson & David F. Wright. Leicester: IVP, 1988, 718-720.

Albrecht, Daniel E. "An Anatomy of Worship: A Pentecostal Analysis". In *The Spirit and Spirituality: Essays in Honour of Russell Spittler*. Edited by Wonsuk Ma & Robert Menzies. New York: T & T Clark International, 2004.

_______ "Pentecostal Spirituality: Ecumenical Potential and Challenge". *Cyber Journal for Pentecostal Charismatic Research*, http://www.pctii.org/cyberj/cyberj2/albrecht.html (accessed 12/10/19).

_______ "Pentecostal Spirituality: Looking Through the Lens of Ritual". *Pneuma* 14 (1992): 107-125.

_______ & Evans B. Howard. "Pentecostal Spirituality". In *The Cambridge Companion to Pentecostalism*. Edited by Cecil M. Robeck, Jr. & Amos Yong. New York: Cambridge University Press, 2014.

Alexander, Paul. *Signs & Wonders: Why Pentecostalism is the World's Fastest Growing Faith*. San Francisco: Jossey Bass, 2009.

Althouse, Peter. "Pentecostal Eschatology in Context: The Eschatological Orientation of the Full Gospel". In *Perspectives in Pentecostal Eschatologies: World without End*. Edited by Peter Althouse & Robby Waddell. Eugene, Oregon: Witf & Stock Publishers, 2012.

_______ "The Landscape of Pentecostal and Charismatic Eschatology". In *Perspectives in Pentecostal Eschatologies: World without End*. Edited by Peter Althouse & Robby Waddell. Eugene, Oregon: Witf & Stock Publishers, 2012.

Alvarado, Johnathan E. "Worship in the Spirit: Pentecostal Perspectives on Liturgical Theology and Praxis". *JPT* 21 (2012): 135–151.

Anderson, Allan H. and Walter J. Hollenweger (eds.). *Pentecostalism After a Century: Perspective on a Movement in Transition*. Sheffield: Sheffield Academic Press, 1999.

_______ "Pentecostal Approaches to Faith and Healing as Signs of the Kingdom". https://www.academia.edu/6068841/Pentecostal_Approaches_to_Faith_and_Healing?auto=download (accessed on 12/08/2019).

_______ "Towards a Pentecostal Missiology for the Majority World". *AJPS* 8/1 (2005): 29-47.

_______ *An Introduction to Pentecostalism*. Cambridge: Cambridge University Press, 2004.

_______ *Spreading Fires: The Missionary Nature of Early Pentecostalism*. London: SCM, 2007.

_______ *To the Ends of the Earth: Pentecostalism and the Transformation of World Christianity,* https://erenow.net/common/to-the-ends-of-the-earth/ (accessed on 30/07/19).

Anderson, Robert M. *Vision of the Disinherited: Making of American Pentecostalism.* Peabody, Massachusetts: Hendrickson Publishers, 1979.

Archer, Kenneth J. *A Pentecostal Hermeneutic: Spirit, Scripture and Community.* Cleveland, Tennessee: CPT Press, 2009.

_______ *The Gospel Revisited: Towards a Pentecostal Theology of Worship and Witness.* Oregon: Pickwick Publications, 2011.

Asamoah-Gyadu, J. Kwabena. "'You Shall Receive Power': Empowerment in Pentecostal/Charismatic Christianity". In *Pentecostal Mission and Global Christianity.* Edited by Wonsuk Ma, Veli-Matti Kärkkäinen & J. Kwabena Asamoah-Gyadu. Oxford, UK: Regnum Books International, 2012.

Atlas of Pentecostalism; http://www.atlasofpentecostalism.net/ (accessed on 01/09/19).

Barrett, David B. & Todd M. Johnson. "Annual Statistical Table on Global Mission". *IBMR,* 23 (January, 1999): 24-25.

_______ George T. Kurian, & Todd M. Johnson. *World Christian Encyclopedia,* 2nd edition. New York: Oxford University Press, 2001.

Bartleman, Frank. *How Pentecost Came to Los Angeles: As it was in the beginning,* 2nd edition. Los Angeles: F. Bartleman, 1925.

Bauckham, Richard J. *Jesus and the Eyewitnesses: The Gospels as Eyewitness Testimony.* Michigan: Eerdmans, 2006.

_______ *The Gospels as Eyewitness Testimony.* Cambridge: Grove Books, 2008.

Bauman, Chad M. *Christian Identity and Dalit Religion in Hindu India, 1868-1947.* Michigan: Eerdmans, 2008.

Bergunder, Michael. "Miracle Healing and Exorcism in South Indian Pentecostalism". In *Global Pentecostalism and Charismatic Healing.* Edited by Candy Brown Gunther. New York: Oxford University Press, 2011.

_______ "Miracle Healing and Exorcism: The South Indian Pentecostal Movement in the Context of Popular Hinduism". *IRM* XC/356, 357 (Jan/April 2001): 101-112.

_______ *The South Indian Pentecostal Movement in the Twentieth Century.* Cambridge: Eerdmans Publishing, 2008.

Berkhof, Hendrikus. *The Doctrine of the Holy Spirit.* London: Epworth Press, 1964.

Bixler, F. "Dancing in the Spirit". In *NIDPCM.* Edited by Stanley M. Burgess. Michigan: Zondervan, 2002, 570-71.

Bloch-Hoell, Nils. *The Pentecostal Movement: Its Origin, Development, and Distinctive Character.* New York: Humanities Press, 1964.

Blumhofer, Edith L. "Consuming Fire: Pandita Ramabai and the Global Pentecostal Impulse". In *Interpreting Contemporary Christianity: Global Processes and Local Identities.* Edited by Ogbu U. Kalu. Grand Rapids, Michigan, Eerdmans, 2008.

Brown, Candy Gunther. *Global Pentecostal and Charismatic Healing.* Edited by Candy Gunther Brown. New York: Oxford University Press, 2011.

Bruner, Frederick Dale. *A Theology of the Holy Spirit: The Pentecostal Experience and the New Testament Witness.* Michigan: Eerdmans Publishing, 1970.

Burgess, Stanley M. "Pentecostalism in India: An Overview". *AJPS* 4/1 (2001): 92-93.

_______ & Gary B. McGee. "Signs and Wonders". In *NIDPCM.* Edited by Stanley M. Burgess. Michigan: Zondervan, 2002, 1063-68.

Cartledge, Mark J. *Testimony in the Spirit.* Farnham: Ashgate, 2010.

Castelo, Daniel. "Patience as a Theological Virtue: A Challenge to Pentecostal Eschatology". In *Perspectives in Pentecostal Eschatologies: World without End.* Edited by Peter Althouse & Robby Waddell. Eugene, Oregon: Witf & Stock Publishers, 2012.

Cerillo, Jr., Augustus. "Pentecostals and the City". In *Azuza Street & Beyond,* 2nd edition. Edited by Grant McClung. Florida: Bridge-Logos, 2012.

Chan, Simon. *Pentecostal Theology and the Christian Spiritual Tradition.* Sheffield: Sheffield Academic Press, 2000.

Cho, David Yonggi . "The Secret Behind the World's Biggest Church". In *Azuza Street & Beyond,* 2nd edition. Edited by Grant McClung. Florida: Bridge-Logos, 2012.

Christenson, Larry. *A Charismatic Approach to Social Action.* London: Lakeland, 1974.

Clouse, Robert G. "Pentecostals". In *The New International Dictionary of the Christian Church.* Edited by J. D. Douglas. Michigan: Zondervan, 1974, 763-764.

Coleman, Simon. *Globalisation of Charismatic Christianity: Spreading the Gospel of Prosperity.* Cambridge: Cambridge University Press, 2004.

Conn, C. W. "Christian Perfection (A Pentecostal Perspective)". In *DPCM.* Edited by S.M. Burgess & Garry B. McGee. Michigan: Zondervan, 1988, 169-180.

Cox, Harvey. *Fire from Heaven: The Rise of Pentecostal Spirituality and the Reshaping of Religion in the Twenty-first Century.* Cambridge, MA: Da Capo Press, 1995.

Cox, Raymond L. *The Four-Square Gospel.* Los Angeles: Foursquare Publications, 1969.

Cross, F. L. and E. A. Livingston (eds.). "Pentecostalism". In *The Oxford Dictionary of the Christian Church,* 3rd edition. Oxford: Oxford University Press, 1997, 1253-1254.

Dasan, Ebenezer D. "Conversion and Persecution in South Gujarat". In *Conversion in a Pluralistic Context: Perspectives and Context.* Edited by Krickwin C. Marak & Plamthodathil S. Jacob. Delhi: ISPCK, 2000.

Dayton, Donald W. "Christian Perfection to the Baptism of the Holy Ghost". In *Aspects of Pentecostal Charismatic Origins.* Edited by Vinson Synan. New Jersey: Logos, 1975.

_______ *Discovering an Evangelical Heritage.* New York: Harper & Row, 1976.

_______ "The Holiness Churches: A Significant Ethical Tradition". *Religion Online;* https://www.religion-online.org/article/the-holiness-churches-a-significant-ethical-tradition/ (accessed on 26/07/19).

_______ *The Theological Roots of Pentecostalism.* Peabody: Hendrick-son Publishers, 1987.

Deere, Jack. *Surprised by the Power of the Spirit.* Grand Rapids, Michigan: Zondervan, 1993.

Del Colle, Ralph. "Schleiermacher and Spirit-Christology: Unexplored Horizons of the Christian Faith". *IJST* 1/3 (1999): 286-307.

_______ "Spirit-Christology: Dogmatic Foundations for Pentecostal-Charismatic Spirituality". *JPT* 3 (1993): 91-112.

_______ "Trinity and Temporality: A Pentecostal/Charismatic Perspective". *JPT* 8 (1996): 99-113.

_______ *Christ and Spirit: Spirit-Christologies in Trinitarian Perspective.* Oxford: Oxford University Press, 1994.

Dempster, Murray W. "Christian Social Concern in Pentecostal Perspective: Reformulating Pentecostal Eschatology". *JPT* 2 (Apr. 1993), 51-64.

_______ "Eschatology, Spirit Baptism, and Inclusiveness: An Exploration into the Hallmarks of a Pentecostal Social Ethic". In *Perspectives in Pentecostal Eschatologies: World without End.* Peter Althouse & Robby Waddell. Eugene, Oregon: Witf & Stock Publishers, 2012.

_______ "Evangelism, Social Concern and the Kingdom of God". In *Called & Empowered: Global Mission in Pentecostal Perspective.* Edited by Murray W. Dempster, Byron D. Klaus & Douglas Petersen. Michigan: Baker Academic, 1991.

_______ "Pentecostal Social Concern and the Biblical Mandate for Social Justice". *Pneuma* 9/2 (Fall 1987): 129-153.

_______ Byron D. Klaus & Douglas Petersen (eds.). *Called & Empowered: Global Mission in Pentecostal Perspective*. Michigan: Baker Academic, 1991.

d'Epinay, Christian Lalive. *Haven of the Masses: A Study of The Pentecostal Movement in Chile*. London: Lutterworth Press, 1969.

Dieter, Melvin E. "The Wesleyan / Holiness and Pentecostal Movements: Commonalities, Confrontation, and Dialogue". *Pneuma* 12/1 (spring, 1990): 4-13.

_______ "Wesleyan-Holiness Aspects of Pentecostal Origins". In *Aspects of Pentecostal-Charismatic Origins*. Edited by Vinson Synan. New Jersey: Logos International, 1975.

Dyer, Helen S. (comp.). *Revival in India 1905-1906*. Akola, Maharashtra: Alliance Publications, 1987.

Etter, Maria B. Woodworth. *Signs and Wonders*, abridged edition. Hants: The Revival Library, n.d.

Faupel, D. William. *Everlasting Gospel: The Significance of Eschatology in the Development of Pentecostal Thought*. Sheffield: Sheffield Academic Press, 1996.

Fee, Gordon. "The Kingdom of God and the Church's Global Mission". In *Called & Empowered: Global Mission in Pentecostal Perspective*. Edited by Murray W. Dempster, Byron D. Klaus & Douglas Petersen. Michigan: Baker Academic, 1991.

Flower, J. Roswell. "Editorial". *The Pentecost* (August 1908).

Frodsham, Stanley H. *With Signs Following: The Story of the Latter-Day Pentecostal Revival*. Gospel Publishing House, 1946.

Gabriel, Reuben Louis. "Reflections on Indian Pentecostalism: Trends and Issues". *Dharma Deepika* 2 (July-Dec 2002): 67-76.

Gaston, W. T. "What Think ye of Christ". *The Pentecostal Evangel* 496 (May 12, 1923): 6.

George, Sherron Kay. "From Liberation to Evangelization". *Interpretation* 55/4 (October, 2001): 367-377.

Glass, James J. "Eschatology: A Clear and Present Danger — A Sure and Certain Hope". In *Pentecostal Perspectives*. Edited by Keith Warrington. Cumbria, UK: Paternoster Press, 1998.

Goff Jr., J. R. "Parham, Cahrles Fox". In *NIDPCM*. Edited by Stanley M. Burgess. Michigan: Zondervan, 2002, 955-57.

_______ "Topeka Revival". In *NIDPCM*. Edited by Stanley M. Burgess. Michigan: Zondervan, 2002, 1147-49.

_______ "Closing Out the Church Age: Pentecostals Face the Twenty-First Century". *Pneuma* 14.1 (Spring, 1992): 7-21.

Graves, R.W. "Tongues Shall Cease: A Critical Survey of the Supposed Cessation of the Charismata". *Paraclete* 17 (Fall 1983): 26-27.

Green, Michael. *I Believe in the Holy Spirit.* London: Hodder & Stoughton, 1975.

Gresham, John L. *Charles G. Finney's Doctrine of the Baptism in the Holy Spirit.* Peabody: Hendnckson, 1994.

Grudem, Wayne. *Systematic Theology: An Introduction to Bible Doctrine.* Leicester: IVP, 1994.

Habets, Myk. "Spirit Christology: Seeing in Stereo". *JPT* 11/2 (2003): 216-228.

Hardiman, David & Gauri Raje. "Practices of Healing in Tribal Gujarat". *EPW* (1 March 2008): 43-50.

Hardiman, David. "Healing, Medical Power and the Poor: Contests in Tribal India". *EPW* (21 April 2007): 1404-08.

Hauerwas, Stanley and R. Bondi. *Truthfulness and Tragedy.* Notre Dame: University of Notre Dame Press, 1977.

Heschel, Abraham J. *The Prophets.* New York: Harper & Row, 1962.

Hesselgrave, David J. *Today's Choices for Tomorrow's Mission: An Evangelical Perspective on Trends and Issues in Missions.* Grand Rapids, Michigan: Zondervan Publishing House, 1988.

Hodges, Melvin L. "A Pentecostal's View of Mission Strategy". In *Azuza Street & Beyond.* Edited by Grant McClung, 2nd edition. Florida: Bridge-Logos, 2012.

Hollenweger, Walter J. "Critical Issues for Pentecostals". In *Pentecostals after a Century: Global Perspectives on a Movement in Transition.* Edited by Allan Anderson & Walter J. Hollenweger. Sheffield: Sheffield Academic Press, 1999.

_______ "Evangelism: A Non-Colonial Model". *JPT* 7 (1995): 107-128.

_______ "The Black Roots of Pentecostalism". In *Pentecostalism After a Century: Perspective on a Movement in Transition.* Edited by Allan H. Anderson & Walter J. Hollenweger. Sheffield: Sheffield Academic Press, 1999.

_______ *Pentecostalism: Origins and Developments Worldwide.* Peabody: Hendrickson Publishers, 1997.

_______ *The Pentecostals.* Minneapolis: Augsburg Publishing House, 1972.

_______ "After Twenty Years Research on Pentecostalism". *IRM* 75/297 (1986): 3–12.

Hong, Young-Gi. "Church and Mission: A Pentecostal Perspective". *IRM* XC/358 (July 2001): 289-308.

http://www.cmalliance.org/about/history/simpson (accessed on 5/7/19).

https://archive.org/details/cu31924052629643/page/n13 (accessed on 27/07/19).

https://www.christianitytoday.com/history/people/denominationalfounders/john-wesley.html (accessed on 25/09/19).

https://www.christianitytoday.com/history/people/evangelistsandapologists/charles-finney.html (accessed on 27/07/19).

https://www.christianitytoday.com/history/people/moversandshakers/phoebe-palmer.html (accessed on 25/09/19).

Hudson, D. Neil. "Worship: Singing a New Song in a Strange Land". In *Pentecostal Perspectives.* Edited by Keith Warrington. Carlisle, Cumbria: Paternoster Press, 1998.

Hughes, Ray H. "The Uniqueness of Pentecostal Preaching". In *Azuza Street & Beyond.* Edited by Grant McClung, 2nd edition. Florida: Bridge-Logos, 2012.

_______ *Pentecostal Preaching.* Cleveland, Tennessee: Pathway Press, 1981.

Hunter, Harold D. "The Resurgence of Spirit Christology". *European Pentecostal Theological Association Bulletin 11* (1992); http://www.fullnet.net/np/archives/writings/epta.html (accessed 1 September 2010).

_______ "Spirit-Christology: Dilemma and Promise". *Heythrop Journal* 24 (1983): 127-140, 266-277.

Hyatt, Eddie L. *2000 Years of Charismatic Christianity.* Florida: Charisma House, 2002.

Jacobs, Alan. *Looking Before and After: Testimony and the Christian Life.* Michigan: Eerdmans, 2008.

Jacobsen, Douglas. *Thinking in the Spirit: Theologies of the Early Pentecostal Movement.* Bloomington, IN: Indiana University Press, 2003.

Jeyaraj, Daniel. "Editorial – Pentecostalism". *Dharma Deepika* 6/2 (July-Dec 2002): 2-3.

Johns, Cheryl Bridges. "Healing and Deliverance: A Pentecostal Perspective". *Concilium* 3 (1996): 45-50.

_______ *Pentecostal Formation: A Pedagogy among the Oppressed.* Eugene, OR: Wipf and Stock Publishers, 2010.

Johns, Jackie David. Yielding to the Spirit: The Dynamic of a Pentecostal Model of Praxis". In *The Globalization of Pentecostalism.* Edited by M.W. Dempster, B.D. Klaus & D. Petersen. Carlisle: Regnum, 1999.

Johnston, Robert M. "Demon Possession and Exorcism in the New Testament". https://digitalcommons.andrews.edu/jams/vol11/iss2/4 (accessed on 12/08/19).

Kalu, Ogbu. *African Pentecostalism: An Introduction.* Oxford: Oxford University Press, 2008.

Kärkkäinen, Veli-Matti. "David's Sling: The Promise and Problem of Pentecostal Theology Today: A Response to D. Lyle Dabney". *Pneuma* 23 (2001): 147-152.

_______ "Missiology: Pentecostal and Charismatic". In *NIDPCM.* Edited by Stanley M. Burgess. Michigan: Zondervan, 2002, 877-885.

_______ "'The Leaning Tower of Mission in a Postmodern Land': Ecumenical Reflections on Pentecostal Mission in the After-Edinburgh World". *JEPTA* 10.2 (2010): 82-93.

_______ "The Pentecostal Understanding of Mission". In *Pentecostal Mission and Global Christianity*. Eited by Wonsuk Ma, Veli-Matti Kärkkäinen & J. Kwabena Asamoah-Gyadu. Oxford, UK: Regnum Books International, 2012.

Keener, Craig S. *Spirit Hermeneutics: Reading Scripture in Light of Pentecost.* Michigan: Eerdmans Publishing, 2016.

Kendric, Klaude. *The Promise Fulfilled: A History of Modern Pentecostal Movement.* Springfield: Gospel Publishing House, 1961.

Ketcham, Maynard. *Tigers That Talk.* Charlotte, NC: PTL Television Network, 1979.

Kgatle, Mookgo S. "Singing as a Therapeutic Agent in Pentecostal Worship". *Verbum Ecclesia* 40/1 (2019); http://www.scielo.org.za/scielo.php?script=sci_arttext&pid =S2074-77052019000100006 (accessed 2/10/19).

Klaus, Byron D. "The Holy Spirit and Mission in Eschatological Perspective". *Pneuma* 27/2 (Fall 2005): 335.

_______ & Loren O. Triplett. "National Leadership in Pentecostal Missions". In *Called & Empowered*: *Mission in Pentecostal Perspective*. Edited by Murray W. Dempster, Byron D. Klaus, Douglas Petersen. Michigan: Baker Academic, 1991.

Knight iii, Henry. "From Aldersgate to Azusa*:* Wesley and the Renewal of Pentecostal Spirituality". *JPT* 8 (1996): 82-98.

Kraft, Charles H. "A Third Wave Perspective on Pentecostal Missions". In *Called & Empowered: Global Mission in Pentecostal Perspective*. Edited by Murray W. Dempster, Byron D. Klaus & Douglas Petersen. Michigan: Baker Academic, 1991.

Kydd, R. A. N. "Healing in the Christian Church". In *NIDPCM.* Edited by Stanley M. Burgess. Michigan: Zondervan, 2002, 698-711.

_______ *Charismatic Gifts in the Early Church*. Peabody, MA: Hendrickson Publishers, 1984.

Lackey, Jennifer. *Learning from Words: Testimony as a Source of Knowledge.* Oxford: Oxford University Press, 2010.

Land, Stephen J. *Pentecostal Spirituality: A Passion for the Kingdom.* Sheffield: Sheffield Academic Press, 1993.

Liardon, Roberts. *Azuza Street Revival: When the Fire Fell.* Shippensburg, PA: Destiny Image Publishers, 2006.

_______ *God's Generals: Why They Succeeded and Why Some Failed.* Tulsa, Oklahoma: Albury Publishing, 1996.

Loder, Allan Thomas. *An Examination of the Classical Pentecostal Doctrine of the Baptism in the Holy Spirit: In Light of the Pentecostal Position on the Sources of Theology.* Allan T. Loder, 2000.

Lovelace, Richard. "Baptism in the Holy Spirit and the Evangelical Tradition". *Pneuma* 7/3 (Fall 1985): 101-123.

Lovett, Leonard. "Liberation: A Dual-Edged Sword". *Pneuma* 9/2 (Fall, 1987): 155-171.

_______ "Black Origins of the Pentecostal Movement". In *Aspects of Pentecostal Charismatic Origins.* Edited by Vinson Synan. New Jersey: Logos, 1995.

Ma, Julie C. "Pentecostal Evangelism, Church Planting, and Church Growth". In *Pentecostal Mission and Global Christianity.* Edited by Wonsuk Ma, Veli-Matti Kärkkäinen & J. Kwabena Asamoah-Gyadu. Oxford, UK: Regnum Books International, 2012.

Ma, Wonsuk. "Asian Pentecostalism: A Religion whose only Limit is the Sky". *Journal of Beliefs & Values* 25/2 (August 2004): 191-204.

_______ "Full Circle Mission: A Possibility of Pentecostal Missiology," *AJPS* 8/1 (2005): 5-27.

_______ "Pentecostal Eschatology: What Happened When the Wave Hit the West End of the Ocean". *AJPS* 12/1 (2009): 95-112

Macchia, Frank D. "Pentecostal and Charismatic Theology". In *The Oxford Handbook of Eschatology.* Edited by Jerry L. Walls. Oxford: Oxford University Press, 2008.

_______ "The Struggle for Global Witness: Shifting Paradigms in Pentecostal Theology". In *The Globalization of Pentecostalism.* Edited by M.W. Dempster, B.D. Klaus & D. Petersen. Carlisle: Regnum, 1999.

_______ "Theology, Pentecostal". In *NIDPCM.* Edited by Stanley M. Burgess. Michigan: Zondervan, 2002, 1120-1141.

_______ *Baptised in the Spirit: A Global Pentecostal Theology.* Grand Rapids, Michigan: Zondervan, 2006.

MacDonald, William. "Pentecostal Theology: A Classical View Point". In *Perspectives on the New Pentecostalism.* Edited by Russell P. Spittler. Michigan: Baker Book House, 1976.

Maddox, Randy L. "Visit the Poor: Wesley's Precedent for Wholistic Mission". *T F Views* (January, 2001): 37-50.

Malek, Sobhi W. "Islam Encountering Gospel Power". In *Called & Empowered: Global Mission in Pentecostal Perspective.* Edited by Murray W. Dempster, Byron D. Klaus & Douglas Petersen. Michigan: Baker Academic, 1991.

Martin, David. *Tongues of Fire: The Explosion of Protestantism in Latin America.* Cambridge, MA: Basil Blackwell, 1990.

Martin, F. "Gift of Healing". In *NIDPCM.* Edited by Stanley M. Burgess. Michigan: Zondervan, 2001, 694-698.

Martin, Lee Roy. "Fire in the Bones: Pentecostal Prophetic Preaching". *Toward a Pentecostal Theology of Preaching.* Edited by Lee Roy Martin. Cleveland, Tennessee: CPT Press, 2015.

May, F. J. "Supernatural Anointing and Church Growth". In *Church Growth the State of Art.* Edited by C. Peter Wagner, Win Arn & Elmer L. Towns. Virginia: Liberty University, 1986.

McClung, Jr., L. Grant. "Evangelism". In *NIDPCM.* Edited by Stanley M. Burgess. Michigan: Zondervan, 2002, 617-620.

_______ "Exorcism". In *NIDPCM.* Edited by Stanley M. Burgess. Michigan: Zondervan, 2001, 624-628.

_______ "From BRIDGES (McGavran 1955) to WAVES (Wagner 1983): Pentecostals and the Church Growth Movement". *Pneuma* 7/1 (1985): 5-18.

_______ "Pentecostal/Charismatic Perspective on a Missiology for the Twenty-First Century". *Pneuma* 16/1 (Spring, 1994): 11-21.

_______ "Spontaneous Strategy of the Spirit". In *Azuza Street & Beyond,* 2nd edition. Edited by Grant McClung. Florida: Bridge-Logos, 2012.

_______ "Truth on Fire: Pentecostals and an Urgent Missiology". In *Azuza Street & Beyond,* 2nd edition. Edited by Grant McClung. Florida: Bridge-Logos, 2012.

_______ "'Try To Get People Saved': Revisiting the Paradigm of an Urgent Pentecostal Missiology". In *The Globalization of Pentecostalism.* Edited by Murray W. Dempster, Byron D. Klaus & Douglas Petersen. Michigan: Baker Academic, 1991.

Mcdowell, D. H. "The Purpose for the Second Coming of the Lord". *Pentecostal Evangel* (2 May 1925).

McGee, Gary B. "Pentecostal and Pentecostal-like Movements (1860-1910)". In *NIDPCM.* Edited by Stanley M. Burgess. Michigan: Zondervan, 2002, 118-119.

_______ "Pentecostal Phenomena and Revivals in India: Implications for Indigenous Church Leadership". *IBMR* 20/3 (July 1996): 112-117.

McGrath, Alister. *The Twilight of Atheism: The Rise and fall of Disbelief in the Modern World.* New York: Doubleday, 2004.

McQueen, Larry R. "Early Pentecostal Eschatology in the Light of the Apostolic Faith, 1906–1908". In *Perspectives in Pentecostal Eschatologies: World without End.* Edited by Peter Althouse & Robby Waddell. Eugene, Oregon: Witf & Stock Publishers, 2012.

Menzies, Robert P. *Toward a Pentecostal Eschatology: Discerning the Way Forward.* Dorset, UK: Deo Publishing, 2012.

_______ *Empowered for Witness.* Sheffield: Sheffield Academic Press, 2001.

Menzies, William W. & Robert P. Menzies, *Spirit and Power: Foundations of Pentecostal Experience.* Michigan: Zondervan, 2000.

_______ "Non-Wesleyan Origins of Pentecostal Movement". In *Aspects of Pentecostal Charismatic Origins.* Edited by Vinson Synan. New Jersey: Logos, 1975.

Miller, Albert G. "Pentecostalism as a Social Movement: Beyond the Theory of Deprivation". *JPT* 9 (1996): 97-114.

Miller, Donald E. & Tetsunao Yamamori. *Global Pentecostalism: The New Face of Christian Social Engagement.* Berkeley: University of California Press, 2007.

Moody, Dwight Lyman. *Moody: His Words, Work, and Workers.* Edited by W.H. Daniels. New York: Nelson & Phillips, 1877.

Mouw, Richard J. "Life in the Spirit in an Unjust World". *Pneuma* 9/2 (Fall, 1987): 109-128.

Nel, Marius. "Attempting to develop a Pentecostal theology of worship". *Verbum Ecclesia* 37/1 (2016); a1661. https://doi.org/10.4102/ve.v37i1.1661.

Neumann, Peter D. *Pentecostal experience: An Ecumenical Encounter.* Eugene, OR: Wipf and Stock Publishers, 2012.

Nienkirchen, C. "Simpson, Albert Benjamin". In *NIDPCM.* Edited by Stanley M. Burgess. Michigan: Zondervan, 2001, 1069-70.

No Author. "Evangelization, Proselytism and Common Witness: The Report from the Fourth Phase of the International Dialogue 1990-1997 between the Roman Catholic Church and Some Classical Pentecostal Churches and Leaders". *AJPS* 2/1 (January 1999): 105-151.

_______ "Pentecostal Conversion in the Popular Perception of the Sacred: Some Methodological Elements for its Analysis". *Voices from the Third World* XIV/2 (December 1991): 51-75.

Noel, Bradley Truman. *Pentecostalism, Secularism, and Post Christendom.* Eugene, Oregon: Wipf & Stock Publishers, 2015.

Oss, Douglas A. "A Pentecostal / Charismatic View". In *Are Miraculous Gifts for Today?* Edited by Wayne A. Grudem. Michigan: Zondervan Publishing House, 1996.

Palmer, Phoebe. "*The Way of Holiness*". In *The Devotional Writings of Phoebe Palmer.* Edited by Donald W. Dayton. New York: Garland Publishing, 1985.

Pate, Larry D. "Pentecostal Mission from the Two-Thirds World". In *Called & Empowered: Global Mission in Pentecostal Perspective.* Edited by Murray W.

Dempster, Byron D. Klaus & Douglas Petersen. Michigan: Baker Academic, 1991.

Pearlman, Myer. *Knowing the Doctrines of the Bible.* Springfield, Missouri: Gospel Publishing House, 1981.

Petersen, Douglas. *Not by Might nor by Power – A Pentecostal Theology of Social Concern in Latin America.* Oxford: Regnum, 1996.

_______ "The Kingdom of God and the Hermeneutical Circle: Pentecostal Praxis in the Third World". In *Called & Empowered: Global Mission in Pentecostal Perspective.* Edited by Murray W. Dempster, Byron D. Klaus & Douglas Petersen. Michigan: Baker Academic, 1991.

Petts, David. "The Baptism in the Holy Spirit: The Theological Distinctive". In *Pentecostal Perspectives.* Edited by Keith Warrington. Carlisle, Cumbria: Paternoster Press, 1998.

Poloma, Margaret M. "Glossolalia, Liminality, and Empowered Kingdom Building: A Sociological Perspective". In *Speaking in Tongues: Multi-Disciplinary Perspectives.* Edited by Mark J. Cartledge. Milton Keynes, England: Paternoster, 2006.

Pomerville, Paul A. *Pentecostalism and Missions: Distortion or Correction?* Pasadena, California: Fuller School of Intercultural Studies, 1982.

_______ *The Third Force in Mission: A Pentecostal Contribution to Contemporary Mission Theology*. Peabody, Massachusetts: Hendrickson Publishers, 1985.

Porterfield, Amanda. *Healing in the History of Christianity.* New York: Oxford University Press, 2005.

Pytches, David. *Spiritual Gifts in the Local Church.* Michigan: Bethany Publishing House, 1987.

Ragoonath, Aldwin. *Preach the Word: A Pentecostal Perspective.* Winnipeg, Canada: Agape Teaching Ministry of Canada, 2004.

Reddin, Opal L. *Power Encounter: A Pentecostal Perspective.* Edited by Opal L. Reddin. Springfield, MO: Central Bible College Publishers, 1999.

Reese, David George. "Demons (New Testament)". In *ABD.* Edited by David Noel Freedman. New York: Doubleday, 1997 (CD Rom).

Reid, D. G. "Powers and Principalities". In *DPL.* Edited by Gerald F. Hawthorne, Ralph P. Martin & Daniel G. Reid. Illinois: IVP, 1998 (CD Rom).

Remus, Harold. *Jesus as Healer.* Cambridge: Cambridge University Press, 1997.

Richie, Tony. "'The Unity of Spirit': Are Pentecostals Inherently Ecumenists and Inclusivists?" *JEPTA* 26/1 (2006): 21-35.

_______ "Neither Naïve Nor Narrow: A Balanced Pentecostal Approach to Christian Theology of Religions". *Presented to the Annual Meeting of the*

American Academy of Religion. Philadelphia, PA (19-22, November 2005). http://www.ncccusa.org/pdfs/naive.pdf (accessed 2 November 2010).

Robeck Jr., Cecil M. "Azuza Street Revival". In *NIDPCM.* Edited by Stanley M. Burgess. Michigan: Zondervan, 2002, 344-50.

_______ "Gift of Prophecy". In *NIDPCM.* Edited by Stanley M. Burgess. Michigan: Zondervan, 2002, 999-1012.

_______ "Seymour, William Joseph". In *NIDPCM.* Edited by Stanley M. Burgess. Michigan: Zondervan, 2002, 1053-58.

Ruthven, Jon. *On Cessation of the Charismata: The Protestant Polemic on Post-biblical Miracles.* Sheffield: Sheffield Academic Press, 1993.

Sahoo, Sarbeswar. *Pentecostalism and Politics of Conversion in India.* New Delhi: Cambridge University Press, 2018.

Sanger, Dale. "Early Pentecostal Eschatologies and their Effect on Shaping the Worldwide Pentecostal Movement". https://www.academia.edu/27187458/EARLY_PENTECOSTAL_ESCHATOLOGIES_AND_THEIR_EFFECT_ON_SHAPING_THE_WORLDWIDE_PENTECOSTAL_MOVEMENT_PENTECOSTAL_SPIRITUALITY_PENT0504 (accessed on 10/09/19).

Shaull, Richard & Waldo Cesar. *Pentecostalism and the Future of the Christian Churches.* Michigan: Eerdmans, 2000.

Shelhamer, E. E. (ed.). *Finney on Revival.* Minneapolis: Bethany House Publishers, 1974.

Shelton, James B. *Mighty in Word and Deed.* Oregon: Wipf and Stock Publishers, 2000.

Sheppard, Gerald T. "Pentecostalism and the Hermeneutics of Dispensationalism". *Pneuma* 6/2 (Fall 1984), 9–10, 32–33, 76.

Shepperd, J. W. "Worship". In *NIDPCM.* Edited by Stanley M. Burgess. Michigan: Zondervan, 2002, 1217-20.

Simpson, A. B. *The Four-Fold Gospel.* A.B. Simpson, 1980.

_______ *The Fourfold Gospel: Jesus as Saviour, Sanctifier, Healer and Coming King.* Orlando, FL: Bridge-Logos, 2007.

Smail, T., A. Walker, & N. Wright. *Charismatic Renewal: The Search for a Theology.* London: SPCK, 1993.

Smith, Calvin L. "The Politics and Economics of Pentecostalism: A Global Survey". In *The Cambridge Companion to Pentecostalism.* Edited by Cecil M. Robeck, Jr. Cambridge: Cambridge University Press, 2014.

Smith, James K. A. "The Closing of the Book: Pentecostals, Evangelicals, and the Sacred Writings". *JPT* 11 (1997): 49-71.

_______ "Tongues as 'Resistance Discourse': A Philosophical Perspective". In *Speaking in Tongues: Multi-Disciplinary Perspectives.* Edited by Mark J. Cartledge. Milton Keynes, England: Paternoster, 2006.

Snell, Jeffrey T. "Beyond the Individual and into the World: A Call to Participation in the Larger Purpose of the Spirit on the Basis of Pentecostal Theology". *Pneuma* 14/1 (Spring, 1992): 43-57.

Solivan, Samuel. *The Spirit, Pathos and Liberation: Toward an Hispanic Pentecostal Theology.* Sheffield: Sheffield Academic, 1998.

Spittler, Russel P. "Pentecostal and Charismatic Spirituality". In *NIDPCM.* Edited by Stanley M. Burgess. Grand Rapids, MI: Zondervan, 2002, 1096-1102.

_______ "Glossolalia". In *NIDPCM*. Edited by Stanley M. Burgess. Michigan: Zondervan, 2002, 670-76.

Stronstad, Roger. "Affirming Diversity: God's People as a Community of Prophets". *Pneuma:* 17/2 (Fall 1995): 145-157.

_______ *The Charismatic Theology of St. Luke.* Massachusets: Hendricksen Publishers, 1984.

_______ *The Prophethood of All Believers – A Study in Luke's Charismatic Theology.* Sheffield: Sheffield Academic Press, 1999.

Studebaker, Steven M. "Integrating Pneumatology and Christology: A Trinitarian Modification of Clark H. Pinnock's Spirit Christology". *Pneuma* 28/1 (Spring 2006): 5-20.

Synan, Vinson (ed.). *Aspects of Pentecostal Charismatic Origins*. New Jersey: Logos, 1975.

_______ "Missionaries of the One-Way Ticket". In *Azuza Street & Beyond,* 2nd edition. Edited by Grant McClung. Florida: Bridge-Logos, 2012.

_______ "The 'Second Comers'". *Christian History* 61 (1999): 38-39.

_______ *Holiness-Pentecostal Movement in the United States.* Grand Rapids, Michigan: Eerdmans, 1972.

_______ *The Holiness-Pentecostal Tradition,* 2nd edition. Michigan: Eerdmans Publishing, 1997.

Thomas, John Christopher. "Pentecostal Theology in the Twenty-First Century: 1998 Presidential Address". *Pneuma* 20 (1998): 3-19.

Tomberlin, Dan. "Pentecostal Worship: The Spirit in the Sacraments". In *Issues in Contemporary Pentecostalism*. Edited by R. Keith Whitt & French L. Arrington. Cleveland, Tennessee: Pathway Press, 2012.

_______ *Encountering God at the Altar: The Sacraments in Pentecostal Worship*. Cleveland, TN: Center for Pentecostal Leadership and Care, 2006.

Tuttle Jr., Robert G. *John Wesley: His Life and Theology.* Michigan: Zondervan, 1978.

Twelftree, Graham H. "Demon, Devil, Satan". In *DJG*. Edited by Joel G. Green, Scot McKnight & I. Howard Marshall. Illinois: IVP, 1992 (CD Rom).

_______ *In the Name of Jesus: Exorcism among Early Christians.* Michigan: Baker Academic, 2007.

_______ *Jesus the Exorcist.* Peabody, Mass: Hendrickson Publishers, 1993.

Van De Walle, Bernie. "A. B. Simpson's Fourfold Gospel: Both Product and Critique of Late Nineteenth-Century Evangelical Theology". https://www.academia.edu/33060050/A._B._Simpson_s_Fourfold_Gospel_Both_Product_and_Critique_of_ Late_Nineteenth-Century_Evangelical_Theology (accessed on 5/7/19).

Vansina, Jan. *Oral Tradition: A Study in Historical Methodology.* Translated by H. M. Wright. New Jersey: Transaction Publishers, 2006.

Volf, Miroslav. "Materiality of Salvation: An Investigation in the Soteriologies of Liberation and Pentecostal Theologies". *JES* 26 (1989): 447-467.

Vondey, Wolfgang. *Pentecostal Theology: Living the Full Gospel.* London: Bloomsbury T&T Clark, 2017.

_______ *Beyond Pentecostalism: The Crisis of Global Christianity and the Renewal of the Theological Agenda.* Michigan: Eerdmans, 2010.

Wacker, Grant. *Heaven Below: Early Pentecostals and American Culture.* London: Harvard University Press, 2001.

Wagner, C. Peter. "A Church Growth Perspective on Pentecostal Mission". In *Called & Empowered. Mission in Pentecostal Perspective.* Edited by Murray W. Dempster, Byron D. Klaus & Douglas Petersen. Michigan: Baker Academic, 1991.

_______ *Look Out! The Pentecostals are Coming.* Illinois: Creation House, 1973.

_______ *Warfare Prayer.* Ventura, CA: Regal Books, 1992.

_______ *Your Spiritual Gifts can make Your Church Grow.* Ventura, CA: Gospel Light Publications, 2012.

Warren, Max. *I Believe in the Great Commission.* Grand Rapids: Wm. B. Eerdmans, 1976.

Warrington, Keith. "The Role of Jesus as Presented in the Healing Praxis and Teaching of British Pentecostalism: A Re-Examination". *Pneuma* 25/1 (Spring 2003): 66-92.

_______ *Pentecostal Theology: A Theology of Encounter.* London: T&T Clark, 2008.

Wenk, Matthias. "The Holy Spirit as Transforming Power Within a Society". *JPT* 11/1 (Spring, 2002): 130-142.

Wilhelmsson, Lars. *The Gifts of Holy Spirit: God's Provision for Effective Ministry.* https://www.pdfdrive.com/the-gifts-of-the-holy-spirit-d23955742.html (accessed 10/08/ 2019).

Williams, J. Rodman. "Baptism in the Holy Spirit". In *NIDPCM*. Edited by Stanley M. Burgess. Michigan: Zondervan, 2002, 354-63.

_______ *Renewal Theology,* vol. 2. Grand Rapids: Academie Books, 1990.

Wilkinson, Michael. "Sociological Narratives and the Sociology of Pentecostalism". In *The Cambridge Companion to Pentecostalism*. Edited by Cecil M. Robeck, Jr & Amos Yong. New York: Cambridge University Press, 2014.

Wilson Jr., J. Christy. *More To Be Desired Than Gold.* South Hamilton, MA: Gordon-Conwell Seminary, 2002.

Wilson, Dwight J. "Eschatology, Pentecostal Perspectives on". In *DPCM*. Edited by S.M. Burgess & G.B. McGee. Michigan: Zondervan, 1988.

Wimber, John. "Signs and Wonders in the Growth of the Church". In *Church Growth the State of Art.* Edited by C. Peter Wagner, Win Arn & Elmer L. Towns. Virginia: Liberty University, 1986.

Womack, David A. (ed.). *Pentecostal Experience: The Writings of Donald Gee.* Springfield, MI: Gospel Publishing House, 1993.

Yong, Amos. "'Not Knowing Where the Wind Blows …': On Envisioning a Pentecostal-Charismatic Theology of Religions". *JPT* 14 (1999): 81-112.

_______ *Beyond the Impasse: Toward a Pneumatological Theology of Religion.* Michigan: Eerdmans, 2003.

_______ *Discerning the Spirit(s): A Pentecostal-Charismatic Theology of Religions, Journal of Pentecostal Theology Supplement Series.* Sheffield: Sheffield Academic Press, 2000.

_______ *The Spirit Poured Out on All Flesh: Pentecostalism and the Possibility of Global Theology.* Michigan: Baker Academic, 2005.

Index

A

Agnes Ozman 62, 92
Aldersgate Street 39, 55
Allan Anderson 8, 18, 26-27, 69, 81, 98, 123, 130, 144, 169
Amos Yong 3, 10, 14, 137-138
Apocalyptic 66, 93, 178, 183-184, 196, 201, 203
Apocalyptic vision 93, 196
Apostolic Faith 43-44, 62, 67, 184-185, 193-194, 197-198
Asa Mahan 40, 60, 98
Azusa Street 22, 37, 45, 62, 65, 67-69, 93, 129, 135, 184, 188, 194-195

Azusa Street 22, 37, 45, 62, 65, 67-69, 93, 129, 135, 184, 188, 194-195

B

B. Simpson 17, 19, 22-23, 25, 41, 98, 188
Born-again 8, 18, 181

C

C. Peter Wagner 12, 80, 111, 116, 118, 164
Candy Gunther Brown 2, 96
Cessationism 82
Charismata 12, 33, 79-80, 82, 85-86, 113, 117, 206
Charismatic XIII, 2, 5, 8, 14, 17, 19, 31-33, 36-38, 40, 45, 55-56, 64, 71, 74, 76, 80-81, 83-87, 91, 93, 96-98, 101, 104, 110-112, 116-117, 119, 133, 136-138, 140-141, 145, 148, 151, 153, 164, 169-170, 172, 174-175, 179, 181, 184-185, 190-191, 200
Charles F. Parham 62
Charles Finney 18, 40, 58
Charles H. Kraft 112, 128, 160
Charles Nienkirchen 22-23
Cheryl Bridges Johns 37, 42, 72, 101, 158, 177
Christendom X, 1, 3, 26, 54-56, 59-60, 72, 78
Christian Missionary Alliance 22
Christian Perfection 19, 36, 38, 40-41, 48-49, 55-58, 61
Christocentric 27, 126
Christology / Christological X, 10-11, 17-23, 25-28, 30-33, 73, 96, 99-100, 106-107, 109, 120, 125-127, 168, 175-176, 193-194, 200, 205
Christoph Blumhardt 50
Church Growth Movement 116, 133, 140
Church of God 40, 139, 164, 185, 191
Church of the Nazarene 40
Conscientisation 44
Conscientization 177
Consecration 40, 48-49, 59
Conversion 9, 11-12, 18, 27, 31, 36, 38-41, 56-57, 60-61, 69, 71, 75, 96, 98, 100, 109, 122, 134-136, 168-169, 180-181, 188, 205

D

D. Neil Hudson 144

D. William Faupel 187
Dalits 8, 29, 46, 131, 175
Dan Tomberlin 147, 150
Daniel Castelo 197
Daniel E. Albrecht 3, 144, 148
David Coffey 32
David du Plessis 118
David Hardiman 109-110
David Hesselgrave 115
David Pytches 94
Dialogical evangelism 139
Dispensationalism 129, 186, 190-192, 199, 203
Divine healing 4, 6, 20-21, 26, 29-30, 62, 81, 83, 96, 98-103, 125, 136, 172, 175, 182, 189, 195-196
Doctrine X, 1-5, 10, 17-20, 23, 26, 32, 35-38, 40, 42-43, 46-49, 53-62, 69, 71, 78-79, 82, 86, 97-98, 125-126, 137, 147, 154, 161, 179, 189-190, 193
Donald Dayton 17, 40
Donald E. Miller IX, 2, 23, 73, 120, 145
Donald Gee 54-55
Donald McGavran 116, 133, 140
Douglas Jacobsen 5
Douglas Peterson 76, 134, 136
Dwight L. Moody 60

E

Ecstasy IX, 1, 155, 157
Eddy L. Hyatt 45
Edith Blumhofer 70
Enduement 55, 59, 91, 122
Eschatology/eschatological VII, X-XI, 14, 45, 86, 93, 101-102, 105, 119, 121, 126-127, 129, 135, 138, 140, 159, 164, 183-203, 206
Evangelical Theology 19, 30
Evangelism VII, 6, 11, 13-14, 23, 76, 79, 81, 83, 89, 95, 98, 115-142, 159, 168, 183, 185, 196, 198, 206-207
Evil spirits 11, 28, 79, 97, 103-104, 106-110, 125, 141, 155, 163, 167, 171, 175
Exorcism 6, 10, 23, 26, 28-30, 79, 81, 83-84, 95, 97, 101, 103-107, 109-112, 123-126, 128, 136, 142, 151, 163, 166, 175, 178, 180, 182, 206
Experiential X, 1-3, 6, 13, 18, 20, 31, 74, 119, 122, 193

F

Frank Bartleman 65-66, 126
Frank Macchia 102
Full gospel VII, X, 9-11, 14, 17-33, 98, 122, 126, 130, 181, 188, 192-193, 196, 198, 205
Full gospel / fourfold gospel / fivefold gospel 17-23, 25, 27-29
Functional Christology 25-26, 28, 31, 33

G

George Whitefield 39
Gifts of the Spirit / Spiritual Gifts VII, IX-X, 3-4, 12, 14, 23, 26, 37, 72, 76, 79-113, 117, 119, 121, 123-124, 141, 143, 150-151, 163, 168, 171, 181, 189-190, 192, 194, 197, 206
Glossolalia 4, 30, 62, 69, 86-87, 152, 195, 200
Gnostic spirituality 27
Grant McClung Jr. 27, 104, 115
Grant Wacker 152, 192
Great Commission 79, 104, 118, 130

H

Harvey Cox IX, 1-2, 120, 145, 152, 156-157, 170
Healer X, 11, 17, 19-23, 25-26, 28-30, 81, 99, 126, 193, 205
Hierophany 148-149
Holiness Movement 17, 19, 25, 37-43, 48, 58, 60-62, 98, 188-189
Holiness VII, IX-XI, 3, 12-14, 17-20, 23, 25, 35-51, 56-58, 60-62, 71-73, 77, 98, 113, 135, 185, 188-189, 202-203, 205, 207
Holy Club 39, 55
Holy Spirit VII, IX-X, 3-6, 9-14, 18-20, 23, 25, 27-28, 31-33, 36-43, 48-50, 53-80, 82-87, 89-91, 93-94, 97, 101, 103, 108-109, 111, 113, 115, 117-119, 121-123, 125-127, 129-130, 132, 135-136, 138-139, 141, 143-144, 146-147, 150-151, 153-154, 156-157, 160, 163-164, 167, 170-174, 178, 184, 189-191, 193-194, 202, 206-207

I

Initial evidence 54, 61-62, 77, 86

J

J. Roswell Flower 119, 129
James K. A. Smith 87, 169
Jeffrey T. Snell 42
Jim Crow laws 63-64
John Christian Aroolappen 68
John Fletcher 39, 56-57
John Wesley 37-39, 55, 57, 92, 188
John Wimber 80, 94, 168
Justice 11, 36, 44, 47, 73, 75-77, 93, 135, 165, 195, 199, 201
Justification 38-39, 44, 152

K

K. E. Abraham 28-29, 69
Keith Warrington 3, 25, 46, 54, 81, 121, 144-145, 185-186
Kenneth J. Archer 9, 25, 28, 171
Kingdom of God X, 4, 7, 12, 43, 50, 86, 95, 97-98, 101-102, 105, 113, 125, 127, 134-136, 138, 159, 164, 166, 177, 196, 198, 200-202, 206
Klaude Kendric 38, 41
Koinonia 77, 203

L

Latter rain 25, 70, 184-185, 189, 192, 195, 197
Lee Roy Martin 165, 169
Leonard Lovett 37, 74
Lesslie Newbigin 5
Liberalism 24
Liberation III, VII, XI, 1-15, 17-33, 35-51, 53-113, 115-161, 163-203, 205-206
Liberation Theology 135
Liberation/liberative IX-XI, 9-11, 14, 18, 20, 28, 33, 62, 71, 73-74, 76, 78-79, 86, 96, 102, 119-120, 127, 141-143, 146, 149-150, 157-159, 161, 163, 168, 179, 185, 191, 193, 200, 203, 205-206

M

Marginalization/Marginalised 25, 117, 135
Maria Woodworth-Etter 173
Mark Cartledge 87, 180-181
Melvin Hodges 131
Messiah 25, 90, 166-167, 187-188
Methodist Church 37-39, 57, 62-63, 65
Michael Bergunder 100-101, 174-175
Miroslav Volf 135
Missiologist 115-116, 119-120, 128-129, 131, 196
Mission Strategies 104, 121, 128, 130-132
Mukti Mission 70
Murray Dempster 76
Myer Pearlman 53-54
Mystical / Mysticism 6, 148

O

Oberlin Perfectionism 40
Ontological 30-33
Oral 3, 104, 156, 168-169, 176-177, 180
Orthopathy 44

P

Pandita Ramabhai 70
Paradigm III, VII, 1-15, 27, 42, 45-46, 48, 51, 71, 102, 115, 127, 135, 164, 196, 199
Parousia 127, 195, 200, 202
Paul Alexander 7, 81, 146, 169
Paul Pomerville 104, 128
Paul Yonggi Cho 93, 122-123
Pentecostal Christology 11, 22-23, 25, 28, 30-31, 73, 96, 99-100, 106-107, 109, 120, 125, 127, 175-176, 193
Pentecostal Evangel 18, 23-24, 43, 81, 88, 102, 127, 129, 189
Pentecostal missiology 12, 81, 115, 123, 126, 137, 144-145
Pentecostal mission 13, 69, 73, 96, 107, 112, 116-129, 131-136, 139-142, 151, 160-161, 199
Pentecostal spirituality I, III, VII, IX-X, 1-15, 17, 27, 30-31, 43, 51, 58, 73-74, 93, 101-102, 115, 130, 139, 141, 143-146, 148-149, 156, 163, 180-181, 183-184, 186, 189, 191, 196, 200, 202, 205-207
Pentecostalism IX-X, 1-3, 6-10, 12-14, 17-18, 22-27, 31, 33, 37, 40, 43, 47, 49, 54-62, 67, 69-75, 77, 79, 81, 84, 96-98, 100-104, 107, 110-111, 115-117, 120, 123, 126-129, 131, 134-137, 140,

144-151, 156-159, 164, 169, 175-176, 180, 183-184, 186-188, 191-194, 196, 198-200, 205-206
Pentecostal churches 5, 7-8, 10-11, 13, 28-29, 35, 40, 45-46, 50, 62, 71, 73-74, 98, 101, 104, 115-116, 126-129, 134, 136, 140-141, 144, 150, 153, 155, 157-159, 163-164, 175-176, 180, 194, 206
Perfection 6, 19, 36, 38-41, 48-49, 55-58, 61
Peter Althouse 183, 190, 192
Pew Research 96
Phoebe Palmer 39-41, 57-59
Pneumatology 26, 31, 54, 71, 80, 126, 137, 190
Postmillenialism 188
Power encounter 12, 79, 104-105, 109, 119, 124-125
Praxis 3, 31, 73, 123, 132, 134, 151
Premillenialism 188
Premillennialism 62, 129, 189-190, 193, 199
Pre-tribulationists 187
Primitive church / Early Church 4, 6, 37, 53, 67, 77, 83, 85-86, 126, 148, 158
Proclamation 24-25, 27-29, 33, 76, 92, 98, 101, 125-126, 128, 132, 164-165, 168, 182, 196, 201, 203
Prophecy 4, 6, 14, 41, 69, 79, 81-84, 86-87, 89-95, 97, 112, 117, 123, 146, 151, 167, 171-172, 186, 189-190, 195, 206
Protestantism 2, 18, 24, 158

R

R.P. Spittler 4-5
Ralph Del Colle 30-32
Regeneration 22, 38, 54-56, 193
Religious pluralism 25, 121, 136-137
Richard Shaull 23, 73, 111, 120, 135
Righteousness 21, 36, 44, 72, 135, 138, 165, 171, 196, 202
Roberts Liardon 62, 174
Roger Stronstad 71, 76-77, 84, 91

S

Salvation Army 40, 42
Sanctification 5, 18-19, 25, 35-46, 48-51, 56, 58-62, 67, 72, 75
Sanctifier 11, 17, 19-20, 22, 25, 126
Sarah Lankford 39, 57
Sarbeswar Sahoo 8-9, 100
Saviour X, 11, 17, 19-23, 25-30, 33, 107, 126, 167, 187, 193, 205
Second coming of Jesus 28-29, 126, 184, 193, 203
Secularization 2
Signs and wonders 11-12, 49, 80-82, 98, 111-112, 117-118, 123-125, 128, 133, 139, 141-142, 146, 163, 168, 171, 173, 182, 191, 193-194, 206
Simon Coleman 170, 179
Smith Wigglesworth 24, 174
Social gospel movement 43
Soteriology 22
Spirit baptism / baptism of the Holy Spirit X, 3-4, 9, 13-14, 19-20, 23, 26-27, 30-32, 37, 39-43, 48, 53-65, 68-69, 71, 74-78, 117, 121-122, 126, 143, 146, 171, 174, 177, 183-184, 190, 193-196, 198-199, 202, 206
Spirit Christology 26-28, 31-33
Spontaneity/spontaneous 65-66, 98, 122-124, 130-133, 143-144, 151-152, 155-157, 168, 170-171, 206
St. John's Syndrome 141
Stanley Frodsham 98
Supernatural 4, 12, 53, 55, 59, 61, 65, 71, 80, 89-90, 97-98, 118-119, 121, 123-124, 132, 151, 164-165, 167-170, 184, 187, 189, 193
Supremacy of Christ 27, 30, 81
Syrian Christians 46, 69

T

Testimony VII, 3, 14, 28-29, 49, 63, 66, 85, 98-99, 101, 126, 132, 138, 163-182, 184
Theophanic 195
Third World IX-X, 7-8, 12, 15, 18, 25, 50, 73, 79-81, 96, 116, 119-120, 131-134, 163, 176, 180, 182, 205
Tongue speaking / Speaking in tongues 4, 6, 14, 18, 25, 54-55, 63, 65, 67, 69-70, 82-83, 86-89, 91, 95, 117, 119, 121, 143, 146, 151-152, 155, 167, 190, 193-195
Tony Richie 137-138
Topeka 62-63, 93

Transcendence 2
Transformation IX-X, 3-5, 8-11, 13, 18, 23, 31, 41-42, 45-51, 55, 61, 71, 75, 87, 95-96, 112, 119, 124, 132, 134, 146, 149, 157, 161, 169, 196, 201-202
Tribals 8, 29, 109, 175
Trinitarian 27, 30-33, 202

U

Untouchable 29, 46
Utopian vision 43, 48, 75

V

Veli Matti Kärkkäinen 11, 26, 119, 121, 135, 137, 151
Vinson Synan 17, 19, 37-40, 56-57, 73, 116, 130

W

Walter Hollenweger 88, 169
Walter J. Hollenweger IX, 37-38, 87, 139, 169, 180, 185
Wayne Grudem 48-49, 84, 147
Wesleyanism 40
Western Protestantism 24
Wholeness 36, 101-102, 161
William Holland 39
William J. Seymour 37, 62-63
William Menzies 118
William Rodman 85
Witchcraft 95, 107, 120, 171
Wonsuk Ma 12, 121, 140, 144, 151
World Christian Encyclopedia 2, 8